ALSO BY JANICE ERLBAUM

—————————●————————— *Girlbomb*

HAVE YOU FOUND HER

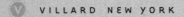 VILLARD NEW YORK

Have You Found Her

A Memoir

JANICE ERLBAUM

A Villard Books Trade Paperback Original

Copyright © 2008 by Janice Erlbaum

Published in the United States by Villard Books,
an imprint of The Random House Publishing Group,
a division of Random House, Inc., New York.

VILLARD and "V" CIRCLED Design are registered
trademarks of Random House, Inc.

LIBRARY OF CONGRESS CATALOGING-IN-PUBLICATION DATA

Erlbaum, Janice.
Have you found her: a memoir/Janice Erlbaum.
p. cm.
ISBN 978-0-8129-7457-7
1. Erlbaum, Janice.   2. Youth shelters—New York (State)—New York—Employees—
Biography.   3. Volunteer workers in social service—New York (State)—New York—
Biography.   4. Homeless teenagers—New York (State)—New York.   5. Problem youth—
New York (State)—New York.   I. Title.
HV1437.N5E75 2008
362.74—dc22
[B]   2007029061

Printed in the United States of America on acid-free paper

www.villard.com

9 8 7 6 5 4 3 2 1

Book design by Dana Leigh Blanchette

For B, of course

Ooh, baby, baby, it's a wild world. . . .
I'll always remember you like a child, girl.

—CAT STEVENS

CONTENTS

Red

There's a redheaded girl panhandling on my corner, sitting on the sidewalk behind a cardboard sign. It reads: *PLEASE HELP ME. TRYING TO GET A PLACE TO STAY. ANYTHING YOU CAN GIVE. I'M JUST A YOUNG GIRL.* I've seen her out there on the street for the past few years, on and off—I won't spot her for weeks at a time over the winter months, but as soon as the sun starts shining in March, there she'll be, all five feet and ninety pounds of her, her back pressed against the stone façade of the Gap Body store on Fifth Avenue, her cardboard sign propped up against her bony knees, her head dropped between her legs, sobbing.

This is what she does. She sits on the sidewalk behind her sign and sobs. Until you put something in her cup, and then she barely lifts her head and mouths *thank you*. And you can see, for a second, how sharp and drawn her face is, how cloudy her eyes; you'll note the sores on her cheeks where she scratches and picks. Heroin sores.

Different drugs leave different scars. I've learned to recognize the signs, since I started volunteering at the shelter, since I started tracking the street kids who migrate around my neighborhood like stupefied antelopes. The girls with the burnt, scabby lips are smoking coke; the meth addicts and junkies have lesions. Except the meth addicts don't look sleepy, like the junkies do; they look rapacious, like starvation-crazed zombies, like they're ready to run up on you and eat your brains. But the redhead's drug is heroin—you can tell by the way she lolls and slumps between crying jags, the way she goes to wipe her runny nose and misses, forgets halfway.

The first time I noticed the redhead, I was on my way to have lunch with my father at an expensive restaurant near Union Square. It was a cold, wet April afternoon, and she was huddled behind her cardboard sign, which was soaked dark brown, the words barely legible. I was going to walk by her, the way I often did in my pre-volunteer days, strode right past kids panhandling on the sidewalk, thinking, *Go back to your middle-class parents in Westchester, girlie, and lay off the dope.*

But the sign—*I'm just a young girl.* And she was shivering, sobbing, her red hair matted into snakes by the rain. Could have been me, once, if things had gone differently.

I stopped and crouched down in front of her, covering us both with my umbrella. "Hey," I said, reaching for her shoulder, cold and bony as a sparrow's wing under her wet sweatshirt. "Hey, it's going to be okay."

She lifted her head and moaned. It sounded like, *Please.* Her body trembled violently under my hand.

Good god, I thought, suddenly urgent. *Somebody has to help this girl.*

I took my hand from her shoulder, dug in my pocket, landed on a crumpled bill. "Hey." I showed her the bill, a five, and put it in the melting paper coffee cup at her side, empty except for some pennies and a quarter inch of rain. She continued to shake and moan—*Please, please.* "Hey, listen, it's going to be okay."

What was going to be okay? Me, I was going to be okay. I was on my way to meet my father at an expensive restaurant; I had on nice pants and heels, nice clothes to prove that I was okay. But *she* wasn't okay, she wasn't going to be okay, and my five dollars wasn't going to make it okay. *Five dollars,* I pled with myself, trying to make myself believe the best: she'd purchase a half hour indoors at a coffee shop, maybe a grilled-cheese sandwich. She wouldn't put it toward her next bag of dope.

I put my hand back on her shoulder—I'd wash it when I got to the restaurant. Other people were streaming by on the sidewalk; I looked at them desperately. Was there a doctor in the house? A social worker? Somebody's mom? Could somebody cover this, somebody equipped to deal with it? It was an emergency, and I had to get to lunch.

She rolled her head back on her neck, tilted her parched eyes my way. Fighting for words like she was drowning. "Pl-ease," she said thickly, her chest hitching. "I'm sick. Nobody helps. . . ."

Her purple lips were stretched into a grimace; she trembled like she might break. *Good god*, I thought again, despite the evidence to the contrary. "I know," I said. "I'm sorry. People want to help, they really do. I want to help. Take this." I took the money from the cup, pressed it into her hand; she grasped it and nodded, still shaking. "Take it, go to a coffee shop, get out of the rain, get something to eat. Okay?"

She slumped forward, her face obscured, the runoff from my umbrella trickling down the back of her neck. A coffee shop wasn't going to help her. One sandwich wasn't going to save her life. Her sharp little shoulder was clammy under my sweating hand. I was going to be late; I hate being late. I cringed at the thought.

"Look, I have to go, but I'm going to come back, okay? I'll be back in an hour. Will you be here? You get something to eat, and I'll come back, and . . . we'll see what we can do, okay?" She nodded into her knees, heaved and jerked. "I'll come back," I repeated stupidly, removing my hand from her shoulder, standing up, backing away. "You take care. I'll see you soon."

I tore myself away, half guilty, half relieved, and stumbled down the block in my unfamiliar heels. Washed my hands, kissed my father hello, and ate my expensive lunch.

An hour later, I walked by her spot. She was gone.

I've seen her I don't know how many times since then. Fifty?

Sobbing behind her sign in front of J. Crew, in front of Esprit, in front of Armani Exchange. Some days I'll pass right by her; other days I'll stop, offer to get her a sandwich or something to drink. She'll lift her weary head and murmur, *"Please, not hungry, spare some change."* I'll bring her some food anyway. Some cookies, a Snapple, anything sweet—junkies crave sugar, that's the lore. I'll crouch beside her, put the offering at her feet; she'll whimper a thank-you, then drop her head again. She does not appear to recognize me from one iced tea to the next.

Samantha knew the redhead. Of course she did—Sam knew all the street kids around Union Square—the blond guy with dreads and a guitar (*STRANDED, TRYING TO GET $ FOR A BUS TICKET HOME*), the brown-haired, slack-faced girl with the scabby lips (*JUST HAD BRAIN SURGERY, PLEASE HELP*). "That guy," she'd say, pointing out a kid who looked like he'd been rolled from hood to sneaker in a fine gray dust, "that guy huffs so much paint and glue, I don't even want to light a cigarette near him."

Sam and I were walking from my apartment to the park one afternoon last summer when I spotted the redhead. I stopped short and nudged Sam, pointing with my chin. "There she is, the girl I was telling you about."

Across the street, in front of the Banana Republic, head between her arms, curled like a porcupine behind her weather-beaten sign. Sam slowed and narrowed her eyes, squinting at the markered words. "Oh, her. I've seen her at StreetWorks a few times. She's a junkie. I mean, obviously." Sam squinted some more, shading her eyes from the sun. "Hah! 'Just a young girl.' She's like twenty-five years old!"

Sam turned to continue walking, but I was still standing, watching a woman deposit some coins into the redhead's cup as she hurried past. The tiny head bobbed up for a second, then dropped back down. *Twenty-five*, I thought—she'd probably been on the street for years now. It must have been the fear on her face that made her look so young.

"Yeah? What's her story? Have you ever talked to her?"

"I don't know, I've just seen her there a few times, getting the free lunch. I think Valentina knows her." Sam wrinkled her nose, bored, ready to move on, to pick up our conversation about cults and EST and Chinese brainwashing techniques. "She's not *that* interesting."

There was that hint of chiding in Sam's voice, the same hint I sometimes got when I inquired after her roommate, Valentina, or when I talked about the girls I'd met volunteering at the shelter that week, the way Sam and I had met. That chiding, like, *What, I'm not enough for you? You want to start seeing other homeless girls?*

I turned away from the redhead and smiled to myself, resuming our pace. *Nobody's as interesting as you, kid.*

It's almost summer again. Sam's been gone for over six months now. I draft her letters sometimes, the kind you can't send. I never get past the first few lines anyway. But the redhead is still here on my corner. It's warm these days, but she's still shivering, teeth chattering in the white sun on the patch of sidewalk in front of the Gap Body store. Sometimes she's crying, other times she appears to be asleep. She doesn't look like she's going to last much longer, but I've been thinking that for years now. Maybe she'll surprise me, and live.

I shade my eyes as Sam did, watch from across the street as people drop coins into the redhead's cup, wishes in a fountain. *I wish I could save you.* And her puppet head jerks and nods, like she fell asleep while praying.

HAVE YOU FOUND HER

Chapter One

How I Became the Bead Lady

It's a Wednesday evening in late May, and I'm at the shelter for my weekly workshop, which is officially listed on the calendar as "Jewelry Making with Janice." This has been my shtick for the past two and a half years—every Wednesday evening, I come uptown to the shelter, and I sit around for a few hours with the girls of the Older Females Unit making beaded bracelets and necklaces and earrings. I am known, colloquially, as "Bead Lady," as in, "Bead Lady, you got more alphabet beads this week? 'Cause last week you was runnin' outa vowels."

All of the volunteers here have a shtick. Some teach ballet, some lead prayer circles; theater groups come in to do presentations about conflict resolution. Out-of-town church choirs give concerts. The Junior League, a group of young professional women committed to volunteerism, sends representatives once a week to lead workshops about things like prenatal health and budgeting. One guy comes in and supervises pickup basketball games in the gym. There's a guy named Carl who's been volunteering on the Older Females Unit for the past fifteen years—a white guy, mousy, quiet, and kind. I have no idea what his shtick is, but the girls seem to like him.

They don't like everybody. I guess when I started, I thought the girls would be so grateful for any kind of sympathy or attention that they'd fall all over the volunteers, but I've seen them turn their backs on a lot of people, watched them size up a bunch of white women in high-heeled shoes, out to do their annual Good Deed for the Poor Little Black Girls, and seen them "put it on frost," as they say, ice up like snowmen. Because the girls at the shelter do not want your charity. They did not ask you to come stare at them with your pity, like they're some fucked-up zebras at the zoo. They know you have some reason of your own for coming, whether it's to burn off your bourgeois guilt, spread the word of Jesus, or pad your résumé—you've got your shtick, and then you've got your angle. *What are you doing here*, the girls want to know. *Slumming?*

They'll still ask me that, directly or indirectly, the new ones who haven't met me before—and there are always new ones, every week. Every Wednesday evening, I'm missing a few girls from the weeks before ("Where's Angela? Where's Zuzu? Where's Grenada?"), and there's a fresh crop of intakes, girls who watch me warily as I dump my bead supplies on the table in the lounge.

"What's this?" they ask, skeptical.

"We're going to make jewelry. You want to make some?"

Invariably: "Is it free?"

"Yeah, it's free. You can make earrings, or a necklace, or a bracelet."

"What about all three?"

That's when I know I've got them. "You can make all three," I tell them, smiling. "If you've got the patience, I've got the time."

"All right then." And the chairs scrape back, and I'll have a table full of girls sitting with me, just like that, asking for a string "big enough for my man's wrist" or "small enough for my baby."

And soon enough, if it's an all- or mostly new crowd, between talking about popular music and cell phone plans and whether or not you can tell the sex of a baby-to-be by the changing breadth and flatness of the mother's nose, the subject will eventually come up: "Miss, Bead Lady, why you come here like this?"

As it has tonight. Tonight's asker is a butch girl of about nineteen, wearing an oversized hockey jersey in black and red, extra-large baggy jeans belted around the upper thighs, do-rag over her braids, and cork-sized fake diamond studs in each ear. She is making a black-and-red bracelet, Blood colors. I always try to dissuade the girls from making gang beads, to no avail. The bracelet has alphabet beads that spell RIP POOKIE.

I concentrate on daubing a finished knot with glue. The glue won't keep the cheap elastic from snapping, ultimately, but it will forestall its demise. "Well," I say, without looking up. "I used to live here when I was a kid."

"For real?" asks the butch girl, eyebrows high. "You lived here?"

"Huh," murmurs someone else. Another girl at the end of the table elbows her neighbor, *Are you listening to this?*

I keep my eyes on the knot, blow on the glue. "Yep. When I was fifteen, I got sick of living with my mother's husband, so I left home, and I came here. I was in the minors' wing for about two months, then they helped me get into a group home, and I lived there for about a year."

"I hate my mother's husband, too," offers the girl to my left, the one with the tattoo of a bleeding rose on her left boob. She hands me an earring in need of a hook.

"Fuck all of them," agrees the butch in the hockey jersey, and turns her attention back to me. "So, wait—so things was messed up at home, and you came here, and then they hooked you up, and then things got better? Things is good with you now?"

I bend the hook with my pliers, smiling to myself. *Succinctly, yes.* "Things are very good with me now. And I'm really grateful to this place for helping me get to a place where I can say that."

She leans back, nods. "So that's how come you came back."

I return the hooked earring to the girl with the bloody-rose tattoo, and she holds it up to her ear, flips her head back and forth like America's Next Top Model, emits a little squeal of pleasure. "Pretty much," I say.

"That's crazy," decrees a girl at the end of the table, pale and haughty, with traces of a Spanish accent. "No offense, miss, but when I get outa here, I am never coming back. *Never.*"

"That's understandable," I tell her. "I didn't come back for almost twenty years."

"So what made you decide to come back, then?" asks the butch girl.

Well, okay. This is a question I've asked myself over and over, ever since I walked through that door again—*What made me decide to come back here, goddamn it?* I'd successfully managed to avoid this place for nineteen years, though I never left New York, never lived farther than a subway ride away. After purposely staying away for so long, why did I decide to return to the scene of the crime? Why couldn't I just leave well enough alone?

Two and a half years later, I still don't know the answer. *Survivor's guilt,* I could say, or, *because I want to help make a difference.* But really, it was something more selfish than that, something I still can't name.

I cut another bracelet length of elastic string, triple-knotting the end.

"Well, you know how it is," I tell her, smiling. "I missed the company."

I'm interested in volunteering here because I'm a former resident of the shelter, and I want to give something back to the place that helped save my life.

That's what I wrote on my application almost two and a half years ago, back in the winter of 2004, when I was all fresh and dewy-eyed. It had been nineteen years since I'd been inside the building, since the day I'd left the shelter for the group home, my donated bag full of donated clothes, a skull and crossbones drawn in eyeliner on my temple, ready to impress my new roommates with my hard-core stories about stabbings and lesbians and twelve-year-old hoes. *See you, wouldn't want to be you. Anymore.*

Then there I was again, age thirty-four, in my pinstriped pants and my good-enough shoes, sitting around the conference table in the volunteer department with my paperwork in front of me, sneaking looks at the other prospective candidates: a young white girl with her hair in braids, looking to earn college credit; a woman in her forties, also going for college credit; and a bald, muscular guy with a big tense grin. When the volunteer coordinator asked him why he was interested in volunteering, he grinned so hard he almost broke a sweat.

"I love kids!" he exclaimed. "I've been a foster parent, and I'm really . . . I love kids. Wanna help 'em out." Grin, grin.

Creep, I decided, for no good reason. *Child molester.* It was something about the muscles; I could picture him shirtless, screaming at his foster kids while he made them do push-ups. He grinned at me, and I smiled back weakly.

The volunteer coordinator put on a videotape about the shelter. "Our crisis center serves two to three thousand kids every year," said the narrator. "Without us, they have few alternatives besides the streets." One black-and-white photo of a sober-faced kid dissolved into another: kids leaning against walls, kids lying curled up on the sidewalk. Then the happy kids, the shelter kids, in color, with smiles and graduation robes. The music swelled. "With your help," the narrator urged, "we can make a difference in their lives. We can give them more than just food and shelter—we can give them hope."

Had this place given me hope? I tried to remember. I remembered the food: white bread, cereal, and milk in the morning; bologna sandwiches for lunch; meat loaf and mashed potatoes out of the box for dinner. SpaghettiOs, canned vegetables, vanilla pudding. Never enough of any of it. I remembered the narrow metal bed frame, and the scratchy industrial sheets, and the bathroom I shared with six other girls; I remembered the paneled drop ceiling over my bed. I remembered the three dollars a week they gave us for spending money, and how every Friday night the counselors would open up the supply cabinet and hand out douches, one for every girl.

I remembered the douches. I didn't know if I remembered the hope.

I frowned, trying to concentrate, but it was distracting, being back in the building again after all that time, the same building I'd dreaded and dreamed of for years after I left. That *smell*—cinder blocks and construction paper, the ragged, musty, wall-to-wall carpeting, the heat coming through radiators thick with cracked paint—it hit me like an old song. *Right*. The night I came here was windy, it was November; I was fifteen years old. I walked through those doors downstairs, went into that office I passed earlier, and talked to my very first nun, who said, "You can stay here, for now, and we'll find you a place to live."

There was another nun on the videotape now, saying, "Your first responsibility with these young people is to listen. First and foremost, you have to listen to them, and you have to take what they say seriously. And they may not always be telling the truth—in many cases, they won't be; they don't know how. But even if you don't believe the *facts* of what they're saying, you still have to believe *in them*, and believe that you will eventually get the facts. Believe in them, and listen to them, and keep listening, and eventually they *will* tell you the truth, and they will tell you how to help them, and how to teach them to help themselves."

Listen, I wrote in my notebook, and underlined it. That's what the first nun did for me, the night I came here. She listened to me, and she believed me.

Now I remembered the hope.

All the remembering was starting to overwhelm me; I was getting dizzy from it, from the heat in the close room, crowded with extra dimensions of time and space. It was nineteen years ago; it was today. It was in that stairwell right over there, three floors down, those girls wanted my eyeliner and I gave it to them. It was thick in here, the air swollen and static, and I knew from experience that the windows didn't open. The Ghost of Janice Past was squirming on my lap. *What are we doing* here? she wanted to know. *And when are we getting a smoke?*

"These young people are suffering," the nun on the tape continued. "Suffering from abuse, addiction, poverty, neglect . . ." I twisted in my chair, tugged the waistband of my pants, slipped my feet out of my shoes under the table and curled my toes. I could feel the bald guy grinning from two seats away. "Heightened risk of gang violence, prostitution, disease . . ." *Oh god. Okay! We get it, all right? We're here! We're here, and we're going to stop all that bad stuff from happening, so let's quit talking about it and get to work.*

Finally, the tape was over, and the volunteer coordinator switched on the lights. "Are there any questions?" she asked.

I slumped in my chair, wrung out. The grinning bald guy raised his hand and asked my question for me. "When can we start?"

I was still flustered when I got back to my apartment that night, pacing the living room with my three cats in tow, their tails crooked with curiosity. I couldn't stop thinking about the kids I'd seen: the young girl waiting for the elevator with me, carrying her days-old baby, smaller than a loaf of bread; the two roughnecks on the corner, with their supersized jeans and their plasticized sneakers shaped like steam irons—I was three feet away from them when I realized they weren't boys. The girl with the pink yarn in her braids, waiting downstairs in front of the intake office, singing softly to herself, that song from *The Little Mermaid.*

I want to be where the people are . . .

Ever since a few weeks ago, when I'd made up my mind to go back and volunteer, I'd been impatient to start making a difference, to start digging through that pile of needy kids and *helping* them, one by one, until they were all good and helped, and I could relax again, knowing they were all right. Volunteering felt like something urgent I'd left undone, something I'd been putting off for years—like the nightmares I had sometimes, where I'd left the cats neglected and unfed for a week and was racing home to see if they were still alive. Now that I'd laid eyes on these kids, I was even more anxious to get back there to the shelter, to help, to *listen* and *believe,* as the nun on the videotape had said.

I plucked a half-smoked joint out of the ashtray and lit it, swallowing a deep drag and holding it in my lungs. Such an old habit, my pot smoking—the only vestige of my drug-addled adolescence. I'd quit all my other teenage habits long ago—cocaine, ecstasy, acid, thumb sucking—but now, in my thirties, I continued to smoke pot daily. Self-medicating, I told myself, against the leftover anxieties of a tumultuous youth; after what I'd been through as a kid, I figured I was entitled to smoke as much as I wanted. Besides, everyone said I was the most productive pothead they'd ever met—I could get up in the morning, run a few miles on the treadmill, then smoke half a joint before going to my editorial job; with a few drops of Visine in my eyes, it seemed that nobody was ever the wiser.

I paced as I smoked, thinking maybe I'd call my boyfriend, Bill; he should have been home from work by then. I took another long hit off the joint, put it back in the ashtray, and dialed his apartment in Queens.

"Our hero returneth," answered Bill, his chair squeaking in the background as he put his feet up on his desk. "So? How did it go?"

I could hear him smiling at me over the phone, could feel it all the way from Queens. Bill and I had been together for two years already, after meeting online, and I still couldn't believe my luck in finding him, this smart, funny, nerdy, handsome guy who adored me, whom I adored. I pictured him—his warm hazel eyes behind his squared-off glasses, his broad shoulders, his long runner's legs propped up on his desk next to a stack of comic books and Macworlds—and I wished we'd made plans for him to come over that night.

"Okay," I said. "I mean, good. They said my application looked really good, and my recommendations were strong. So now I just have to pass the criminal-background check, and then they can place me on a unit."

"Excellent," he said, sounding very satisfied. "That's great, Shmoo."

I flopped down on the sofa, disarmed as always by Bill's support. Even after two years, it was still hard to get used to the idea that I had a partner I could lean on and trust, someone who responded to my plans and ideas with "That's great, Shmoo," instead of "Well, the only problem with *that* is . . . ," like the voice inside my head, like every jerk boyfriend I'd ever had.

"I'm so proud of you," continued Bill. "You feel good about it, right?"

"Yeah, I feel good. I feel . . ." *Tired.* I felt tired all of a sudden, like I'd run out of adrenaline, like it was three in the morning instead of nine-thirty at night. "I just . . . I don't know what I'm supposed to do for these kids. I don't know what the hell I think I'm doing. I'm not a social worker, I'm just some person off the street."

Bill cut right through this, authoritative. "Babe, you're more than just some person off the street. You lived there. Nobody's going to understand these kids better than you. And they'll train you, right? I mean, once you're placed on a unit"—he threw a little extra relish on "on a unit," like I was going to work at Oz Maximum Security Prison, and I was buoyed for a second by his vicarious excitement—"I'm sure they'll give you instructions, tell you how the whole system works. You'll be—"

"I wish you were here," I said abruptly. "I love you and I miss you and I wish you were here."

He paused, restarted carefully. "I wish I was there too, Shmoo."

All I had to do, I knew, was ask Bill to move in with me, and he could be there every night. I didn't know why I was balking. He was ready to give up his lease in Queens; he was sick of schlepping his overnight bag to work every other day, of trying not to let the milk in his fridge go bad, of missing the three cats he and I had adopted together on nights he spent alone. Two years—that was more than enough time to decide whether or not you wanted to move in with somebody, especially in New York, where rent usually dictates the course of a relationship, and it's not like I didn't have enough room; I had more than enough. I just had to ask him, already.

"Anyway," I demurred, "I won't know more until I hear from this woman Nadine, she's the head of Older Females. And it might take her a while; they're really busy over there."

"I'm sure they *are* busy," said Bill, and yawned. The desk chair squeaked again; his feet landed back on the floor. "Listen, I'm going to eat something, maybe throw on the hockey game—you want to call me back before you go to sleep?"

The nightly before-bed phone call—another amazing feature of the Bill and Janice deal. I was crazy for not asking him to move in. I rose from the couch, and the cat on my lap made an exasperated noise. Me and my wanderlust.

"Yeah, okay," I told him. "I love you, Shmoo."

Nadine Daniels, head of the Older Females Unit, was as busy as predicted. Her phone was ringing as I entered her office, ten minutes early for our seven o'clock appointment, nearly knocking over a counselor on her way out, with a girl hot on my heels, pleading, "Miss Nadine! Miss Nadine! I got to talk to you about my roommate!" There were foot-high stacks of manila folders on Nadine's desk; had she not been standing, she would have been invisible behind them.

"Don't forget to call Charmaine!" she called after the counselor, picking up the phone. "Hello? Come in! Not you!"

It took five minutes for everything to be resolved—"No, Officer, we had no knowledge of any out-of-state warrants. We'll transfer her belongings in the morning. Thank you. And you—I told you, we're not moving your room again. Well, I'm sorry she disrespected your religion, but we don't have any open beds. You've got to learn to get along. Now go."

She turned her attention to me, like, *You're still here? Okay, then—welcome to air-traffic controller school.* She stood five feet nine or ten, broad and imposing in her smock dress, her hands on her hips, unruffled.

"Busy night," I observed.

"Not unusual," she said.

She indicated the visitor's chair, and I sat, as she did, pushing two stacks of folders to the side. She shuffled through some loose papers on her desk until she found my application, and frowned at it like she hadn't seen it before. I doubted she had. She looked up at me, clearly dubious about this small, freckled white girl with hoop earrings and ponytail and backpack. Her eyebrows gathered, and her brown eyes locked on mine.

"So, JuhNEECE. Why do you want to volunteer with us here?"

JuhNEECE. Her lilting West Indies accent, the backward pronunciation of my name—it brought me right back to the age of fifteen, when I was living at the group home, and the meanest counselor, Mavis, would bellow at me from under her batik head wrap, *JuhNEECE!* That word, said in just that way, meant bad things—I'd been busted smoking a cigarette out the window of my room; I was getting raked over the coals in group therapy; I was getting double chores that week and no phone privileges. Nineteen years later, it still made me want to flinch.

I smiled instead, keeping my eyes steady on Nadine's. "Well, as I said on the application, I'm a former resident, and I wanted to give something back—this place did so much for me when I was fifteen."

"Really." Nadine's eyebrows unknotted, and she tipped her head to the side. "That's interesting."

"Nineteen eighty-four," I confirmed proudly. "Two months in the minors' wing."

"Okay." She nodded, holding my gaze for a long moment. She had a stare like a hypnotist, or a detective; I wanted to break down under it and confess everything. *The truth is, I'd be a terrible volunteer. I don't know what the hell I'm doing here. I smoke way too much pot. I'm thirty-four, and I still act like I'm fifteen.*

I laughed a little and started babbling. "Of course, I mean, a lot's changed for me since then—I reconciled with my family, got a lot of therapy—I'm a pretty solid citizen these days. I have a nice apartment and a good job, and I guess I feel like I'm at a place in my life where I'm ready to give something back."

She nodded again, more decisive this time. Now that she knew my angle, she could afford to be maybe 10 percent less wary of me. I could still hear the 90 percent circumspection in her voice as she continued. "So you're familiar with our population—you know the types of clients we serve. Runaways, throwaways, addicts, kids who just got out of foster care or jail. The girls on this floor are ages eighteen through twenty—a lot of them are pregnant, or have children of their own staying with relatives, or in the system. A lot of them are emotionally disturbed. They have post-traumatic stress. They've been abused, they've been in the sex trade. Some of them are illegal immigrants. Some of them are HIV-positive. You know that, right, Juh*neece?*"

Her eyes stayed locked on mine, watching me for signs of fear or squeamishness. I hoped I was doing a good job of masking them. "I'm aware," I said.

"And did they tell you the rules for volunteers? No physical contact with the residents of any kind. You're not allowed to give them anything, including money, and you're not allowed to accept anything from them. Try not to play favorites; treat everyone the same. Everything they tell you is confidential, unless they're going to hurt themselves or someone else; if so, you tell staff right away. And you don't ever try to break up a fight; you back away and call for security."

I nodded seriously, acknowledging each item on the list as she detailed it—"Uh-huh, of course, right."

I was in way over my head, and we both knew it. I was completely unprepared to deal with a bunch of pregnant immigrants with criminal records and post-traumatic stress. And if there was a fight, I was going to hurl myself under the nearest piece of furniture and sit there with my ass sticking out like an ostrich until help came. Her unspoken judgment of me was right; I was a poser, a well-intended cream puff looking for some street cred; I was flaky, I'd never make it. *Just let me get through this interview*, I told myself. *I'll worry about the rest of it later.*

"All right," she said. She leaned back in her chair, faintly smiling. "So when do you want to start. Tomorrow?"

"Oh! Wow." Nadine's smile broadened at my obvious surprise. I'd been dying to get started, but now I felt unprepared somehow, like I needed to shop for supplies, or pack a suitcase, or get a degree in social work or something. "Well, I have some commitments after work tomorrow, but—"

"Uh-huh." There was a knock on the door, and she looked up, ready to be done with me and move on. "Just a minute!"

"But I could start next Wednesday. I could come in after work, around five-thirty? Would that be good?"

The knocking continued. "Miss Nadine!" She picked up her pen, hovering over her calendar, and looked at me with a devilish grin, like, *Last chance to change your mind.* I looked back at her, earnest and unblinking.

"Wednesday at five-thirty," she said, writing it down. "Juh*neece.*"

Nadine rose from behind her desk, and I rose as well, my backpack sliding awkwardly off my lap onto the floor. I stooped to get it, laughing at myself, saying "Whoops!" like an idiot. I managed to collect myself and shook her outstretched hand.

"You know," she said, almost incredulous, as she put her hand on my shoulder to steer me out. "I think you might do all right here."

My first shift: an abject failure.

I showed up early and eager and knocked on Nadine's door, ready to present myself for service, but she wasn't there. So I turned to check in at the counselors' office down the hall, where I interrupted a heated discussion between two girls and a young female counselor regarding whose fake hair belonged to whom.

"Hi," I said. "I'm the new volunteer."

The counselor did not address me; the two girls ignored me as well. Another young female counselor was on the phone; a third counselor, a twenty-something guy with glasses and a shaved head, glanced up from his paperwork and looked at me. "Uh, okay, why don't you hang out in the lounge for now, and see if anybody needs anything."

He turned back to his paperwork, and I backed out of the office, obviously in the way. There was nobody in the lounge when I entered, just a large-screen TV playing a rerun of *Full House* on mute. I lay my coat on a grimy, beat-up sofa and sat down.

Now what.

Nothing, for a while, and then two girls came down the hallway speaking Spanish to each other. The only words I could make out from my undergraduate days were *ahora* and *también*. Now and also. "*Veinte dólares*," said one. I lingered by the lounge entrance and smiled in their direction as they passed. I didn't know how to say, *So, ladies, is there anything I can help you with?* in Spanish. *Any outstanding emotional issues you'd like to discuss with a total stranger?* They giggled, pushed open the door to the stairwell, and were gone. So much for helping them.

I sat and sat, alone in the lounge as the TV went from *Everybody Loves Raymond* to *Family Matters* to *The Parkers*, perking up the few times I heard voices in the hall. Once, a girl nearly entered the room—she poked her head inside for a second, then yanked it out. "She ain't in there," I heard her say to whomever she was traveling with. "Ain't nobody in there right now." Then silence for another half hour. I hadn't brought anything to read—I wasn't supposed to be reading, I was supposed to be *helping*—but no girls were making themselves available to be helped. I sat and listened to the *clunk . . . clunk* of the second hand on the old school clock on the wall.

Finally, at seven o'clock, I couldn't stand it anymore. I'd said I'd stay through nine, but I couldn't imagine sitting there a single second longer, in that terrible, inert air, on a sofa that stank like feet, doing nothing besides proving my own existential uselessness. So I left. I just hopped up and walked out. Didn't stop by the counselors' office to say good night, just blew past the sign-out sheet at the front desk. The two Spanish-speaking girls were sharing a cigarette on the corner. They didn't notice me as I hurried by.

Stupid, I told myself, rocking back and forth in my seat on the subway home. I shouldn't have given up so easily. I should have at least stayed. I mean, what was I going to do now? After weeks of yammering to everyone about my plans to volunteer, and how profoundly life-changing it was going to be, I couldn't just flake out after my first shift.

Two days later it came to me, the thing that would help me get in with the girls: beads. I'd worked at a bead store when I was in college, and I still had a shopping bag full of supplies in my closet—all my old tools and materials, packs and packs of seed beads, perfect for making friendship bracelets, earrings, necklaces, what have you. I could bring my beads with me, set them up in the lounge; maybe people would spot them on their way past and stop in to see what was up. And okay, it was tantamount to bribing the girls to sit and talk with me, but I didn't see any other way to get them close enough for me to *listen to* and *believe* them.

That night, I went digging in my closet. The cats, initially attracted by the noise, scattered as I hefted the shopping bag full of rattling plastic boxes, bags, and vials, a few loose beads raining from a small hole in the bottom. I used to spend hours making jewelry when I was these girls' age—it was therapeutic, especially during my college-era depression, but I burned out on it in my early twenties. Still, it looked like I had enough supplies on hand to keep a whole flotilla of girls handily occupied for a week. I started sorting through the contents of the bag, gloating over my own ingenuity.

My second shift: an unqualified success.

I was nervous, coming down the block with my heavy, clattering bag of beads, but I kept my head up, smiling at the two butch girls on the corner, one with a pick stuck in the back of her picked-out 'fro. This time I was prepared to sit all night in the empty lounge if I had to, but I'd also prepared myself to be more assertive in my volunteering. "How you doin' tonight?" I asked the girls as I passed.

There was no audible reply.

I checked in with the counselors again—they, barely, duly noted my presence—then headed into the empty lounge to set up shop on the long conference table in the back. I'd just started unpacking my supplies when a short, gap-toothed girl in a head wrap strode past the entrance, saw me there with the glittering pile of beads, turned around, and came over to the table.

"How you doin', miss? What's this, arts and crafts? It's free? TENEISHA! TENEISHA! Come over here, we got arts and crafts today!"

Her name was Precious, and she and her roommate, Teneisha, sat right down next to me at the table and started sorting through the beads like old ladies at a swap meet. Precious, I quickly learned, was from Brooklyn, and she worked at McDonald's. Teneisha was from North Carolina, and she wanted to become a model.

I glowed, thinking about it the next day—talking with them, how self-aware they were. Precious, making a crystal-colored bracelet, telling us about her abusive father—"I am *not* my mama, and I am *not* my aunt, and I am *not* my grandma neither; I will not let *any* man put his hands on me, or my child when I have one. Not me. I'ma have a *better* life." She waved her arm to indicate the dingy room, the cinder-block walls. "I'd rather come kick it here, do what I gotta do. It's grimy, but it's better than where I came from." She was so motivated, so full of faith and optimism that life was going to get better. The shelter was just the first step for Precious.

Precious stayed at my side all night, making bracelet after bracelet, even after Teneisha was distracted by a gentleman caller from the boys' floor—literally a caller, who stood in the hallway outside the forbidden Older Females Unit calling, 'NEISHA! YO TENEISHA! until she slammed her beads down on the table and went to go deal with her admirer. Precious and I talked about her job in the Mickey D's kitchen (hot, she said, but better than working the counter, where you had to deal with the public), her lifelong desire to be a writer/producer/TV host ("Like Oprah," she elaborated; "that's me in ten years"), and her disappointment with the ongoing Michael Jackson child-abuse trial. "I *know* Michael is innocent," she swore. "I just *know* him. I've been listening to his music since I was a little girl."

Which was when? I wondered, looking at her wide brown eyes, the baby fat under her chin. *Two weeks ago?*

The next Wednesday seemed like such a long time to wait to see her again; I thought about maybe dropping by the shelter on Friday after work for an hour or two, just to volunteer a little more. I might have even mentioned the possibility to Precious—"Maybe I'll stop by on Friday and we can hang out." It wasn't against the rules to volunteer a few extra hours a week, was it? I figured I should be welcome to drop by anytime, even if I wasn't on Nadine's schedule. It would just be extra credit.

Nadine had warned me: *Don't play favorites; treat everybody the same.* That probably meant I shouldn't go by on Friday to hang out with Precious. Right? I thought about it all day Thursday—her shy smile with the gap between her teeth; the way her face lit up when I told her I'd bring some Michael Jackson CDs with me next time. I thought about it on my way to the grocery store that evening, passing the shoeless guy lying on the street wrapped in a filthy blanket, the hunchbacked woman, face obscured by a plastic bonnet, with her shopping cart full of empty cans. I thought about it as I mixed a special old-school Michael Jackson compilation, including a song Precious had mentioned as a favorite, "She's Out of My Life."

And I smiled, remembering how she'd helped me clean up the loose beads at the end of my shift. How she'd grabbed the broom and dustpan—"I do this every night, at my job"—and made short, efficient work of sweeping the floor. How she shook my hand on my way out and called after me as I headed down the stairs—"Bye, Bead Lady!"

What the hell, I thought. I'd known it since the interview: I was in over my head.

Chapter Two

New Favorite Alert

Nine months later, nearly Thanksgiving, and I was still breaking the no-favorites rule. I'd been breaking it since my second week of volunteering, when I went to the shelter on that unscheduled Friday to bring the CD I'd burned for Precious. But Precious wasn't there. Her friend Teneisha saw me lurking around the block and told me the good news: Precious had been moved to a different program, at a better, longer-term facility. She was, as Michael Jackson sang, out of my life.

You might have thought I'd have learned from that day, dragging my feet back down the block in a daze, bereft; maybe I might have figured out that playing favorites was going to hurt me more than it hurt anybody else. And then I met Amaryllis. A member of the Latin Queens, a reforming cokehead with six months in Rikers Island under her belt, she threw herself down at the bead table with a whoop—"Ho-oh! What's this? What's this all about? I want to make me some beads!" She had that throaty voice, that wild energy, and she was razor-sharp, dispensing wisdom to the rest of the girls who floated by—"Girl, don't let them put you in the mental-health program. You got nothing wrong with you, you don't need no Section 8 voucher. You want to go live in the projects with all the other Section 8s? Once you go Section 8, what happens when you wanna get a job, get a real place? Tell me you never gonna wanna get a job. You wanna live in the pj's all your life? Not me, miss. I want to live good. I want to live for real. They ain't gonna put me in mental health, not me."

I loved Amaryllis. She sat with me for four weeks at the bead table, always right there at my shoulder, making long black-and-yellow necklaces, her old gang colors, which I never saw her wear. I made her promise me that nobody was going to get shot because of the gang beads—"Please, miss," she assured me, rolling her eyes. "The beads is the least of it. Once you bangin', you bangin'. If anything, these protect you."

Then she relapsed, hard. I came in one night, and she was being carried out in an ambulance, with a police car behind it. The counselors had discovered her coked to the gills, raving with paranoia and shaking, and they sent her to detox at a hospital on Staten Island. I would never see or hear from her again; I'd never know what happened to her after that. Just, good-bye, Amaryllis.

After Amaryllis came Jerrine. Jerrine broke the no-hugging rule for me right away. "Miss, I love you," she told me, throwing her arms around me for a squeeze. How could I not hug her back? Jerrine had a two-year-old son who'd been permanently placed in foster care; she'd met her abusive ex-husband here at the shelter when they were both minors. Now she was back, solo, working at Subway, making a baby-blue bracelet with the name HECTOR on it. It was too tight, but she wore it anyway, rolling it up and down her arm, rubbing the indents it left on her wrist. She was supposed to move to a better program, and then she went AWOL. Good-bye, Jerrine.

After Jerrine was Belinda, from Ecuador—she got so good at making earrings, I bought an extra set of pliers just for her to use, and the rest of the girls clamored for her to make something for them. "Do one for me, Belinda, like you do, with the loops; it looks fancy that way." Belinda and I spent a month of Wednesdays with each other over that summer; I even dreamed of taking her on a day trip to

Coney Island with me and Bill, but I knew it would never happen—the rules expressly forbade it. Then she graduated to Independent Living. *Adiós*, Belinda.

It didn't stop hurting, and I didn't stop doing it, finding new favorites. Coming home and raving to Bill, "Tiffany, her mother died of AIDS when she was sixteen. And she's so funny—'That motherfucker's so white, he's blue!'" "Hazel, she's my new favorite, she's the sweetest thing, making a necklace for her stuffed elephant." "Mimi, she's this teeny-tiny stone butch, and she rules the lounge—she made everybody clean up their beads and tell me thank you at the end of the night."

Breaking the favorites rule, breaking the confidentiality rule, telling Bill everything the girls told me. Justifying it by telling myself that Bill wasn't ever going to meet these girls, as curious as he was about them. And he was curious—every week, he'd ask me, "So how's Brenda? How's Priscilla? How's St. Lucia?" and I'd run down the list. "She's all right; she just found out she's having twins; she got discharged for fighting." And every week there was the unspoken question behind it, the one I didn't know enough to ask myself—*Have you found her yet? The one who reminds you of you?*

They all reminded me of me. Black, Latin, Indian, it didn't matter what color they were; whether they were gay, pregnant, Christian, or all three. They were fierce, they were confused, they were striving, they were in pain. And yet none of them reminded me of me. None of their stories matched mine. I had yet to meet a middle-class white girl, not pregnant, no kids, not too much of a drug addict yet, who just couldn't hack it at home. More than that, none of them *felt* like Little Janice to me.

Until Sam.

I met her right around Thanksgiving, sitting alone in the cafeteria—this tall, rangy, white girl with a shaggy mop of brown hair, a grunge-butch affect, and a cast on her hand, cheerfully shoveling meat loaf and mashed potatoes into her mouth. I hadn't seen her the week before; she was probably new. Probably in need of someone to eat dinner with.

"Can I join you?" I asked, motioning toward the empty seat across from her.

She continued chewing, eyebrows slightly raised, and signaled a welcome with her busted hand. I sat.

"How's that doing?" I asked, pointing to the cast.

She waved her hand, *So-so*, and swallowed. "It hurts a lot. I snapped a ligament in my wrist. I have to have surgery before I can go to rehab."

"Ouch," I said, wincing in sympathy. "How'd it happen?"

"Punched a wall." She grinned a little. "I thought it was just Sheetrock, but it turned out to be concrete."

She had a hint of a West Coast accent, or something, I couldn't exactly place it, and there was a frankness in her voice, something knowing and wry. The way she said "rehab"—so matter-of-fact, with no dread, no shame—she might as well have said, "I have to have surgery before I can go to the bank." Rehab was just a place she had to go. And she met my eyes easily, her own eyes large and clear. Most of the girls avoided eye contact; that's why the beads were such a handy trick—they didn't have to be looking at anybody while they talked; they could look at their hands. This girl looked at me like she was studying me, memorizing me, and unafraid to have me do the same.

"You gotta be careful about punching unfamiliar walls," I cautioned, smiling. "Apparently, some of them punch back."

She raised the wrist as proof that I was right. "When I was a kid, my dad used to punch out all the windows. Then he'd put boards over them, and then he'd punch out the boards."

"Sounds like a great dad."

She smiled with one side of her mouth, her eyes still on mine, and I felt that instant rapport, that excitement—*new favorite alert*. In truth, I never chose any of my favorites; my favorites were the ones who chose me, the ones who acted like they'd just been waiting for me to sit down next to them so they could spill their stories: "I don't tell anybody this, but I trust you, miss." And maybe they'd told someone before and maybe they hadn't, but right now they were choosing *me*, because I made them feel safe; they were going to imprint on me for the next three hours, or five minutes, whatever it was, while I sat there feeling honored and astonished and vitally important for as long as it lasted.

So it went with Samantha—"Sam," she introduced herself, formally shaking my hand with her good one. She was nineteen, she said, and had been on the streets since she was twelve. I asked her where she was from, and she laughed. "All over." Her father cooked crystal meth for a living, and whenever the heat got too hot or the kitchen blew up, the family would move—Sam, her brother and sister, their meth-cooking dad, and their junkie hooker mom. From the Florida Panhandle to the outskirts of Chicago, through Arizona, Texas, and Colorado—that's where she ran away from, Colorado. She was tired, she said, of what her parents did to her, what they made her do for money and drugs. "I figured, fuck it, I can get my own money and drugs."

I walked out of the cafeteria with her, and we paused under the scaffold that surrounded the building so she could smoke a cigarette. She told me about Portland, Oregon, and the street scene there; about how easy they made it to be homeless in San Francisco. She told me how, just a month ago, she was sitting in a doorway in Cheyenne, Wyoming—

"And it was that half rain, half snow, the kind that really stings when it hits you, you know? And it was coming in from all sides, even in the doorway, I couldn't get away from it, and all my clothes were wet, and I was freezing, and dope sick, I really needed another hit, but I couldn't get any because I didn't have any money or any way to get any, and I said to myself, 'I am tired of living this way.'"

Her brown eyes still met mine as she spoke, her voice clear and sincere. Nearly six feet tall and as hard-assed as any of the kids I'd met, and yet there was something so vulnerable in her face.

"And all night that night, I did the 'poor me' thing, and I got mad at my parents and my fucked-up life and everything, and I just felt so fucking sorry for myself. It was the worst night of my life.

"So I tried to figure out what kind of life I wanted. And the first thing I knew was that I wanted to get a place to live indoors. And then

I knew I needed to get a job to get money for rent, and that nobody was going to hire a junkie. So I decided to quit using."

Over the next week, she said, she put together some money from meth deals and got on a bus to New York. She figured the meth scene wasn't as big in New York, she wouldn't know any dealers here, she'd be forced to kick it. Within two hours, she'd scored a bag of her second-choice drug, heroin, and snorted it. But she was trying not to shoot it, trying to keep increasing the hours between fixes, sleeping on the street around Port Authority during the day.

One night a woman walked by and saw her sitting on the sidewalk, dope sick. She shook her head, assessed her, and told Sam to go to the shelter, right down the block; she said they'd help her there. And Sam peeled her sick, aching bones off the cement and came in from the cold, for the first time in seven years.

"I'm really glad you came here," I said.

"So am I," she said, earnest. "It's hard, dealing with all the rules and the other residents and stuff, but this is, like, the best place I ever been."

I was late in reporting to the floor after dinner, and the rest of the girls were probably waiting upstairs for the Bead Lady, but I lingered while Sam carefully stubbed out her cigarette, saving the few unsmoked centimeters in her near-empty pack. Together we trudged back inside and up the stairs to the Older Females Unit.

Samantha had been at the shelter for ten days already, she told me as we huffed up the stairs, and had used heroin twice. They didn't catch her, so she went to the drug counselor, Jodi, and told on herself. "Listen," she told Jodi, "I don't want to keep using drugs; please help me get into rehab soon." Jodi congratulated Sam on her honesty and gave her a full house restriction. Sam was not allowed to leave the premises, all day and all night, except for doctor's appointments, but she was okay with that. "It's what I gotta do right now," she said with a shrug. Then she took a seat at the bead table and, even with the cast on her hand, started making a key chain for Jodi the drug counselor.

It was a busy night at the bead table, but I pretty much neglected everyone else—the shy Panamanian girl from the week before seemed to be adjusting well. One girl made six pairs of earrings, put the clips on herself, no help from me, didn't say a word but looked satisfied. A girl named Heaven showed off her sonogram photo. There was a bossy girl from Baltimore named Ellenette, and another girl who made earrings that said SEXXY, except the Y was upside down. Ellenette asked me to read her horoscope from the paper—not because she couldn't read but because her eyes hurt.

Sam bantered easily with the other girls, praising the shy girl's bracelet-in-progress, busting on Ellenette for believing in astrology. ("You don't believe in astrology?" asked Ellenette. "Naw," said Sam. "I believe in astrophysics.") Every once in a while she looked up at me and caught me looking at her, but she didn't seem to mind. She just gave me that half-smile, her lips flattened like she was trying to suppress it.

"This is pretty meticulous work," she observed.

Meticulous, I noted. Where the hell did she get *that* word from?

I could have stayed forever that night, but I'd learned to set limits for myself long ago, back in the days when I used to hang out with Amaryllis until it was time for the nightly floor meeting, until I was starving and mentally fried and practically weeping on the subway home. "Almost time to pack up," I told the girls regretfully.

A few of the girls sauntered off; I got a shy "Good-bye, miss" from Panama. Sam pushed her chair back and started sweeping the stray beads into piles, bagging the reds and yellows as best she could with her one and a half hands. She must have spied the notebook sticking out of my tote bag as she handed me the beads. "You write?" she asked.

"Every day," I replied. "Keeps me from going insane."

"Me too," she said. "You wanna see something I wrote?"

"Uh, *yeah*. I'd love to."

She fished a folded piece of paper from her back pocket, dirty around the creased edges, like she'd been carrying it for a while, and passed it to me. It was a poem. Stern and plain, exactly metered—like Dickinson, or Donne, if Dickinson or Donne were a homeless teenage junkie—and short, maybe twelve lines long. The last two lines:

Let me live how I want to live;
Let me die when I want to die.

My eyes filled with tears. She observed. I knew I wasn't supposed to be hugging anybody, it was against the rules, but it was tempting as hell to put my arms around her. Not that she was asking me to.

"This is great," I said, passing it back to her. "It's really great."

She shrugged again, nonchalant, as she stuffed the poem back into her pocket, but I could see the half-smile trying to break through. "Thanks."

I looked around for any last few beads to corral, but the table was clean; it was time to go. I put on my coat, picked up my bag, patted my pockets, shuffled my feet. "Well, it was great meeting you, Sam."

She gave me a funny wave-salute with her cast hand. "Nice to meet you, too. And . . . thanks."

Thanks. It pierced me, that one word. She shouldn't have been thanking me—I was the one who'd been favored. She didn't even know how much.

"Thank *you*," I told her, smiling. "I hope I'll see you next week."

I was still dumbstruck when I got home that night, petted the swarm of cats at my shins, and kissed Bill hello.

"Welcome home, Shmoo."

Bill had moved in with me just weeks before, at my invitation—one of the many signs of the progress I'd made since I started volunteering. He was my family, I'd realized; I couldn't watch him walk around like a man without a country anymore, schlepping his overnight bag full of essentials everywhere he went, like the kids at the shelter did. It was time for him to come home.

"How'd it go tonight?" he asked, grating cheese for the dinner he'd started.

I put my stuff down, kicked off my shoes, and lit the longest roach in the ashtray, waving the smoke away from him—Bill didn't share my fondness for the stuff. "Well, I can't even believe the girl I met tonight."

He grinned at me. "Oh yeah? Tell me about her."

I shook my head. "Oh my god. Worst life story! She's been homeless—like hard-core, street homeless—since she was twelve years old. Totally fending for herself, living the life, dealing drugs—anyway, the thing is, she's a genius. She's unbelievable. She's this amazing writer, and she's read everything; she's quoting the *Tao Te Ching* to me—"

"A junkie savant," he observed. "Interesting."

I kept it up through dinner, talking about my amazing discovery, my priceless find. Bill listened patiently, taking seconds as I rambled on, barely touching my food. "And she's got this homemade tattoo, it just says, PSALMS 22—you know, 'My Lord, My Lord, why hast thou forsaken me—'"

"Wow," he finally interrupted. "Sounds like you had an intense night up there."

I'd been talking nonstop about Sam since I got home—not a word about Bill, or anything else, for that matter. "Yeah, it was," I said, sheepish. "But. Anyway. How was your day?"

"Okay." He smiled a little. "Not as interesting as yours."

"Oh, honey." I wrinkled my brow, guilty. Of course I was interested in Bill's day. He always had stories from his job at one of the city's daily papers, stories that featured guys with names like "Big Jim" and "Duke." You could practically smell the ink on Bill at night, though the printing press was a borough away from his desk.

"Well, there were definitely some shenanigans in the morning meeting . . ."

Seven years, I thought. *She's been on the streets for seven years. She's practically feral, and yet she's so tame. I wonder if anybody realizes how intelligent she is. I wonder if she knows. She certainly must have figured out that she's not like other people, she's not like the other girls there. They seem to respect her—they can tell she's been through hell, that's why. She's more hard-core than most of the girls in there, the gangbangers and the jailbirds. . . .*

"Anyway." Bill waved his hand, sweeping it all away. "That's the report. Same bullshit, different day."

"Well. Huh. That's . . ." I couldn't think of anything to say. "Huh."

He poured himself another glass of wine, regarded me over its rim. "So, this girl—how long has she been there now?"

A pent-up rush of air escaped me. "Ten days. They've lined up a bed for her in a yearlong rehab program; she'll go there sometime after her wrist surgery. I'm not sure where they send them—Staten Island, I think, or Westchester."

"So will you get to see her next week? Or will she be gone by then?"

I bit my lip. "I don't know. I'm hoping she'll still be there." A selfish hope, as always—if I cared about this girl, I'd want her to get to rehab as fast as she could. But how often did you meet somebody like this? She was a rare specimen, a real unicorn. You couldn't blame me for wanting to hang out and hand-feed her some carrots for a while.

"Well, she sounds pretty interesting. Sounds like you're really impressed with her."

"I am," I confessed. "I mean, I just met her, but I have this feeling . . ."

Bill smiled at me, rueful. He knew the feeling; it was written all over my face. Love at first sight, I believe they call it.

He raised his wineglass and toasted me. "Well, babe, I hope it works out for you."

No *favorites*, Nadine had told me. And *no presents*. And yet there I was, stopping at the drugstore on the way to the shelter the next Wednesday, buying a spiral-bound notebook just like the one I carried in my bag, and a box of blue ballpoint pens. There I was, resting the notebook on my knee as I balanced against the wall outside, opening the notebook to the first page, writing:

Dear Sam,
I want to let you know that you are an amazing writer,
with great talent, and I've been thinking about your poem

all week. I know things are very hard right now, but I also
believe that if you hang in there, you will succeed in
everything you want to do, and that I will read your work
in books someday. I hope you know how very special and
talented you are, and I hope you know that I'll be thinking
about you wherever you go.
    Janice

I put the notebook in my bag and soldiered on toward the shelter.
It was doubtful that Sam would still be there today, doubtful that
she'd just go through withdrawal right there in the middle of the
lounge, detox with no support while waiting to go to rehab. I'd met
girls who were waiting for rehab before—there was Jill, the crack-
head from Pennsyltuckey; she wound up using here and there just to
keep the edge off, or so it appeared to me. I wondered if others saw
what I saw—the dull, red eyes, the bleary stare—and turned a blind
eye. I mean, Jill followed all the shelter rules, except for maybe the
one about not smoking crack; she was honestly trying to make it to
rehab so she could quit, on account of her being pregnant. But I don't
know what happened to Jill in the end—if she made it to rehab, or if
she was sent to detox with a police escort behind her ambulance, or
if she simply wandered away one day, tired of waiting for her bed to
come up.
    I waved at the guard in the booth out front, signed in at the front
desk, walked past (but not through) the metal detector, and went into
the cafeteria. There was Sam, sitting alone at a corner table, staring
at a Styrofoam cup of fruit punch like it was ipecac.
    "Hey!" I approached her gleefully, there was no hiding my excite-
ment, but she didn't look well—her skin was pale and sweaty, and
there were purple circles under her eyes. She looked up at me,
caught my eyes with her plaintive ones, and she looked *strung out*,
like she really would have appreciated some heroin right about then.
And all I had for her was a notebook with an inspirational message
instead.
    She gave me a brave smile, then winced and put her hand on her

back, as though the smile had been too strenuous. "Hey, how are you?"

I dropped into the chair next to her, alarmed. "I'm fine, but you don't look so good. Are you all right?"

She started to nod, then corrected herself and shook her head. "Well, yeah . . . no. They're gonna take me to the hospital after dinner, as soon as someone can go with me."

"Oh, no way!" *No hugging*, I reminded myself sternly. Especially not the ones who looked like they were about to puke. "What happened?"

"Well . . ." She looked reticent for a minute, like she didn't want to tell me, like she was going to think up a lie. I watched her turn it over in her head, saw her face soften a little. She leaned toward me, dropped her voice. "I kind of did something I wasn't supposed to."

"What's that?" I asked, sympathetic.

"Well, you know, I been trying not to use, I been here on house restriction all week, but last night, it got real bad, and this kid from the guys' floor had these hypnotics on him—"

"Wait, what are hypnotics?" I interrupted. Galling, that they kept inventing new designer drugs after I'd quit doing them.

"Like, downers. Vikes, Oxys, stuff like that. Anyway, I was going crazy in here, so I bought a bunch of pills from this kid, and . . . I took 'em. And I kinda OD'd a little bit." She flashed me a hangdog smile, like, *Oops. Don't be mad.* "I wasn't trying to kill myself or anything, I just wanted to be out of it for a little while, you know?"

Yeah, I knew. If we'd had hypnotics back in my day, I probably would have spent a lot of my time hypnotized. "So what happened? They found you unconscious?"

"No, see, I took 'em before bed, and this morning, when I didn't respond at first, they didn't know what it was. I mean, they knew I was real sick, but . . ." Here she leaned in farther, and her voice lowered even more. "See, I have these bad kidneys, from all the meth and the other stuff I did, and they know my kidneys are bad, so I just told them that's what it was, my kidneys acting up, and maybe it'd get better. But they still want to take me to the hospital, 'cause I been trying to play it off, but . . ." She gestured helplessly and grimaced with the pain it caused her, then flashed that hangdog smile again.

I wanted to squeeze her shoulder, pat her head, tell her it was going to be okay, tell her how glad I was that she was going to the hospital, as scary as that might be. Tell her I knew how hard she'd been working to stay at the shelter, how much she didn't want to mess up her chance at rehab. She'd been so forthright with them, even asked them to make her stay indoors all day, just so she wouldn't be tempted to use, but it wasn't enough—they couldn't protect her, in the end.

"Well, I hope it goes okay at the hospital. And I hope they'll let me know how you're doing. I know we just met last week, but . . . you know, I brought something for you."

Her face brightened. "Really?"

"Don't get excited—it's not an Oxy or a Vike." I mugged at her as I dug in my bag and fished out the notebook, put it on the table with the box of pens. I pushed them toward her casually, like we were conducting a drug deal in a restaurant.

"Wow, for me?" She waited until I nodded to take the notebook, holding it carefully as she read the inscription. "Wow. Wow, this is so nice of you. Thanks."

So sincere, her thanks, her voice clear and sweet, high with surprise. She sounded like a girl, for a change, and for a second the audible pain was gone. Then she winced again and groped for her back.

"You're welcome," I said, wincing along with her.

One of the counselors—Rina, a thin young woman who always held her arms folded over her chest as though she were cold—came over to collect Sam. We traded how-you-doin's. "You ready to go?" Rina asked Sam.

"Uh-huh. Just gotta take my notebook." Sam caught my eye and smiled. She rolled the notebook and stuffed it into one of the giant pockets of her cargo pants, tucked the pens in there, too. "All right. Maybe I'll see you next week, I hope."

"I hope so, too," I told her, holding that look. "Good luck, and take care."

• ■ •

The rest of the shift went by without incident, not that I would have noticed anything short of a shooting or a stabbing, and only if it was right in front of my face. The week—the week dragged on interminably. I worked (freelance these days, from my desk at home), petted the cats, watched hours of TV after dinner with Bill.

Finally, finally, finally, finally, Wednesday. Finally.

I knew better than to hope Samantha would still be there; I'd had my heart broken before. How many times had I practically skipped down the block, thinking *Precious, Amaryllis, Jerrine, Belinda*; how many times had I been wrong? Sam could have still been in the hospital, for all I knew; she could have been discharged for smoking a cigarette in her room; she could have decided she was sick of this shit and walked away. I knew better than to hope, but it didn't stop me from doing it anyway.

I showed up ten minutes early for dinner, landing at the top of the stairs on the Older Females Unit out of breath, too anxious to wait for the elevator.

"Bead Lady!" yelled Ellenette, the bossy girl from Baltimore, from her seat in front of the TV. "You came early!"

"I sure did," I agreed, smiling at her. *Yell louder,* I thought. *So everyone in their rooms can hear.*

Samantha came around a corner with a small bag of clean laundry in her cast hand. "Hey!" she said, pleased. "I forgot you came tonight. Cool."

"Yeah." I grinned. She didn't forget, I could tell; she was just trying to play it cool. Which proved how much she liked me. "How's it going? I was worried about you."

She nodded. "It's good, thanks. Better. I was only at the emergency room for a few hours. My kidneys are still messed up, but they're not so bad right now. They told me in a few years I might need dialysis. But I'm okay right now."

"Oh, wow. Dialysis. Jesus."

"Yeah." She looked downcast at the possibility but quickly perked back up. "Hey, thanks for the notebook. I been writing in it a lot; do you wanna see it?"

I laughed, giddy with the pleasure of her company, her enthusiasm, her writing. "Of course!" She put down her laundry and fished the notebook out of its cargo pocket. Its cover was worn, and it had already acquired a satisfying curve from being curled up and stuffed in its place. She flipped through it, located a page she liked, and handed it to me.

That handwriting—careful, shaky, spiky, every letter distinct, straight up and down, like it took hours to etch, and that was with her good hand. The poem was about watching the stars from the back of a pickup truck, hitchhiking by the constellations. You could feel every bit of it: the piney smell of the Oregon trees, the jolt of the rocks in the road. I cleared my throat, which had gone froggy, and closed the book.

"This is great," I understated. "I mean, this could get published. I'm serious. I could even help you. I know people—"

She reached out for it, demurring, and I didn't want to hand it back to her, but I did. "Naw," she said. "It's just for me. And . . . people I choose to share it with."

I basked in the glow of the compliment as she went off to stash her laundry in her room, and the rest of us filed downstairs for dinner and lined up outside the cafeteria. The other girls clamored in her absence—"Miss, we gonna do beads after dinner? How late you stay till? I gotta go meet my man, but I'ma come up and make some beads with you before you go. Bead Lady, you got more pink this week?"

I got my tray and grabbed the corner table; Sam came along shortly and joined me. Ellenette put her tray down at the next table, observing the two of us already gabbing away—"So, who do you like to read?" "Kerouac's all right, and I like Bukowski." "Have you ever read Augusten Burroughs?" "No, who's that?"

"Miss, Bead Lady," Ellenette said, pouting. "Why you love the white girl so much, and not me?" She was kidding, but she had a point, and she'd made it loud enough for everyone to overhear. "Why don't you pull up your chair with us," I suggested. "I can't love you so much if you're all the way at the other table."

And so Ellenette was glued to my side all evening, from the cafeteria to the bead table, where I had an unusual number of takers; every seat around the table filled up fast, and the action was spilling over to the couches. The girl they called St. Croix took the seat immediately to my left, the seat Sam wanted. "Move down," Sam insisted, trying to poke her chair between mine and St. Croix's.

"Move yourself, heifer," said St. Croix genially. "Don't sleep, next time." But she scooted over a few inches to her left, and Sam shoved her long legs between our short ones.

"Can I have a J, an O, a D, and an I?"

I passed Samantha the box full of alphabet beads. I'd never met Jodi the drug counselor, but I'd heard about her from some of the other girls—she was one of those tough-but-fair types, like Nadine; the girls trusted her. Jodi had been an addict herself, like all the best drug counselors; with more than twenty years sober, she hadn't lost a single bit of empathy, or any of her street smarts. It was obvious that Sam had bonded with Jodi, the first adult she'd bonded with in a long time.

Funny, that I'd feel jealous of Jodi when there was a table full of girls entreating me—"Bead Lady, help me tie this? Lemme get a long string for a necklace? Can you put the hook on for me? Who's got the letters? Someone pass me the letters." It should have been enough attention for me; sometimes, in fact, it was too much. Sometimes I was so busy cutting and tying and hooking and gluing, I felt more like a shoe salesman than anything else. Nights like these, I barely even got to talk to the girls, barely got to *listen* and/or *believe*.

Still, I got to sit there, with Sam at my side, and even if we weren't all having the deepest conversation ("Usher is not gay, don't you dare say that about my boo"; "He's gay, son, I saw it in a gay magazine"), I could tell she was watching me, listening to me, observing everything I did. So when my golden moment came, as it so often did— "Miss, you pay for all these beads you bring? Out your own pocket? Why you do that?"—I took it and ran.

"Because I remember how boring it could be when I used to live here," I said, eyes on the string I was tying. "So I like to bring something with me when I come to hang out with you all."

"You used to live here?" The question didn't come from Sam, but it might as well have; I could read it all over her face, and I wasn't even looking at her.

"You didn't know that?" bellowed Ellenette from the chair on my right. "Bead Lady is old school."

"When were you here?" asked Sam politely.

"Twenty years ago," I told her, launching into my spiel. "Nineteen eighty-four. Right around this time of year—from November to January. Then I went to a group home for a year or so. I'm really grateful to this place—"

She interrupted me, incredulous. "Wait, *how* old are you?"

"Thirty-five. I was here when I was fifteen."

"You're *thirty-five*? You're only one year younger than my mother!"

Oh, the joys of volunteering. Having ten girls drop their bead projects to crane their necks and get a better look at you, insisting that you couldn't possibly be thirty-five, you couldn't be any older than twenty-five—"Miss, first time I saw you I thought you was a resident!"—there was no greater reward. I mean, most of it was the way I dressed in my downtime, with my scruffy jeans and Pumas, but when it actually worked—when one of the boys loitering outside whispered "'Sup," as I passed—well, I was probably a little bit too complimented by being mistaken for a twenty-year-old homeless girl.

"Thirty-five," I confirmed. "I am *seriously* old school."

Yeah, volunteering has always been a selfish enterprise for me. If I didn't recognize it before, I definitely felt it that night, sitting around feeling downright cozy in the company of my girls. *My* girls. I could use the possessive, couldn't I? Sure I could. I mean, who sought them out, who tended to them? Who was one of their own? Me! Carl the volunteer might have been there for fifteen years, but I was there *as a resident*. Plus, look at them. I gazed over the table beatifically, choosing to ignore the argument bubbling at the end of the table about the "sin" of homosexuality ("What you mean, you don't believe in being

gay? I'm gay and I'm sitting right here, you don't believe I exist?")—
look at how industrious they were, how young and sweet their faces
looked, their mouths slightly slack with absorption. How everything
else had melted away for them, except for the moment.

Sam, at my elbow. I looked up at her and she was looking at me;
she grinned a little and went back to the key chain she was making for
Jodi. It was one of the more intricate creations I'd seen, woven like a
braid with four separate strands of elastic. "This will be good," she
told me, "because it won't be, like, some stupid piece of jewelry she
feels like she has to wear or something."

"It's cool," I agreed. "And it's useful."

She shrugged one shoulder. "And if she doesn't like it, she can
just stick it in her drawer and forget about it."

"I bet she puts her keys on it," I said. I knew I would.

Samantha stayed at the bead table until cleanup time—until
about fifteen minutes after cleanup time, actually, because once
again I didn't feel like cleaning up and leaving. While most of the
girls had already made their fill of jewelry and wandered off, Sam
stayed put, helping me to bag the loose beads that other people had
neglected to put away. I went to the counselors' office to grab the
broom and dustpan, then made a last-minute detour and knocked on
Nadine's office door.

"Come in."

I didn't catch Nadine in her office very often, not that I tried to. I
knew she was there at all hours—nights, weekends, Fourth of July—
but it was still hard to get an audience with her. I entered her office,
crammed as usual with the recorded evidence of human misery, and
she turned briefly from her computer to greet me.

"Juh*neece*. How is everything?" She glanced back at her computer, like she'd prefer the short answer.

"Great," I said. "It's great. Listen, I was just wondering about
Samantha. . . ."

Now she looked right at me. "What about her?" she asked, half
suspicious and half amused. Fully intimidating, as ever.

"Well, I know she's on house restriction—"

"When she's not in the hospital." Nadine shook her head. "That girl has got to make it to rehab soon. They can't take her until her wrist is healed, and they had to postpone the wrist surgery because of her kidneys." Her voice softened and lowered. "To tell you the truth, I don't know how long she's going to make it here. She's got a very tough case."

I nodded seriously, honored to be vested with Nadine's confidence. "Yeah, actually, that's why I was wondering, maybe if I could escort her, we could just go to the coffee shop on the corner for ten minutes or so—it seems like she's got a lot to talk about, and it must be hard for her to be here day in and day out—"

Nadine shook her head. "Juh*neece*. I appreciate what you are trying to do for Samantha, but you know, if you take her out, everybody else is going to want you to take them out, too."

Of course. The rules. No favorites. And no buying them stuff. So why didn't I just knock on Nadine's door and ask for permission to break both at once? That was bound to go well. "Right, I know, I just . . . I thought maybe because she was restricted, you know, they'd understand."

Nadine was still shaking her head at me. "If one of these girls gets an extra canned peach in her dessert cup, we have a riot on our hands. I know you want to help her, just like you want to help all the girls . . ." Here she paused, to let this sink in.

"Of course," I said, smiling, shaking my own head—what was I thinking? "You're right. I'm sorry to bug you, I just . . . thanks, Nadine."

I turned to go, but her voice stopped me. "Listen, Juh*neece*. I really do appreciate what you want to do for Samantha. I'm glad she's talking to you. She's a very . . . unusual girl."

"She is," I enthused. "Unusually bright."

"Unusually damaged." Nadine was dead serious now, pinning me with that stare. "Some of the things that have come up with her drug counselor—she's got very serious issues. If she feels comfortable talking with you, I think that's a good thing; I just want you to be careful with her, you know? A little bit goes a long way with these girls. They can't always handle a lot of emotion, even if it's good. They don't know how to react. And you might not know how to react to some of the things she might tell you."

"I . . . I guess that's true." Of course it was. I recognized it with a shiver. What Sam had endured, the amount of pain she'd absorbed — she was a junkie street kid, an addict since childhood, abused every second of her life. I liked to think I could relate to the girls, that I'd been just like them once; but I'd never been through anything like what most of them had been through, and Sam was an unusually hard case. And now I was acting like this was a talk-show makeover or a Lifetime movie; like I'd buy her a notebook, and then there'd be this montage of her struggling through rehab, and then she'd come out the other side perfectly cured, and the two of us would go off laughing in the sunshine. When really, this was going to be years and years of trying to convince this girl not to kill herself; this was going to be relapses and crises and bottomless sorrows, and there was no guarantee of success.

Nadine kept up the penetrating stare. I tried not to wither, tried to appear capable and strong. "I know you mean well, Juh*neece*. And you do a good job. You know, the girls look forward to the beads every week. They're very grateful that you come."

Subtext: *And isn't that enough? They don't ignore you in the lounge anymore. Instead they pout when you don't sit with them at dinner—what more could you ask for? You always wanted the girls to accept you, even back when you were a resident; now they do. You're the Bead Lady. So why don't you just keep being the Bead Lady, and leave the rest to us.*

"I know. I'm grateful, too." I shifted my weight, stepped back a step. "Thanks, Nadine. Sorry again to bug you."

She swiveled back to her computer. "Okay, Juh*neece*. Good night."

I took the broom and dustpan and went back to the lounge, where Sam sat, casually guarding my bag.

"Thanks," I told her. "Had to pee."

"Oh." She reached out her good hand for the dustpan. "Can I help?"

We swept in near silence for a minute—"Man, these things get everywhere, don't they?"—then I returned the broom to the counselors' office. Then back to the lounge, where Sam watched me zip up my coat, shoulder my bead bag, and put my knit hat on my head. I stood there awkwardly for a minute, like at the end of a first date.

"So listen," I blurted. "I was thinking of coming by on Saturday. I've got some old books and clothes to get rid of, and I want to drop them off at the donations room. Probably about one o'clock. You think you might be around then?"

She gave me her suppressed smile, her top lip pressed flat against her teeth. "I'll check my calendar," she said. "Yep, looks like I'm free."

I laughed. "All right. Well, I hope you'll stay out of trouble until then—no more hospitals, okay?"

She indicated her cast. "Well, not until my surgery, anyway."

"Okay. Well." I cleared my throat, re-shouldered my bag. Took one last look before walking away, just in case. There she was— stooped, her head hung, but looking back at me. "Take care."

It wasn't like I didn't listen to Nadine that Wednesday; I did. But I didn't feel like I could stay away. I promised Sam that I'd be there that Saturday. So as soon as Bill left for a weekend shift at the paper, I grabbed a bunch of books and clothes earmarked for donation and headed uptown, heart fluttering like a hummingbird in my throat.

When I got off the elevator, Sam was right there, pacing the hallway in front of the counselors' office. She looked furious, fists clenched, wearing her hardest and most menacing face. "What's up?" I asked, immediately concerned.

She shook her head, wouldn't talk, so I nodded respectfully and entered the lounge, where a cluster of girls—Pinky, Leticia, St. Croix, Preggo, and Ellenette—were watching the movie *Belly* for the ninety-ninth time in a row. Ellenette yelled, "Hey! Bead Lady! What you doin' here on a weekend? You got beads?"

"No, I just came to drop off some clothes and books—figured I'd stop up and say hello."

I put the bags down on the table, and the girls dropped everything to run over and pick through them. "What's this? This looks like it'd fit me. Miss, you got any books by Teri Woods?"

They were distracted, so I headed back to the hallway to check on Samantha—still pacing and muttering outside the closed door of the counselors' office. She had her street accent on, I noticed. "I'll kill the bitch, fuckin' bitch."

"Who's that, now?" I inquired gently.

She shook her head. "Fuckin' bitch all up in my face, sayin' 'What you gonna do about it?' I'll show you what I'ma do about it. Let her come out that office."

I nodded, agreeing with her without even knowing the story. "I'm sorry she's in your face," I said. "You don't need that."

"Fuckin' right I don't. I'll lay that bitch flat." She stalked away, the girl with the cast on her hand from punching a wall.

I wandered over to Ellenette. "What happened?"

Nutshell: A discussion about vegetarianism got heated, people sucked their teeth at each other, one girl told Samantha to "shut up, you skinny white crow." Sam told her to fuck off; the girl laughed in her face. "What are you going to do about it?"

And Samantha, who was detoxing her ass off after seven years of homelessness and addiction, after nineteen years of intermittent abuse, rose and said, "I'm going to beat your ass, bitch," and stepped toward her with murderous intent.

And the girl ran into the counselors' office. "Samantha's going to kill me! Samantha's going to kill me!"

"Damn right I'ma kill her," said Sam, pacing, snarling, flexing her fists.

Rina the counselor came out of the office, her back to the closed door, and started telling Sam to calm down. She didn't want to be discharged, right?

"I don't give a shit, I *will* get discharged, fuck that, I'ma lay that bitch flat."

Rina warned her, "You could get discharged just for threatening her. You can't let her get to you, Sam. That's what she wants."

It was a little too late for that, I noted; the mystery girl had already gotten to Sam. But I didn't want to contradict the staff; their job was impossible, Sisyphean. I hung back and watched Rina handle it, and offered noises of support in the background. At one point I said, "Look, this was a shitty day anyway. You're stuck in this place for a month now, going through withdrawal, people in your face—it sucks. It sucks to be here, and this made it worse. I don't blame you for wanting to get kicked out. Let's go smoke a cigarette and talk about it."

It was the closest Sam got to going outside since she was on restriction, standing downstairs under the scaffolding for a smoke. She insisted that she didn't want to go, she wanted to stand there until the "bitch comes out the fuckin' office, so I can beat her ass." But then Jerome, the bald counselor with the glasses, came out of the office with his arms folded, and he had a look on his face that spelled trouble for Sam.

"You can leave the floor now, or you can leave the building for good," he stated.

"Let's go smoke," I urged her.

She didn't agree, but she stalked away, and I chased after her.

She had to wait while I ran across the street and bought a pack of Marlboros—definitely favoritism, definitely against the rules. I ran back, and we stood under the scaffold as she smoked and paced and talked.

First she ranted, spit flying from the corners of her mouth, her customary hunched-over walk exaggerated into a pimp stroll. She told me how hard-core she was, banging herself in the chest—"What do I care if I get discharged, I been sleeping on the street since I was twelve! They think I give a fuck? I been stabbed, shot, stabbed some more, stuck up—look at this." She hiked the leg of her cargo pants, and I could see a deep two-inch gouge on the back of one heel. "Achilles tendon. Someone cut it when I was a kid after I burned 'em on a drug deal." My eyes widened in horror, and she let the pant leg drop, satisfied. "I don't need this place, shit. I'ma smoke this cigarette, go upstairs, and beat that bitch's ass, then grab my stuff and heave-ho."

Then she started talking about respect. I told her, "I respect you one thousand percent. I think all the adults here respect you, a lot." She rolled right over this. She was still working that pronounced 'hood accent, but it was a combination of about eleven different hoods—Wyoming, New York, Texarkana. If there was a ghetto, she'd been there.

Ice. That was her nickname. She was talking about guns she'd carried, a dog she had. She mentioned her old street families, people named Turtle, Tiny, and Pyro. I asked, "What did they call you?" Ice.

She was done with her cigarette, stomping on it and scowling at it. We sat on the concrete loading dock under the scaffold, swinging our legs. It was cold, and she had no coat on, so I gave her my sweatshirt to wear. I had my down coat.

Philadelphia was her favorite city, she told me—no, Washington, D.C., because of the free museums. Her face was starting to relax; though she still wouldn't look directly at me, I could see it peripherally. She had the notebook in her pocket; she showed me some new drawings. A faceless girl on a cloud embraced a broken mirror; her reflection bowed her head. An exquisitely detailed pair of bound hands, blood pouring from the slit wrists. I cleared my throat and wiped my runny nose. "These are really good," I said.

We sat out there for a while; she smoked another cigarette. At one point she said, "I'm cold." And without saying anything else, we walked back inside.

Rina was waiting for us. They conferred, and Sam agreed to "chill," she said. "As long as that bitch stays away from me, I will stay away from her." That was good enough for Rina. I was betting the mystery girl would stay away from now on—everyone in the lounge was already talking about how Sam jumped up "like she was gonna kill somebody!" and how the other girl cowered in the office for an hour while Sam calmed down.

It was time for me to head home—I had groceries to buy, phone calls to make. "Are you really going to be okay?" I asked Sam, searching her eyes, which were finally turned toward mine. They were soft around the corners again, wide and warm. She even smiled.

"Yeah. Hey, good thing you came up here today, huh?"

I brushed this off, though I was thinking the same thing—my timing was perfect, I'd pretty much rescued her from being discharged, and what might have happened had I not dropped by to handle the situation? She could have been bounced; she could have been halfway to nowhere by now. I straightened up, stifling a smile of pride. "Always glad to see you," I said, and passed her the pack of cigarettes. "I'll see you Wednesday. I *better* see you Wednesday."

She laughed. "All right."

I waved and headed for the staircase, wondering, as I always wondered when I left her side, whether I'd ever see her again; whether she'd make it to next Wednesday, much less rehab, or anyplace beyond. Each time I let her out of my sight, it seemed more likely that she might disappear from my life entirely, and more vital that she stay. But walking that day toward the subway home, the image of her laughing fresh in my mind, I had hope.

The next Wednesday, Sam wasn't there.

I showed up at the shelter early again and found Ellenette and St. Croix in front of the TV with two new girls, holding hands on the couch, despite the rule against physical affection among residents. Ellenette put out the call—*Bead Lady!*—but there was no response. No Sam coming around the corner, no Sam galumphing down the stairs two at a time when Rina called for dinner. No Sam in the cafeteria.

I sat with Ellenette and St. Croix, trying not to swivel my head around like an owl, listening to them tell the story of how they went to eat at T.G.I. Friday's, and Ellenette spent the whole meal fucking with the waitress. "Every time she turned around, we were like, 'MNUGH!'"—here Ellenette made an inhuman grunting groan. "She did not know what the hell was going on!"

Where is Sam? I wanted to ask. I was agitated beyond reason, digging my nails into my sweaty palms. I'd worried she wasn't going to make it another few days here; it was exactly as I'd feared. She'd dematerialized, the way the girls always did when I decided I loved them. "Where is everybody tonight?" I asked. "Seems kind of empty."

Of course the cafeteria was just as crowded as it had been for weeks, ever since it turned cold for the winter. Ellenette didn't even dignify the comment with a response. "MNUGH!" she said, and St. Croix cracked up.

I wasn't in the mood for Ellenette and St. Croix, or for the girl they called Mocha, with her bitchy gossip, or for the butch girl who ignored me, came over and started ordering the other girls to make her something, and when I said to her, "Why don't you join us? What do you want to make?" she acted like nobody was speaking.

"Yo, make me a bracelet—blue and black, son, blue and black."

Finally I ducked into the counselors' office, ostensibly for the broom, though it wasn't even close to the time when I'd normally clean up. I peered up at the list of residents on the whiteboard the counselors used to track the active residents, and there was her name, Samantha Dunleavy, listed in the row underneath her caseworker's name, Ashley.

"Hey, Janice," said Ashley, who happened to be sitting right there. "How's it going?"

God bless Ashley, a tall, broad white girl from Texas—the only counselor who'd ever come over to the bead table and struck up a conversation with me. Most of the counselors still tended to give me a wide berth; they were exceedingly busy, it seemed, and it wasn't like I went out of my way to talk to them, either. I was afraid they thought I was weird, coming back here as an ex-resident, or I was fishy, or I was trying to do their job for free, not that anybody had ever indicated any of the above. Ashley, for instance, had been nothing but friendly, sometimes to a fault—when she sat down at the bead table for a chat, the needle would go skidding right off the record, and all conversation among the girls would halt.

"It's good," I said. "How's by you? Busy around here?"

"As always," she said cheerfully, rolling her eyes.

"So . . . how's that girl Sam, is she still around?" I bit my lip, but it was too late; the words had already spilled out.

Ashley raised her hand, shook it like she was showing off a bracelet. "Wrist surgery," she said. "Should be back tomorrow."

"Oh. Huh." I nodded, grabbed the broom, fought the urge to break into a grin, or a song. "Well, I'll bring this right back."

"No problem," said Ashley, already back to her files.

The rest of the night passed quickly. Suddenly I was able to banter with everyone—"MNUGH!" I said to Ellenette, which won me big points, in the form of whooping laughs from around the table. Sam was all right, she hadn't split; she was exactly where she was supposed to be tonight—in the hands of the professionals. She was in a clean room, in a freshly made bed that went up and down when you pressed the button. And her pain, for a change, was the pain of healing.

Chapter Three

The Twelve Days of Christmas

Two weeks later, the Wednesday before Christmas, and the cafeteria at the shelter was decorated with freshly handmade construction-paper signs in red and green and black: MERRY CHRISTMAS. HAPPY HOLIDAYS. HAPPY KWANZAA. As I walked in, I saw Nadine coming my way, two girls dogging her heels like she was the Pied Piper. I raised my hand and smiled in greeting, and she stopped short, nearly causing her followers to collide with each other.

"Juh*neece*. You know your friend Samantha is back in the hospital."

"Oh no. What happened?"

I'd seen Sam the previous Wednesday, her hand recast from the successful surgery the week before. She had been wincing occasionally, making do without much in the way of painkillers, but her spirits had been high. She'd spent most of the night by my side, talking about what she wanted to do after her stint in rehab—maybe she'd become a vet, she said, or a mechanic. When there was a lull in the bead action toward the end of the night, she'd confessed to me that she was scared to go away; scared, after seven years of complete autonomy, to commit the next year of her life to an institution where they'd dictate her every move. But, she told me, she trusted Jodi the drug counselor—for the first time in her life, she was trying to trust an adult for longer than the duration of a drug deal—and Jodi said that rehab was the way to go. So she was going to trust rehab.

I hadn't known, at the end of the night, if they'd be moving Sam upstate to rehab that week, if it would be the last time I'd see her. I'd wanted to hug her good-bye, in case, but she'd slipped away as I was leaving.

The two girls tailing Nadine got distracted and moved on; Nadine moved closer and dropped her voice. "She got an infection, her hand, from the surgery. Bad fever, really sick. She waited a long time to say anything; you know she doesn't like to show pain. The doctors hope they got to it in time to save the hand."

"Oh my god." I thought of Sam handless, trying to become a vet or a mechanic. "What hospital? Is she nearby?"

Nadine caught my eye with that all-knowing look of hers, her forehead furrowed with concern. "Well, officially I wouldn't say anything, but you know, off the record, she's at St. Victor's. I'm telling you because it's the holidays"—here she gave me a warning look, and I nodded, *Right, the holidays, special once-a-year dispensation, not a policy change*—"and I know you've been important to her."

"Well, I . . ." I didn't know what to say. I was important to Sam, trustworthy to Nadine. Nadine, who once almost canned me on the spot in my first six weeks for taking a camera-phone picture of one of the girls, at the girl's request—*Juh*neece! *What are you doing! You don't take pictures of the girls, you compromise their security.* "Thanks, Nadine."

"Off the record," she reminded me. Her followers were coming our way to resume their pursuit.

"Miss Nadine, we got a situation in our room, Miss Nadine!"

She gave me a droll smile, raised her voice for the girls behind her. "Upstairs, ladies." One more emphatic look, and she forged on.

It was all I could do not to declare bead time canceled for the evening and run straight down to St. Victor's before the end of visiting hours, whenever those might be, but I'd already been spotted—by

Ellenette, of course. She waved me over to her table to give me the good news—she was getting her Section 8 housing voucher, her free pass to the projects. "I am gonna be set *up!*" she declared, holding up her palm for me to slap.

"Congratulations," I said, trying for enthusiasm. Thinking *Welcome to welfare, Ellenette. Good luck enjoying your shitty, limited life.*

It was an all-right night, I guess; who knew, who cared. All I wanted to do was go see Samantha; everything else felt like a waste of time. So Ellenette would make it to the pj's with one more pink-and-purple bracelet; St. Croix would make the seventeenth pair of earrings that said ST CROIX on them—would any of it make a difference in their lives? Would it help them get jobs, or find self-esteem, or save them any suffering? I spent three hours every Wednesday at the shelter, an extra hour to run to the bead store during the week for supplies; I'd been spending four hours a week volunteering, for ten months now. I should have cured homelessness already. Instead, I had decorated it.

And then there was Sam.

"She's in the hospital again," I told Bill as soon as I got home that night, all hyper and distraught.

He didn't have to ask who I meant. "Jesus. Poor kid. Kidneys again?"

He started shuffling through the take-out menus, and I started rolling myself a joint. "No—hand infection, from the surgery. They might have to amputate it; they don't know yet. I thought maybe I'd run by the hospital tomorrow and see how she's doing."

"Yeah?" His eyebrows were raised as he handed me the menu from the Thai restaurant. "That's kosher with everyone?"

"Well, Nadine's the one who basically suggested that I go—off the record, of course. She said, you know, because it's the holidays, and because I've become *important* to Sam." I rolled my eyes at myself, mocking my own "importance," smiling ironically to cover up the real smile that wanted to bust through. "Anyway, since Nadine mentioned it, and I have some extra time this week . . ."

Which I did. Work was slow over the holidays, and I'd already finished all my gift shopping—a jacket for Bill, tennis lessons for my father, an herbal eye mask for my stepmother, Sylvia. Cash for my twenty-one-year-old half-brother, Jake, my mom's kid, still in college in Boston; a card for my mom, to whom I hadn't spoken much in the past few years. I loved my mom, but dealing with me made her anxious, and dealing with her made me sad. I sent her cards twice yearly, for the holidays and for her birthday; maybe every other year she sent a reply.

"God," said Bill. "The kid just can't catch a break, can she."

She never should have punched that wall was what I'd been thinking. But what if she hadn't? She'd have gone straight from intake to rehab; I never would have met her. I certainly wouldn't have had the chance to get to know her, to become *important* to her. And the reason she'd punched the wall, she'd told me, back in our first week of conversation, was because she was about to punch this girl Dime, and that would have gotten her thrown out. So she'd *chosen* to punch the wall instead. Even with the broken wrist, she told me, she was glad she'd done it.

Secretly, so was I.

"You came," said Sam, sitting up in her hospital bed, amazed.

The hospital, like the shelter, was decorated for the holidays; there were candy canes at the information desk downstairs, where I'd given her name, Samantha Dunleavy, and they'd told me where to find her. I had a candy cane in my fist, along with a bag of cookies; I brandished the booty in front of me as I came around her bedside toward the empty chair.

"Bearing gifts." I put the stuff on the table next to her bed, stepped back to look at her. She looked like a dead fish that had been left in the sun, so pale she was almost pearly, dark bruises on her arms and under her eyes. The hand in question was swathed in white gauze, the arm was hooked up to a beeping IV, and there was an angry red line shooting from her wrist to her elbow. Her skinny arms stuck out from her hospital gown; for the first time, I saw the thin, pink, parallel scars she'd carved into her own shoulders, above her tattoo. I hadn't known she was a cutter, on top of everything else; but of course, why wouldn't she be? "How are you feeling?"

"I'm . . . I'm really happy you came to visit me. I didn't think . . ." She shook her head a little, like she was trying to clear a hallucination, then looked at me again. I was still there. "Thanks for coming. Here, pull up this chair."

She leaned over, her face strained. "Don't reach," I ordered her as I settled myself into the visitor's chair. "You're here to rest. You've got to get this damn hand fixed, already! How's it going?"

She indicated the twin bags of antibiotics flowing into her arm, the infected vein, vivid with poison. "It hurts like hell. And they're trying to keep me off the opiates, but they're giving me a little bit today, 'cause the pain's . . ." She trailed off.

"Pretty bad," I said. "It looks like it. God, I'm sorry you're going through this."

"It's all right. I'm just really glad you're here. It makes it a lot better." She breathed deeply, trying not to flinch.

"Yeah, obviously." I frowned. "Is there anything they can do for you? Do you want me to talk to your doctors? I mean, who's been dealing with them—Nadine?"

Unlikely, I realized, with Nadine's caseload; Jodi's was just as full. So who was this teenage girl's medical advocate? Who was holding her remaining good hand throughout this, helping her make decisions? Was there anybody who could stand up to the doctors and say, *Recovering junkie or no, how about you guys up the painkillers?* Or, *What the hell is she going to do if you have to cut off a limb?*

She shook her head again, with difficulty. "No, I'm dealing with them, but it's cool, I understand what's going on. They been good about explaining it to me. It's this blood infection called sepsis, but hopefully the antibiotics will kill it. Right now they think it looks pretty good that it's working."

"That's good," I said, freaking out inside. *Jesus Christ, people die from sepsis.* I wondered if they'd been fully honest about that with her. She didn't seem like someone who'd been informed of the potential consequences of her condition—coma, amputation, death. She seemed like someone who was told she had a really shitty flu and was bummed that she might miss Christmas dinner.

Well, if they weren't telling her, then neither was I. "I'm glad they're taking care of it," I said.

"Me too," she agreed. She fixed me with her wide brown eyes. "And I'm really glad you came."

Her voice—so childlike, so blunt. So unlike the hard-ass 'hood rat who'd been stalking the counselors' office that Saturday just two weeks ago, bragging about how easy it would be for her to get a gun and lay a bitch out. "I'm glad I came, too," I said, smiling.

"I mean, I didn't think anybody was going to be able to visit me. You know, the staff's real busy, and I called Hericka's cell"—Hericka was St. Croix's given name—"just to see if she could bring me some of my clothes and books and stuff from our room, but she hasn't called me back." Sam looked genuinely hurt. "I mean, I know we're not best friends or anything, but we been roomies for, like, a month now, and we talked a bunch of times in our room at night, about guys we been with, and shit we been through . . ."

Guys? I could have sworn, up until that moment, that Sam was gay—with her baggy clothes, her loping stride, and her jutting lower jaw, she was as butch as the hardest butch dykes on the floor (AG's, they called themselves, for "aggressives"). That'd teach me to judge by appearances. "Well, you know, it's only two days until Christmas. She's probably running around."

"Yeah, I know. Everyone's busy." She nodded, almost to herself, and cast a glance up at the IV monitor. It was getting toward empty, I noticed, wondering if maybe someone should be doing something about that. She turned back toward me, her pale face and glassy eyes on mine. "That's why it's so awesome that you're here. I asked Nadine to tell you, in case you might be able to come, but I didn't think—I mean, I know you're probably busy, too."

"Here I am," I assured her. "And if you thought hanging out with me at a homeless shelter was fun, you've never hung out with me in a hospital."

She smiled, and this time there was no grimace behind it, just a smile. "Thanks," she said again, relaxing back into her pillow. "I hope you don't mind if I close my eyes a minute . . . I'm real tired."

"Of course," I told her. "I'm glad just to be here with you."

"Thanks." That syllable again, the one that hit me right in the heart. *You're welcome, Sam; you'll always be welcome.* Her eyes fluttered closed, and for a second, she looked like she was at peace.

"You *came*," she said again.

Same amount of amazed as the day before. But slightly less pallor today, I noted as I walked into the room. There was a nurse by her bedside, refitting two new bags of antibiotics to the pole of Sam's IV, resetting the monitor so it dripped on schedule.

"This is my friend Janice," Sam told her. "The one I was telling you about."

The nurse smiled at me as I lowered myself into the visitor's chair, beaming. "That's nice," she said.

I peered at the writing on the bags, a discordant mix of syllables, *clindamycin, aztreonam.* It all sounded horribly toxic, like floor cleaner, and it was going right into her veins. *Well,* I thought, *her veins have seen worse.*

The nurse left—"I'll be back to check on you soon," she promised—and Sam inspected the IV, straightening a tube so it flowed more evenly.

"How's it going?" I asked, noting the bruises on her inner arm where the IV was taped, the crease in her forehead, her hair, damp with sweat around the hairline.

"Okay. She had trouble finding the vein. They usually do." She tried to smile. "The good news is, they said I'm doing better today."

"That's great. So the medication is working."

"Looks like." She frowned, leaned over, and restraightened the tube. Her voice got perky again. "And I'm probably not going to lose my hand, so . . ."

"That's good." I laughed, relieved, and picked up an empty

Styrofoam cup, tapping it against an empty juice cup in a toast. "Merry Christmas Eve!"

"Merry Christmas Eve," she agreed. "Thanks for coming."

"Thanks for having me." I reached into my bag and pulled out the small stack of reading materials I'd gathered—some memoirs; a comic-book anthology called *Hothead Paisan, Homicidal Lesbian Terrorist*. I hefted the stack in front of her and placed it on her nightstand.

"Wow," she said, scanning the spines. "That's so cool. I haven't had anything good to read in weeks."

"Well, this should keep you busy overnight."

She looked from the books to me, her eyes full of gratitude. "Thanks, Janice. You been so awesome to me, I can't even—"

"Oh, stop thanking me. I'm glad to be here. I just want you to feel better soon."

"I know." She sank back into her pillow and smiled. "It's just, it's Christmas Eve, I'm sure you got better things to do."

I cocked my eyebrow. "As a matter of fact, I'm Jewish. Therefore, I have nothing 'better' to do tonight. My boyfriend, Bill, went to visit his family on Long Island for the night, and I've got no family plans until tomorrow. I'm actually going up to the shelter later, bringing some movies with me—I figured I'd see if they'll let me spring for some Chinese food for everyone. So this is the perfect way for me to spend the afternoon."

She nodded, approving and a little wistful. "That sounds fun, tonight. I wish I was gonna be there."

Yeah, she'd be missing so much—sitting around the shelter eating greasy takeout and watching the *Blade* movies. "Well, this isn't so bad, either—this is like a one-on-one Christmas party." I toasted her empty cup again. "Cheers."

"Cheers," she said.

She wanted to know more about my holiday plans, about Bill. "Bill? Let's see. He's six years younger than me, but you can't tell by looking at him. He's prematurely mature, you know? He's a newspaper designer. He's so smart, and *so* funny, and he's so good to me. We've been together almost three years; he just moved in two months ago."

I had a Polaroid of Bill tucked into my notebook, one of the extra snapshots I had taken to send to my mom with her biannual update—*Here's a picture of Bill, all moved in; here are the cats—look how big and greedy they are.* I pulled out the picture and showed it to Sam. She took it carefully by the edges with her fingertips and studied it.

"He looks nice," she decreed. "He looks . . . normal."

I laughed again. The glasses and the short hair fool everyone. "He is, on the outside. On the inside, he's got his stuff. He had his own abusive dad; he's survived some shit. But he's managed to have a good life," I emphasized. *Just like you will.*

She passed the picture back to me, thoughtful, her gaze slipping to the far wall as though she were in a reverie. "What about tomorrow? Are you doing anything for Christmas?"

I hesitated—I wasn't sure I wanted to tell her all about the fun, fantastic things I was going to be doing while she was here, gnashing her teeth in agony. "Bill and I are seeing my dad and stepmother and some of their old friends for dinner—they're like my honorary aunts and uncles. It's a little Jewish Christmas tradition we have. It's nice, it's low-key."

She nodded, still with that faraway look. "I guess you and your dad made up, after . . . everything that happened in the past."

I'd filled Sam in on the troubles I'd had with my dad in my childhood, troubles he'd atoned for long ago. "He went to a lot of therapy," I said. "And so did I. A few times we even went together."

"Wow." Her eyes closed, like she was trying to imagine her father walking into a therapist's office, as mine did, saying, *I know what I did, and I'm sorry for it.* I tried to imagine it, too. I pictured a tall, weathered man, with a hard, scarred face, brown teeth, and evil, brilliant eyes, wearing a mesh ball cap over his overgrown hair, clothes soaked in fumes. Just conjuring his image made me want to shudder.

"I really hate Christmas," said Sam, eyes still closed. "One year, when I was eleven, my dad disappeared for a couple weeks—which wasn't always a bad thing." She stopped and took in a deep breath, opened her eyes. "But we didn't have any money, because my mom was useless without him."

I sat and squeezed the arms of my chair as Sam told me the story of Christmas Eve 1996, when her mother made her hustle in downtown Scottsdale, Arizona, until she'd made enough money for dinner from McDonald's, drugstore toys for her younger sister, and a bundle of dope for Mom. Her mother bought one of those foot-high novelty singing trees for the table, and wrapped the toys, and sang carols all over the apartment until 4 A.M. In the morning she wasn't speaking to Sam anymore, lavishing attention on the other kids instead. She told Sam that she was a whore and didn't deserve any presents.

"And any time I see one of those fake trees . . ."

Her eyes, still unfocused, were fixed on the far wall; I was free to look straight at her. She was as white as a vampire, bloodless with grief. This was my chance to say something, something epic and profound, something that would undo some of the violent damage that had been done to her.

"That will never happen again," I promised. "Nothing like that will ever happen again."

"I know," she said softly. Two tears rolled out of the far corners of her eyes, still staring at the horror of the past now playing on the far wall.

I wanted to reach over and take her good hand, but I stayed very still, kept my voice low and steady. "It won't. That's over. You're going to be protected now. Now that you've asked for help, you're going to get as much help as you need. You went to the right place, and they're going to help get you to the next right place. And you've met some people who are going to keep helping you, right? Now you've got some people who really care about you—you've got Jodi, and you've got me, and you're going to keep meeting people who want to help you, who recognize how special you are . . ."

She pressed her head back against the pillow and squeezed her eyes closed, more tears tracing the tracks of the first. Her good hand was right there for the taking. I had never hugged her, not once yet, not even when I left the hospital the night before. The tears slipped from her closed eyes, her body barely moving as she suppressed what sound she could.

"It's okay," I said. I moved my chair closer, put my hand on her shoulder, right above the tattoo, over the self-abuse scars. "It's going to be okay."

She continued to cry, and I kept my hand there on her shoulder, drinking it in through my palm like a faith healer, the waves of pain and exhilaration, contraction and release. Pressing the message into her, as she pressed back against me:

Let it out. They can't hurt you anymore. This is today. You're going to be okay.

"No way," she said as I entered her room on Christmas Day.

"Merry Jewish Christmas," I replied, smiling, shaking off my coat. "And Happy Chanukah, and Kwanzaa, too."

She was sitting up in bed today, far rosier than the day before, and the TV was on, a repeat of *Law & Order*.

"You got TV?" I asked, surprised.

"Yup, and phone." She grinned, a decent approximation of her old, pre-hospital grin. She must have sweet-talked someone into turning them on for free, unless Medicaid was now footing the bill for hospital extras, which seemed unlikely. "I'm feeling a lot better, too. I even ate those cookies you brought the first day. They were *good*."

"I'm glad." I glanced at her arm on my way to my chair—it looked much improved, and the mitten of gauze around her infected hand had been reduced to a fingerless glove. "Have the doctors said anything new?"

She raised the hand to show me the fresh bandage. "They're saying I'm healing really well, and the infection's pretty much under control, so that's good. Pain's still pretty bad, but I might get to go home sometime next week. Well, not *home*, but . . ." She grinned again, flush with satisfaction.

"Fantastic. That's fantastic. See? You're totally a superhero, you're kicking this thing's ass."

And here I'd been worrying to Bill all week, "She's so sick, and her kidneys; what if she doesn't make it?" Chewing my fingernails, smoking joints, trying unsuccessfully to calm myself down. "The stories she was telling me, babe—I don't know even how she's lived this long." Pacing around last night like I was waiting for Santa, waiting for the next day to dawn so I could unwrap the present of seeing her again, the privilege of sitting by her side. There was no question this afternoon when I started to make noises about "maybe, just for an hour, before we go to the folks', just running over to say hello."

"Go," said Bill. "And give her my best."

Today's was an upbeat visit all around. I told her all the gossip from the shelter the night before—"Dime went AWOL with that girl Trini three days ago. Princess Jasmine told me. She said Trini was about to get her Section 8 but now she's blown it. And Hericka says hi. She's sorry she hasn't been able to visit." Here Sam pouted for a second. "But Nadine said if she doesn't get a job by the New Year, she's gone, so as soon as she gets a job she's coming to see you. And I told everybody you're doing well—I told them you have your own room with a private bathroom, and now everybody wants to get in here."

She smirked, gloating over the others in absentia. "This *is* kind of a nice setup, right? Food's not bad . . ."

"And you get to eat it in bed."

"I know!" She gestured grandly around the room with her good arm. "And now I got a private phone and TV—I even get drugs every couple of hours, and I don't gotta go out and score!"

I laughed. "This is the life, all right."

"And here, the Bead Lady comes every *day*. Even on Christmas!"

And all she had to do to enjoy it was almost drop dead of an infection. How sad, that this was the highlight of her year, a near-fatal attack of sepsis; that for her, St. Victor's was the Ritz-Carlton. Her overwhelming gratitude for everything—the food at the shelter, Jodi's full house restriction, a nurse who didn't stab her for a full half hour before getting the IV inserted, a visit from me—it was kind of sickening, actually. I tried to smile, but it came out flat.

Sam saw it cross my face; she immediately pulled back. "I mean, I know you won't be able to come *every* day, I don't expect—"

"Ah ah ah," I warned her. "I've told you, I want to come, and I will come whenever I'm able, and when I'm not, I'll let you know in advance. All right?"

She smiled grudgingly; she'd let me have this one, for now. "All right."

So we talked about the books I'd brought; about feminism, the sex industry, victimless crime, and vigilantism; about whether or not people were essentially good or essentially bad. "What do you think about Nietzsche?" she asked, and I said, "Uch, fuck that sociopath." Soon enough, I had to pull out my cell phone to check the time. She noted it with a quick, involuntary frown. Another hour in her company had sped by; it was time for me to leave.

"I've got to go," I said with regret. "But I'm glad you're feeling so much better today. Take it easy, and keep improving, okay?"

"I will," she promised, her voice small and high again. A sad look down at her lap, then a smile for me. "Thanks for coming."

"Thanks for having me." I shrugged on my coat, fished my hat from the pocket. I'd be running home through the fresh snow on the sidewalk; even so, I'd be a few minutes late.

I stood at the foot of her bed, not knowing how to say good-bye. Yesterday I had held her shoulder, clasped it when it was time to go, and she had reached up and grasped my hand. Today I was all the way down by her feet.

"Have a good time with your family," she said.

I reached out and grabbed her foot, squeezed it for a second, let it go.

"I'll see you tomorrow," I said.

"Just an hour," I told Bill the next day. I don't even know how I justified it to him, taking time away from our postholiday Sunday to go be with Sam, but he didn't ask me to. He just said, "See you in an hour."

I ran the blocks through the fresh snow, sweating in my down coat, ripping off my hat, catching my breath in the elevator. A young male doctor was in Sam's room, unpacking the dressing from the wound, picking out chunks of pus like cottage cheese with a pair of tweezers. She had a brave face on, but when he hit a nerve, she writhed and gagged in pain.

It was a down day; her infection had flared, her organs were inflamed again, her kidneys throbbed and ached. She didn't want to talk about anything, not books, not the essential nature of humankind, not how good things were going to be when she got out of rehab in a year, sporting her GED and some vocational training, a year of therapeutic sobriety under her belt. She had no appetite, no patience for TV. "I'm sorry," she said, "I just feel crappy right now."

"I understand," I said. I didn't know whether to stay or go. I wanted to let her know that she didn't have to entertain me, that I'd be by her bedside through the rough days as well as the good. And yet I wasn't sure she wanted me there. She seemed almost angry, or maybe it was the frustration of the setback. Maybe it was the pain. It was palpable in the room, the way she gritted her teeth, the whimpers as she thrashed around, looking for a position that would give her relief. The doctors were still being stingy with the painkillers—she wanted them to be stingy, she didn't want to undo whatever progress she'd made, however many sober days she'd been able to collect. But in the hours between meds, she was in agony.

As was I. I sat in the visitor's chair, watching her eyes dart around behind her closed lids, then fly open wide, then shut in exhaustion again. Sat there saying meaningless things, like, "I wish there was something I could do for you." Worrying—*She's crashing again. The sepsis is recurring. Her kidneys can't take the stress. She's not going to make it after all.*

She rolled over, moaned. I couldn't stand the pain, and I was three feet away from it. "Do you want me to call the doctor again?"

She shook her head. "There's nothing they can do, I just gotta . . ."

Speaking was too much effort. She collapsed against the pillow. "Maybe . . . you should go."

"I'd rather not leave you like this." Another stupid thing to say; what was I going to do, wait until she felt better? She was in a hospital; I was going to have to go home at some point. She was telling me to go.

I felt like I could see her watching me through her closed eyelids, like she was just waiting for me to leave so she could write me off. Meanwhile, the clock in my pocket was ticking; Bill was waiting for me at home. If she really didn't need me, I knew somebody who did. Somebody, and three cats, and a long list of people to call to say *Happy holidays, I love you.* Suddenly, sitting there in the visitor's chair—yet another uncomfortable chair, in yet another institution, that smelled yet again like disinfectant and pain—I felt unbearably homesick for our apartment, just a few blocks away.

"All right," I said, rising, though she hadn't said anything. "I'll let you get some rest. I hope it gets better by tomorrow. I'll come by and check on you, okay?"

Sam's jaw clenched in confirmation, or maybe it was a nerve twinge. She kept her eyes closed, shifted her drowsy head, and muttered, "Right."

Was that supposed to be sarcastic? Or did she mean "all right"? I'd never promised her something and not delivered; I never would. I would be there tomorrow, and we both knew it.

"Okay," I said. I reached out tentatively for her foot, but she shifted again, and my hand fell short of it. "All right. I'll see you tomorrow."

The door to her room was closed when I arrived the next day.

I knocked softly in case she was sleeping or didn't want company. Yesterday had been a bad day; maybe today was worse.

Sam's voice, cheery and airy. "Come in."

I entered, bearing today's books and cookies, and grinned at Sam, sallow but happy, propped way up in her adjustable bed with pillows.

Then I stopped short. There was a woman in the visitor's chair, *my* chair. She was in her mid-forties, with graying, shoulder-length hair and a wry smile on her face. She held out her hand. "I'm Jodi," she said, in her thick Brooklyn accent. "Lemme guess, you must be the Bead Lady."

I beamed at her, shaking her hand. Here she was, my competition for Sam's affection; totally likeable, of course. Not to mention: a grown-up, with real credentials, who might actually be able to help Samantha in a substantive way, who'd already helped her so much. I was instantly grateful for and relieved by her presence—I'd been starting to feel overwhelmed by the extent of Sam's emotional damage, wondering how I was going to single-handedly see her through to rehab and beyond, but now Jodi was here, in person, ready to take over and show me how it was done. "I'm Janice. I've heard so much about you. It's great to meet you."

"You too," she said, raising an eyebrow toward Sam. "This one talks about you all the time."

Sam glowed with happiness—again, she'd turned 180 degrees from the day before. Yesterday she was moribund; today she was as chipper as a chipmunk. "Janice visited me *every day* since she found out I was here. Even *Christmas*."

Jodi's eyebrows climbed even higher, and I felt a little busted. "Work's been slow for the holidays," I offered, sheepish.

"Uh-huh," said Jodi. Probably thinking *Child molester*.

I stood there, chairless, biting the inside of my cheek, trying to decide if I should stay or leave them alone. They'd obviously been in the midst of something deep and important; maybe I'd interrupted an important revelation. Maybe Sam was telling Jodi the Christmas Eve story. Maybe Jodi had already heard it.

"I should give you guys a chance to talk privately," I said. "I'll take off; I'll come back tomorrow."

"Are you sure?" asked Sam. She wrinkled her forehead, apologetic. "I feel bad—yesterday I wasn't feeling so good, and now you came all the way back here today . . ."

"I'm just a few blocks away," I assured her. "It's no problem. I'm glad you guys are getting a chance to catch up. I'll come back tomorrow, and you'll tell me what you think of these." I showed her the books I'd brought for her to read, two novels and another memoir.

"Thanks, Janice. I really appreciate it." She looked happy and guilty in equal measure, like she'd been caught having some kind of affair, and she wanted to get back to it as soon as possible. "Thanks."

"It's okay." I zipped up my bag, stood straight again. "Okay!" I sort of bowed to each of them. "It was great to meet you, great to see *you.*"

"Same here," said Jodi. "I'm sure I'll see you around again."

"Either here or there," I said, smiling and pointing north, toward the shelter. "Okay."

There was Sam's socked foot, sticking up at the end of the bed. I grabbed it, shook it, and walked out of the room.

Me again. It was getting to be a routine, coming to the hospital in the evening after work. The guard downstairs nodded at me now, and the nurses recognized me in the halls. I smiled as I passed—*That's me, the noble volunteer, going to visit that poor homeless girl who's been so sick over the holidays.*

Nothing else really existed for me in that lost week between Christmas and New Year's. I got up in the morning, ran a few miles, and poked around at my desk until it was time for me to visit Sam. Then I'd visit, come home, and write about it in my notebook until my hand wanted to fall off—the things we'd talked about, bits of dialogue, the way her face looked in varying lights. Then I'd start making dinner, and Bill would be home around eight. Over dinner, I would talk about Sam. When we turned on the TV, she was all I saw.

Still, I was trying for moderation. I set time limits on my visits, even if I broke them most days, and I didn't call between visits, as tempting as it was. I was preoccupied with her, but I knew I couldn't let Sam take over my life.

Sam, Sam, Sam. Her grateful eyes as I entered her room. Today she was feeling okay, the wound was starting to close at the ends, her appetite was back. They were stepping down her painkillers some more, which made her a little flinchy, but aside from exhaustion and nausea and body aches and a hot throbbing in her hand, she was doing all right. I was getting the brave face again today, tinged with sadness. I sat right down in my chair and we got to work.

What was on her mind? Something that girl Dime at the shelter had said. The reason Sam was going to punch her that day she punched the wall instead, the reason she snapped her wrist in the first place. *What's the matter, you miss your daddy's dick?*

"Oh, wow," I said. "Them's fighting words."

"Why would Dime say something like that?" Sam asked. Maybe she had her own issues, I suggested. Sam gnawed her bottom lip, looking at the far wall again. "Maybe," she said. "But . . ."

It was like she was trying to tell me something, or ask something. I thought I'd read enough survivors' lit to guess what it was.

"Listen," I told her, "sometimes when people are molested or raped, their bodies decide to do what they can to protect them from the trauma. Physiologically, you know what I mean? Their bodies go along with it, and react as though it's not so bad. It doesn't mean the person liked it or wanted it, it just means their body decided to try and make it better for them any way it could. It's a survival mechanism."

She nodded, eyes on the far wall, still gnawing her lip.

"It's science," I said. "I'm not blowing smoke. It's a recorded phenomenon. You can look it up."

She nodded again, unconvinced, but dropped it and moved on to subject two. The illness had screwed up her spot in rehab. Jodi broke the news to her last night—the yearlong treatment place upstate wasn't going to be able take her, with her kidneys in the shape they were in, not to mention her chronic asthma. She was too much of a medical risk; they were a rural facility with no contingency for serious ongoing illness. So once she was released from the hospital, she would go back to the shelter for an indefinite period, until they could find another program.

"Oh, wow," I said again. My chest felt heavy, like I'd swallowed a rock. I tried not to show the extent of my dismay. Sam had to get to rehab, soon, and it had to be at least a year—the amount of intensive therapy she was going to need was staggering. It was what we'd been planning on, all we'd been talking about: how she'd get to rehab with everyone's support, how she'd find more people there like Janice and Jodi who'd care for her, how I'd write letters and visit on visiting days, how much better off she'd be in just twelve months. If she didn't get into a decent program, quickly, she might decide to give up; she could wander away and get lost again. "But they'll find you another program, I'm sure."

She wasn't so sure. What if her health continued to suffer? What if she needed dialysis sooner rather than later? All these health problems were her own fault; one of the night nurses had indicated as much. Why bother to patch her up, when she was bound to relapse and ruin whatever they'd managed to do for her? And if she ever needed a transplant, she knew she'd die—nobody was going to give a kidney to a junkie. She was still gnawing her lip, staring at the dreaded far wall of doom.

"Hey," I said sharply, to get her attention. "You're in good hands. They're going to find the right place for you."

They'd better, I thought. *I can't take much more of this.*

Our conversation wandered all over the map that day. She was worried about her younger sister, Eileen, who'd almost died after a suicide attempt and was now living in a group home somewhere in Colorado. Sam didn't know how to contact her, and wouldn't be allowed to even if she did. Then she was talking about her brother, older by one year—he'd left home around thirteen, cleaned up at seventeen, and joined the navy. They were so close as kids, ran the streets together for a few years; now that he was sober, with a new life, he wanted nothing to do with her.

One thing at a time, I told her. Take care of your health, and deal with your trauma, and then, if you want, you can find your family.

Her face softened as I talked, telling her the success stories I knew, friends who'd overcome abuse and addiction. "And now she's an actress, and she writes screenplays, and she has a day job that pays well; she has a boyfriend and an apartment and two cats." Telling her how I quit cocaine at the age of seventeen by going on a monthlong

marijuana binge, smoking about eighteen joints per day while waiting for the cocaine urge to subside.

This really piqued her interest—she knew I'd had a dalliance with
drug addiction, but we hadn't discussed it at length. "So you've been
sober since then?" she asked.

I fingered the callus on the side of my right thumb, the one I had
from flicking the wheel of my lighter, lighting and relighting joints.
"Well, not *entirely* sober," I admitted, then immediately kicked myself. I shouldn't have said that; I was setting a bad example, still acting like a juvenile delinquent at the age of thirty-five. "I still smoke
pot. Too much, actually. But I barely drink, and I never do any hard
drugs anymore—I haven't in years and years."

It looked like she was going to ask me something else, but she was
distracted by the door opening. *Probably the doctor,* I thought, turning in my chair. Good, I wanted to talk to him. Instead it was Ashley,
Sam's caseworker from the shelter, the big white girl from Texas.

"Surprise!" Ashley's face was tan and her nose freckled, like she'd
just come back from a vacation in the sun. She waved at Sam and
then pointed at me, her broad smile showing a dimple on one side.
"And look who else is here! You've got so many visitors!"

"Hey, Ashley!" Sam's face perked right up. "I can't believe you
came!"

Ashley put her hands on her hips and bugged her eyes out at Sam.
"Of course! Soon as I got back from vacation! And I was thinking
about you when we were down there; we had the most fun, I was
wishing you could see it."

I deferred to Ashley, scooting out of the visitor's chair and seating
myself on the wide ledge of the windowsill. She unwrapped her outer
layers and sat down in the chair, still jabbering about her vacation.
Apparently, she and her family had gone to Disney World, and they
took the Disney cruise, too. "Which is great, because you get to hang
out with Mickey and the rest of the characters. . . ."

Sam was rapt, nodding and smiling. I hadn't been aware that she
liked Ashley so much. There had never been any extracurricular
mention of Ashley, no key chain made for her. Most of the girls at the

shelter thought Ashley was okay but no great shakes—kind of bossy, kind of dorky, kind of into the Lord. Now Sam was beaming at her, laughing. "That sounds so fun, oh my god."

And I was smiling along, but I was thinking, *Maybe ix-nay on the isney-Day thing, Ashley. Maybe don't come all busting in here, talking about your fancy vacation to the Happiest Place on Earth with your big old intact family, to this girl who thinks it's a treat to lie in a hospital with every antibiotic known to science shooting into her elbow. How about that.* But Sam seemed interested enough, nodding as Ashley described the rides, the parades, and the fireworks.

I could picture Sam in the Magic Kingdom, where my dad had taken me when I was a kid, and where my mom and I took Jake when he was young. Who would appreciate it more than Sam? I could see her staring in wonder at the spectacle of it all, the richness of every detail; I pictured her running her hand, amazed, over the fake rocks of the fake mountains, gaping at the colored lights playing over the castle at night. We'd trade her grungy ball cap for a pair of mouse ears; she'd get off Space Mountain for the fifteenth time and run right around to the entrance for the sixteenth. Ice cream in one hand, fudge in the other. The works.

Ashley stayed for only a half hour or so—she had laundry and unpacking to do—but on her way out she pressed upon Sam the copy of *Cosmopolitan* she'd bought for the plane ride home—"Just something for you to flip through," she said. Not exactly a present, so she wasn't breaking any shelter rules. I wondered if Ashley was visiting "off the record" or not—she probably was, I guessed, whereas Jodi had come on business.

"Good to see you, Janice. Maybe I'll see you up there tomorrow? And Sam, you better get better soon, okay? We all miss you a lot!"

"Okay," said Sam. "Thanks, Ashley." Her little-girl voice again—funny how it would come out at times. So disarming, you just wanted to reach out and muss up her hair, which was always already mussed. Ashley beamed at her with maternal pride as she left. She was the *caseworker*.

The door swung shut behind her. Sam turned her head to me and gave me a bemused look. "*Cosmopolitan?*" she asked, emphasizing every syllable. "Do I look like I read *Cosmopolitan?*"

I laughed, louder than I should have. She still liked me better than Ashley, thank god. "Don't you want the latest eyeliner tips for more orgasms?"

She held my eye, exaggerating the drollery. "Do I *look* like I wear *eyeliner?*" She made a tossing gesture with the magazine, and I laughed again. Maybe Ashley could help Sam find a new rehab program, but I knew what reading material to bring.

I had to leave soon, according to my internal schedule, but I wound up staying almost forty-five minutes more, talking about Ellenette and her welfare checks, about Sam applying to college when she was out of rehab. Now that her mood had lifted, she wanted to tell knock knock jokes, dead-baby jokes, guy-walks-into-a-bar jokes. Every time she saw my hand go into my pocket for my phone, she started a new topic of conversation—"Oh, hey, I really liked that one book you gave me, the one about the girl who lived in Grand Central station. You know she wrote it with the social worker who helped her get sober?"

Finally, I had to tear myself away—I was hungry, and Bill was on his way home, and I'd been there for two hours of up-and-down intensity. Between the sexual abuse and the near-dead sister and the rehab delay, I was emotionally spent. "Listen, I really do have to go," I told her. "But you know I'll come by again tomorrow, right?"

Her lower lip poked out for a second, but she reined it in quickly. "I know. And you know you don't have to come! If you're busy after work, or whatever."

I stood up, folding my arms in mock exasperation. "Samantha Dunleavy. What do I have to do to convince you that I want to be here?"

She squirmed a little, dug her chin into her chest, trying to suppress a smile. "I know, I'm just saying—"

"I told you, I'm going to be in your life from now on. That's a threat, *and* a promise. You're not getting rid of me."

"All right." She gave in and smiled.

I stood there at the end of her bed and decided. I came around the side and half hugged her across the chest with one arm, my cheek resting on the top of her head. She reached up with her gauzed paw and hugged back.

"I'm here," I said.

I love you, I thought.

"Thanks," she said, as a tear hit my shoulder. "Janice, thanks."

Chapter Four

Gone

The streets were empty on New Year's Day, strewn with muddy confetti and slush as I trudged to the hospital to see Sam. I was still hungover from the bottle of champagne that Bill and I had split the night before, but I was looking forward to seeing Sam, as I always did, my heart quickening in the elevator like I was about to go onstage. *Okay.* Time to be that person again—the strong, steady adult, the one who said all the wise, profound things, the one I'd always imagined I could be.

I walked down the hallway to her room and stopped short in the doorway. The room was dark and the bed was empty, flat as a slab, neatly made with fresh white sheets. There were no books on the night table; her name tag was missing from outside the door. A ghost room, like she'd never been there at all.

She's dead, I panicked, then scolded myself. *She's not dead, don't even think that.* Why did I always have to jump to the worst conclusion first? It was like I enjoyed freaking myself out. I backed up and headed down the hall to the nurses' station, breathing quickly, trying for an obsequious smile. "Excuse me," I began, but the nurse with the phone to her ear did not acknowledge me. I spun around, spotted a doctor I recognized coming down the hall, and put myself directly in his path. "Excuse me, Doctor, I'm looking for Samantha Dunleavy — she was in that room over there. . . ."

The doctor paused, annoyed at the interruption. "And who are you?"

"I'm . . ." I was stumped. I was nobody. I was no relation; I'd just met the girl six weeks earlier. *I'm the Bead Lady*. Nobody — just the person who'd been sitting in that visitor's chair every day for the past week and a half, praying for her to survive. "I'm her friend."

"Oh, right." He gave me the barest recognition, started to move past. "She was discharged this morning."

"Oh! Okay. Can you tell me if she was with anybody when . . ."

No, he couldn't, because he was already halfway down the hall.

"Okay!" I said to nobody. The nurse on the phone regarded me oddly. I turned and headed toward the elevator.

I felt so weird and weightless, walking back home, like my arms were too light, like I'd forgotten my bag somewhere. *Discharged*. Okay. So she was better, she was fine, her health was all right. I was off duty now. I was dismissed. She was probably back at the shelter already, watching Jerry Springer on the TV in the lounge, playing cards for cigarettes, bitching at her roommate, St. Croix, because she never came to visit.

I could go up there. I stopped in the middle of the sidewalk, ready to turn and walk toward the subway, then started toward home again, defeated. I couldn't go up to the shelter just to see Sam, and I couldn't pretend I was there for any other reason. Even if I did go up there, I wouldn't be able to sit and talk with her for hours the way we'd been doing, not at the shelter. I'd have to wait until Wednesday, and see her around the bead table, with ninety other girls all hollering for me, "Miss, glue this? Hook this? Tie this? Miss, how you spell *lesbian*?"

My feet dragged all the way home, where I surprised the cats; they blinked at me like they hadn't expected me for a while. Called Bill at work, told him the news.

"Discharged," he mused. "Well, I guess that's good news, right?

She's all better, and now you can take a breather." He knew the every-day visits had been wearing on me; I'd just been complaining to him the night before. *It's unbearable to witness that much pain, and the stories she's told me . . .*

"If she really is all better," I fretted. "I mean, yesterday she still had an IV in her arm, and today she's back on the street? This is how she got the infection in the first place. It's our goddamned health-care system—they push you out the door before you've recuperated."

"Honey, she's fine," I heard Bill say, but I rushed past it.

"And how do I know she even made it back to the shelter? She was sick, she could have collapsed somewhere! For Christ's sake, she had a blood infection, she almost died, and now they're giving her subway fare and sending her on her way?"

"You could call the shelter," he suggested. "Make sure she got back okay."

"I could, but they wouldn't let me talk to her. The residents can't receive phone calls; they can only get messages. And I can't leave her a message with my phone number. *The rules.*"

I knew I should listen to Bill; I knew Sam was fine, and I was just panicking. And still, I started to cry. Told Bill that he was right and that I loved him, put down the phone, and started to cry. Why? Not for her. She was fine, she was better than she'd been in weeks. But I wasn't fine. I'd been cut off, abruptly and without warning, from something I hadn't even known I needed six weeks ago. The rush of her company, the high of holding her hand. Her addictive grin.

The next forty-eight hours were all thumb twiddling, waiting for Wednesday night. I tried to concentrate on work, on my friends, on whatever Bill was saying at any given moment, but I was too anxious. Precious time was slipping away! The urgency—it was like high school again, where a relationship could live or die depending on whether or not you skipped homeroom one day, where hanging out with someone for ten days in a row was practically a common-law marriage. Every day that I wasn't with her, that intense bond we'd forged weakened; if I didn't see her again soon, I'd be consigned to the past—*Oh yeah, remember Janice? Whatever happened to her?*—like a one-night stand at a sophomore kegger.

My heart started its pronounced thumping early on Wednesday, while I was still on the subway uptown; by the time I'd walked from the station to the shelter, I was working up a little sweat. *What if she's not there? What if she was sent to rehab already? What if she doesn't like me anymore?*

The next two and a half hours were miserable, sitting in the cafeteria, craning my neck around like an attention-deficit giraffe, looking for a sign of Samantha, who did not appear. Sitting around the bead table with a new girl called Frenchie, an old-timer called Dagger, and a girl they called Klepto, who smelled like pee—still no Sam. Most of the girls who knew her before the hospital were gone; her erstwhile roommate, St. Croix, had been discharged for overstaying her deadline without getting a job. "Have you seen that white girl, Samantha?" I asked a few girls, to no avail.

The counselors' office was locked; I knocked and got a no-nonsense "We're in a meeting" through the door. So I couldn't peek at the whiteboard; there'd be no clues about Sam's whereabouts from Ashley. I waited an extra half hour before cleaning up, hoping Sam would materialize from somewhere, or the counselors' meeting would end. Finally, my cell phone buzzing in my pocket with messages from Bill ("Hey, Shmoo, thought you'd be home by now; let me know if I should start dinner"), I loaded up my bead bag and prepared to go.

I was dawdling by the elevator when the door to the counselors' office opened and Nadine walked out.

"Hi, Nadine!"

Nadine was pinching the bridge of her nose. She looked like she'd just been through a tour of Iraq. "Juh*neece*," she acknowledged, on her way to her own office.

"Nadine, I was wondering . . ." She stopped and looked at me, almost incredulous. Now was obviously not a good time. "I know Samantha was discharged from the hospital on Wednesday; I was hoping to find out—"

"Samantha is not here right now." Nadine started toward her office again, finished with me. I took the risk of following her, like I'd seen the girls do.

"Is she back in the hospital?" I asked, trotting up alongside her. "I mean, is she all right?"

Nadine didn't turn to look at me. "She is in a hospital, yes."

I *knew* it. I *knew* she wasn't fine; I could *feel* it. It was just as I'd predicted: the doctors had discharged her too soon, and now she was lying in a septic coma, fighting for her life. "What happened? Is she back at St. Victor's?"

We stopped at the door to Nadine's office. She put her key in the lock, turned it, then straightened up and faced me. "She's not at St. Victor's. She's in a hospital on Staten Island. And she's not allowed any visitors. She'll be out in a few days."

"Oh. Okay." *No visitors—Jesus!* What kind of near-death ward was that? And how did Nadine know when she'd be released? "I just . . . is there any way I could—"

Nadine exhaled hard. "Samantha is in a lockdown detox facility. She relapsed and used heroin the day after she left the hospital. She will probably be allowed to come back here once the detox program is through. I don't know yet."

She waited a second, then pushed the door open, like, *All right? Are we done here?* I stumbled backward a step or two, thrown by the news.

"Oh. Well, thanks, Nadine. Sorry to bother you. I'll just—"

Nadine cut me off, final. "Listen, Juh*neece.* Don't get too involved with Samantha. It's not a good idea. She's got too many problems for you to deal with. Okay?"

"I . . ." My throat froze. Twenty years melted away, and I was a resident again—chewed out for breaking the rules, still determined to keep breaking them. "I understand. Thanks, Nadine."

"Okay." She stepped into her office and closed the door. "Good night, Juh*neece.*"

I was numb when I got home. Then I was despondent. This could be the end of the friendship, I thought—if the shelter didn't take her back after detox, or if they sent her straight to rehab before my next shift; if she decided she was tired of trying, and she walked away—that would be it. I'd never see her again. She'd have no way to contact me, even if she wanted to; she had no last name or address for me—I was just Janice the Bead Lady. She'd never know that I was still her supporter, her friend; that I was still thinking of her, waiting to see her, just like I said when I left her bedside on New Year's Eve, saying *See you tomorrow.*

I couldn't lose her the way I'd lost all my old favorites—not again, not this time. I had to find a way to get her a message in detox. *Hang in there; don't give up, I'm still on your side. Don't run away.* But patients weren't allowed any contact in detox, damn it. I'd just have to wait until she was discharged and pray that she made it back to the shelter.

I called Jodi the drug counselor the next morning.

"Bead Lady," she hailed, flipping papers in the background. "What's up."

I got right to the point. "I hear our friend Samantha's in a lockdown detox."

"Huh," she said, like she was considering it. The flipping stopped, and there was a pause. "Well, whoever told you told you right. She's gonna be on Staten Island through tomorrow, and then I'm fighting to get her readmitted here." She sighed a little. "Then I gotta find a rehab that's willing to take her, with all her health issues."

Thank god for Jodi, for her calm, reassuring voice. As bad as all this was, at least Jodi was on the case. She sounded harried but by no means overwhelmed; this was her job, this was what she did best. Jodi would fight for Sam; she'd find her a rehab. I realized I'd been holding my breath, and I let it go, *phew.* "What happened?"

Her voice dropped, confidential. "Well, *I* think they didn't step her down off the pain meds slow enough, or they discharged her too soon, while she was still in pain. Either way, I think both the pain and the withdrawal got to her. She copped on the way back from the hospital."

"Wow." I laughed, though it wasn't funny. "That didn't take long."

"She's an overachiever," said Jodi. "She works fast."

I could see why Samantha liked Jodi so much—her deadpan delivery, her slow, unruffled way of speaking—she exuded an air of resigned humor, like she was expecting the worst, so she was almost amused when it happened. I wished I'd had a counselor like her when I was a kid; someone who'd have understood me and fought for me. An adult I could trust to help me, even when I'd made a mistake.

"So," I ventured, "the thing is, you know, I was spending a lot of time with Sam over the holidays. . . ."

"Oh, I know," she said wryly. Then her voice warmed. "You were very dedicated. It meant a lot to her."

I closed my eyes, pressed my lips together, heart surging. *I meant something to her.* "Well, I won't be around when she gets out of detox, and in case I don't get to see her before she goes to rehab, I just wanted to send her a note, or a card or something, like a message of support."

Jodi was considering again; there was a pause and then an exhale. "Well, I guess I could pass along a card. Like a get-well card, right?"

"That's it," I agreed. Nothing rule-bending, not a gift, just a *get out of detox soon!* card. "And I'll leave the envelope unsealed, so . . ." So Jodi could see that I wasn't a child molester.

"All right." She seemed to like this caveat. "So drop it off anytime, and I'll make sure she gets it when she gets back."

I hung up the phone, relieved, and got back to work, humming to myself. On my lunch break, I went out card shopping. *Dear Sam,* I wrote inside the card. *I'm sorry things have been so shitty for you, but I want you to know that I'm still on your side, and I can't wait to see you soon. Keep fighting the good fight!*

I ran up to the shelter after work, slid the unsealed card under the closed door of Jodi's office, then turned right around and left before I could run into any of the other girls. I didn't have the wherewithal to hang out and mentor anybody today.

I got the message the next afternoon: "Hey, Janice, it's Jodi. Sam's back here at the shelter, she got your card, it made her very happy. She says she's gonna really try to stay sober this time, and make it to rehab as soon as she can, so we're working on that. So everything's good, and we'll see you on Wednesday."

Great. I could picture Sam sitting in Jodi's office, her wide brown eyes scanning the card I'd sent, her lopsided half-smile as she tucked it carefully into the pocket of her cargo pants. No doubt Jodi would put her on restriction until she got to rehab; she'd spend the next few days in the lounge, writing to herself in her thin, scratchy hand, tearing through the slim collection of battered paperbacks scattered on the bookshelves. I'd come into the lounge on Wednesday before dinner, and her face would brighten like a bulb; I'd ignore the rules and give her a hug.

If I could last the five days until Wednesday. "I don't know," I told Bill that night over dinner. "Maybe I'll drop by there tomorrow while you're at work, bring some more donations. I got some more books to give away, and there's some stuff in the closet I'm not wearing. . . ."

"Uh-huh," said Bill, his eyebrows only slightly raised. He'd been watching me fret and fume all week, since Sam's surprise discharge from the hospital; he knew this trip was about more than donations. I could see the concern on his face, the tension in the corners of his eyes—*Don't get burned out,* he wanted to say; *don't overdo it, okay?*—but he refrained from saying anything besides "I'll check my closet; I think I have some pants that shrunk in the wash."

So I walked into the lounge that Saturday with my prop bag full of donations and my eager heart pumping hard against my chest. A roughneck named Melissa ("Call me Mel") hollered at me.

"Bead Lady! What's poppin'?" She stuck out her fist for me to pound, and I hit it lightly with mine. "What you got in the bag, beads?"

Mel would have been my new favorite these days, if I'd had time for new favorites. Funny, manic, and thoroughly sincere, she'd run away from her parents in North Carolina at the age of fifteen to go live with her girlfriend, who was moving to Florida. The girlfriend's parents quickly threw her out, so she lived on the beach for a while. Since then, she'd bounced around to various people's houses, institutions, beaches, and parks, through various states, with various girlfriends; now, at eighteen, she was trying to get a job and a place to live.

I put the bag on the table. "Not beads today, just some clothes and books and whatnot." The other girls in the lounge immediately clustered around, chattering—*Ooh, clothes.* "How's things been with you?"

Mel lifted one scrawny shoulder. "A'ight. Boring. I got an interview at Key Food tomorrow."

I smiled absently. "That's excellent. I hope it works out. Hey, do you know that girl Sam, tall white girl, she was in the hospital. . . ."

"Oh, yeah." She nodded. "She's not around. Actually, I think she mighta left this morning—her roommate was giving away her shampoo and stuff."

"Oh. Huh."

My stomach flipped over. *No way.* She couldn't have left the shelter, not since her return; she just couldn't have.

"Be right back," I said.

I headed toward the counselors' office as the girls started claiming their seats at the table in the lounge. Knocked, entered, noted the counselors on the phones, engaged in conferences. No Ashley. I looked at the whiteboard. No Samantha Dunleavy.

Oh, no. No, no, no.

I stumbled back into the lounge. A six-foot-two stunner named Ynnhoj (pronounced "ee-nazh"; also the name Johnny spelled backward), with broad shoulders and a prominent Adam's apple, was holding up a pair of Bill's old pinstripe pants—"Oh, I could make a *fierce* pair of shorts out of these."

Mel shuffled up to me, wearing her eager smile. "Bead Lady, you hangin' out?"

Any other day I'd say, "Yeah, I'm hangin' out, where's the party at?" and I'd sit right down with Mel and Ynnhoj to shoot the shit, to dissect the days-old newspaper someone had left behind, the faces on the front page already vandalized beyond recognition. "No, I gotta go see a friend. I'll be back Wednesday with the beads, though."

She scowled and waved one arm at me—*Forget you, then.* "I'ma have a job by Wednesday!"

I smiled at her as best I could. "I'll miss you, then."

"A'ight," she said, arm dropping to her side, disappointed.

I started crying on the subway home. And there's nothing like crying on the subway, shielding your eyes with your hand and folding into yourself, trying to stifle the sobs so they look like coughs—you're never supposed to show weakness on the subway. I pulled it together well enough, but by the time I'd emerged at Union Square, I was in the onset of a full-blown panic attack, reduced to muttering to myself as I race-walked, spastic, *It's okay, it's all right, everything's okay, I'm okay.* Looking over at the redhead's corner by the Gap Body store, empty for the winter. Where could she be? Where did they all go when they disappeared—winter homes? Other cities? Detox wards? Early graves?

I got home and e-mailed Bill at work. *Sam's gone. I don't know where. This fucking SUCKS.* Then I called Jodi—no answer, of course, since it was the weekend. I left her a message. "Hey, it's Janice. I saw that Sam's not there at the shelter anymore; can you tell me what happened? Thanks."

I drummed my fingers on the desk. Nadine might be in her office, but I couldn't call her; she'd told me to back off from Sam. Nadine probably didn't know where Sam was anyway—she'd been discharged. Sam's name wasn't on her whiteboard; Sam was not her problem anymore.

Think. I could call the shelter and pretend to be someone else looking for her. A police officer! At least they'd tell me the last time they saw her. But probably better not to impersonate the police. I could call all the hospitals and morgues—isn't that what people did when their loved ones were missing? Or maybe I could call the cops. *Hi there, I'm missing a homeless girl—well, she was last seen at a hospital, then a detox, then a shelter. She's about six feet tall, and she has a tattoo that says* PSALMS 22 *on her left arm. Her right hand has a three-inch scar, one of her Achilles tendons was slashed, and her kidneys are about to fall out. Can you help me?*

Nobody could help me that night—not Bill, not my friends, not the joint and a half I smoked, hoping to quell the terrible panic. I'd lost her; Sam was gone. Bill tried his best to talk sense to me—"Jodi will call you back on Monday," he said. "You'll find out something. She probably got sent to rehab, and they forgot to let you know. If she's back in the hospital, you'll find her, and she'll be okay. Get some sleep. Jodi will call you back."

Eventually, and against my will, I got some sleep. *She'll be okay,* I repeated to myself. *Jodi will call me back.*

I got up on Monday, ran a few miles, and got to work, checking my cell phone every ten minutes. Ten o'clock . . . ten-thirty, and still no call. Maybe Jodi was coming in to work late today. Maybe she wasn't coming in at all. Eleven A.M., I called again. No answer. I didn't leave a message. She'd get the first one. I called again at noon, at one—still no answer. At two, I left another message. "Hi there, Janice again, I'm sure you're busy and I hate to bother you. . . ." Nothing. Three-thirty, my cell phone rang, and I jumped out of my skin like a skeleton to get it, but it was just Bill: "Heard anything? Well, hang in there."

By 6 P.M., I was crying, smoking, and trying to hug the cats, who wanted none of it. I decided to try the counselors' office; maybe Ashley would be there. Maybe she'd take pity on me and break confidentiality and tell me where Sam had gone. A counselor named Tamara answered the phone.

"Hey, Tamara, it's Janice! Bead Lady! How are you?"

"Good," she said, businesslike. I could hear a knot of girls arguing in front of her desk. "What's up?"

"Well . . ." I faltered. I didn't want to ask for Ashley—*Hi there, Tamara, could I talk to the* white *counselor, please?* And I couldn't just ask Tamara about Sam; she wasn't allowed to give out information about residents, even discharged ones. I'd have to try the back way, the way the girls always went when they wanted someone to tell them something. *Yo, I heard about what happened with that girl, yo. . . .*

"Well, I heard about what happened with Samantha Dunleavy—"

"Again," said Tamara into the phone. Then, phone askew— "Ladies, I will discharge all of you if you do not stop."

Again. What did that mean? Hospital or detox? I chuckled, like, *That rascally Samantha! Doing "it" again!* "Is she back at St. Victor's?"

There was no chuckle in Tamara's voice. "I can't say. *Ladies!*"

"Oh, sure. Well, thanks anyway."

"All right," she said, and hung up.

I sat back in my chair. *Again*—that was my clue. Sam had never run away from the shelter, or been discharged—*again* meant either a hospital or a detox. If she was in an institution, I could find her. I jumped online, started searching for all the hospitals in the city, already dialing St. Victor's with one hand.

I didn't have to dial anyone else. The woman at Patient Information said she was there: Samantha Dunleavy, on the Weiss Pavilion, third floor. She'd been admitted Saturday morning.

"Oh!" I gasped with relief, a vision of Sam's grinning face swimming into view. *Hooray, she's in the hospital!* I sprang from my chair, ready to grab my keys and go see her right away. "Great. Thank you so much."

"Looks like you just missed visiting hours," said the woman. "Tomorrow's six to eight."

I looked at the time—6:30 P.M. I'd seen Sam at six-thirty before—it was prime visiting time. "I'm sorry, I thought visiting hours were two to ten."

"Not the psych ward. Today was five to six-thirty, tomorrow's six to eight."

The psych ward. Well, this was a new one. I sat down again, heavy. "Oh! Of course. Thanks, thanks so much."

I called Bill, my hands shaking with leftover adrenaline.

"Found her. She's at the St. Victor's psych ward. I can see her tomorrow between six and eight."

He let out a deep, grateful breath. "Hey, that's great, babe. That you found her, I mean. And that she's someplace safe."

"Yeah." I was solemn again. I mean, the psych ward? Something bad must have happened. *What if she'd tried to kill herself? Or somebody else?* My head dropped into my free hand. "Perturbing, though. What do you think you have to do to get into the psych ward?"

"I don't know," said Bill. "Practice?"

Chapter Five

Psych

It had been almost two weeks since I left Sam's bedside, saying, "I'll see you tomorrow." Now, walking along the same old course to the hospital, I felt like I'd aged a year. Surely there were new crow's feet in the corners of my puffy eyes, still swollen from the previous night's posttrauma meltdown. "Look, you found her, and she's all right," Bill had said, trying to soothe me, but I was having none of it. She wasn't *all right*, I snapped; she was in a psych ward. She'd gone from the hospital to a detox to the nuthouse in under two weeks—how did that make her *all right*?

St. Victor's psych ward had its own entrance, with its own awning and its own locked elevators. I waited with a group of other visitors for the clock to strike six before the guard would let us sign the register and receive our passes. One gentleman was particularly agitated by the short wait; he paced a two-foot square of the lobby, muttering and fuming. I was only slightly less impatient.

The attendant took us upstairs in the elevator, and the door to the ward was opened. And there was Sam, standing a few yards down the hallway, wearing a pair of hospital slippers under her cargo pants and an expression of surprise, almost alarm, on her face upon seeing me.

I burst into a huge grin, putting out my jazz hands as I came down the hall, *Ta da!* "I *told* you you weren't getting rid of me."

"Oh my god." She covered her face with her hand and doubled over with embarrassment, but underneath the hand, I could tell, she was smiling. "I told Jodi not to tell you where I went."

So Jodi had known. As frustrated and freaked out as I'd been, trying to get ahold of her all day the day before, I had to admire Jodi for keeping Sam's confidence. "She didn't tell me. I found you anyway. You want me to go?"

"I just . . ." She twisted around some more, still trying to hide the upturned corners of her mouth, then gave up and let out a sheepish grin. "I didn't want anybody to know I was in here! I didn't know what you'd think."

"Oh, for fuck's sake," I assured her, pshawing. "It's not like you're the first person I've ever visited in the psych ward. I mean, you're special, but you're not *that* unique."

She laughed ironically, *hah*, and I followed her down the hall toward the patients' lounge, studying her peripherally. She looked okay—her color was better than the days when she was at death's door, and her wrist bore a long, wide scar like an earthworm, but there was no dressing on it, it was fully closed. She was still too thin, but she probably always had been. Then she looked over at me, and I saw the exhaustion in her eyes, and the hard line between them, the one that came out when she was suffering. It looked like someone had hit her in the forehead with a chisel.

We found two seats together in the lounge, where a woman in a flowered housedress was mumbling to herself in Italian, and a young Korean girl stared intently at her reflection in the window. The girl wore thick green eyeshadow up to her brows and no other makeup. The agitated man from downstairs was yelling at a mousy brunette about how hard they made it to visit; she was cowering next to him on a battered sofa. I sort of hoped someone would come over and throw a straitjacket on him.

Sam watched me look around, taking it all in. She gave me a half-shrug. "Well," she said to me, like we were adulterers at a motel. "Here we are."

There we were. I smiled at her. "It's good to see you. I missed you."

"I missed you, too." She tried to smile back, but her head drooped forward, and a tear threatened to bust out of the corner of her eye. She rested her elbows on her knees and let her head hang. "It's . . . been a hard time."

"I bet it has. You want to tell me about it?"

A tear splashed onto her thigh, then another. I reached out and put a hand on her shoulder, the blade poking through her orange sweatshirt. I felt her heave a few times, felt how hard she was trying to repress it. She straightened up, and I removed my hand.

"I don't even know how I wound up here," she said, miserable. "I mean, I know, but . . ." Her voice trailed off, another renegade tear sliding down her cheek and onto her thigh.

I smiled again, supportive. "Well, I wasn't going to ask, but I am curious."

I got a wan chuckle and a sideways peek. *Look at me all you want,* I thought, *I'm right here.*

Her mouth twisted again; she was deciding something. She sighed. "Okay, well, last time I saw you, I was still in the hospital, right?"

"Right. New Year's Eve." We'd talked about books, about gun control, about free will versus determinism. She'd told me about hiking in the Rockies with her late dog last summer, her last attempt to get clean. We'd watched a rerun of *Law & Order.* "Then the next day, they discharged you, and you went back to the shelter."

She hunched her shoulders and cringe-smiled. "Except, I kinda made a stop along the way."

She looked up at me from her hunch—*Please don't be mad*—and I shrugged at her—*What are you gonna do.* I'd already forgiven her for it, not that it was mine to forgive. "And that's how you wound up in detox."

She rolled her eyes heavenward. "*That* sucked."

"I bet."

"But I guess I had to go, because otherwise I just woulda been . . . right back where I started."

She gestured at the floor with her arm. Right back to a square of sidewalk, a cup, and a needle. "You're probably right," I agreed.

She nodded. "That's what I said to Jodi; I said I don't want to go back to it. And part of the reason is, like, for the first time, I would be *losing* something if I went back. I mean, in the past, my life was always that bad, so who cared if it stayed that bad? But now I feel like maybe there could be something better." She was staring hard at a patch of linoleum, her eyes narrowed. "I mean, I got high, and it took the sick feeling away, but then I knew I was just going to get sick again in a few hours, and I didn't know what to do."

So she went to Jodi's office, and she waited on the busted green chair outside until Jodi was off the phone, and she went in and told Jodi what was up. And she let Jodi convince her that she should check herself in to detox and start again, fresh.

"I'm really proud that you did that," I said.

"I don't know why." She ducked her head again. "I mean, when I got out of there, and I got your card, I couldn't even believe it. Like, why would you want to be my friend, after I'd fucked up like that?"

I wanted to reach up and pet her hair, but she was about ten inches taller than me; even with her slouching, it felt like a stretch. I must have grown used to seeing her lying down in the hospital bed; I'd forgotten how much bigger than me she was. "I'm proud of you because you made a mistake but then you did the right thing to try to fix it."

She nodded at her lap, just once. Then she raised her head and looked at me with those giant eyes of hers.

"I'm glad you found me," she said. "I'm glad you came."

My turn to stifle a tear. "So am I."

It was too hard to stare at each other. We had to break it somehow, laugh about something. A short, balding guy in a gown was humming the theme song to *Jeopardy!*

"I get that song stuck in my head all the time," I confessed. "I should probably get locked up, too."

Her grin switched on. "Oh, man! Guzman. That guy's hilarious." And she was off on a string of anecdotes about her ward mates: who was all right and who was creepy, and who was never getting released. And the staff—she especially liked this one orderly, Milton, who'd been very cool with her. He'd given her a forbidden cigarette, which she'd smoked in the shower.

"See, the air vent is right there in the shower, so I shut the bathroom door and turned on the cold water, because I knew the cold air would force the warm air in the room upward and out through the vent, so I could smoke without anyone smelling it."

Rrrrright. She knew the cold air would force the hot air upward. That was, like, elementary physics. Or . . . science, of some sort. I probably should have known that, shouldn't I. "Ah-hah," I said. "Pretty sneaky, sis."

Then she was on to a story about climbing onto the roof from the deck where they got recreation time every day—"So everyone's, like, 'Where's Samantha?' And my feet are dangling right over their heads! It was so funny—"

I didn't want to interrupt her, but I had to ask. "Okay, so, you got through detox, and they sent you back to the shelter. So how'd you wind up in here?"

Okay. She reared back a little and rolled her eyes again, mortified this time. "Well . . . it's complicated." She sighed, deciding how to tell it, different expressions shifting across her face. She tilted her head, started to say something, shook her head no, then made up her mind.

"Well, really, it's all Ashley's fault. She's the one who said I had to come here. And now they don't want to let me out!"

Ah, of course, it was Ashley's fault. There was scarcely anything bad that happened at the shelter—nay, in the world at large—that the girls could not trace back to Ashley's fault. "Okay, but *why* did Ashley say you had to come here?"

Sam threw out one arm. "I don't know, because she hates me?

Because she's a stupid bitch, who doesn't know how to do her job? I don't know, *she's* the crazy one, she should be here, not me! Alls I said is, I was having a hard time and I was depressed. Which is normal, if you consider my circumstances!"

I nodded in sympathy. "But did you say you were going to hurt yourself?"

She pressed her lips into a hard, flat line. *Yes.* "No! Alls I said was, I think about it sometimes. But who doesn't? You told me you thought about it in the past, right, and you didn't kill yourself, did you? Just because you think about robbing a bank doesn't mean you're going to do it."

Yeah. I used to believe that, too. It's funny, though—the more you think about robbing that bank, the better the idea seems. But Sam was on a tear now, head high, voice loud, gesticulating all over the place.

"And Ashley totally lied to me, too. She told me I'd just be in here for the weekend. Because ordinarily, if I was feeling real bad, I'd just go talk to Jodi, you know? Except it was the weekend, and Jodi was gone until Monday morning—"

"So you went to talk to Ashley—"

"And she made me come here. But they lied! They said if I committed myself, I could get out in a few days! And now they don't want to let me out, even though I *told* them, I'm not going to hurt myself! And besides, if I really wanted to hurt myself, I could do it in here as well as anywhere else, they can't stop me if I really want to do something. I could stab myself right here in the throat with this pen—"

"Please don't," I offered.

"I'm not gonna! That's what's so frustrating. I mean, sometimes I want to, but I already said I won't!"

She hung her head and scowled. I didn't say anything.

"They're not helping me here, anyway. They're just giving me meds, and they can't even figure out which ones I should take. It sucks."

"I bet." Pause. "I'm sorry to hear it."

The girl with the green eye shadow was staring at us, I realized.

I turned my head and smiled at her. She stared back at me, then rose and shuffled over to our chairs. Sam muttered something under her breath: *Great, here we go.*

"You sisters?" asked the girl. Her voice was slurred and faint. "This your sister?"

"No," said Sam, trying to be patient. "Friend."

"Like a sister," I added, still smiling. "Hey, I like your eye shadow."

The girl turned toward me suddenly, as though I'd just reminded her of something, but when her eyes locked on my face, it was clear that she'd forgotten it. Sam groaned to herself, then cleared her throat and said politely, "Hey, Dawn, me and my friend are talking right now, and I don't mean to be rude, but—"

Dawn stared at Sam like she was reciting the Pledge of Allegiance. "Sister?" she repeated.

"Like a sister," I said again.

Sam shook her head in despair. "Everybody here is crazy," she said.

Dawn wandered away, which was good news, because Sam and I had a lot to cover before the end of visiting hours. I wanted to find out what her diagnosis was (a mix of borderline personality disorder and posttraumatic stress leading to suicidal ideation, she said), what meds they were giving her (a mix of antidepressants and antipsychotics), and when the doctor said she'd be getting out. She sighed in frustration at the last question.

"I get out when I don't feel like hurting myself anymore, which could be forever, as far as I know."

"It won't be forever," I told her. "I promise." I reached out for the pointy shoulder blade again, and this time my hand felt right there. "I swear."

She nodded at her lap. A few more tears dripped onto her thigh.

"Okay," she allowed. "I'm trusting you. But if things don't get better, I'm gonna be *real* mad at you."

"Okay." I laughed. "I'll totally accept that."

It was almost time to go, and I wanted to use the ladies' room. "I'll be right back." I rose and placed my bag on my seat—my way of say-ing, *I trust that I can leave this here with you.*

"All right," she said, moving over to the busted old upright piano that was sitting there, somewhat incongruously, hosting a collection of board games with scattered pieces on its bench and top. Her way of saying, *You'll hear that my hands are occupied, so you know I'm not going through your bag.*

She lifted the lid and cracked her knuckles, and as I closed the door to the bathroom across the lounge, I heard her begin to play.

It was Beethoven—fucking Beethoven!—"Für Elise." She played it perfectly, fluidly; the notes lingered and rushed and got louder and softer as she caressed each key, feet urging the pedals. I froze. She *could not* be playing this right now; she *could not* be playing like this. This was *not believable.* This called into question everything she'd told me about herself so far. How could she have been homeless since the age of twelve, neglected and abused since birth, living in squalor and poverty, and have learned to play the piano like this?

I washed my hands, dried them, and walked out to where she was hitting the crescendo. She swayed a little as she put the finishing touches on it, leaned over with one hand to hit the last note, and put her hands in her lap.

She looked at me. I bugged my eyes at her. Her lips pursed as she tried not to smile.

"Dude," I said. "You did not just play that like that."

She sat there with her pursed lips, enjoying my reaction as I con-tinued to stare at her, mouth agape.

"Where the hell did you pick that up?"

She shrugged, *no biggie.* "I used to sell dope to this guy who had a jazz bar in Oklahoma City. Sometimes he'd let me crash there. He showed me how to read music." She squinted at the sheaf of sheet music on the rack, played a few bars of Bette Midler's "The Rose." "Once you learn how to read the notes, you can play just about anything."

So she'd learned how to sight-read from a jazz and dope fiend in Oklahoma City. "Yeah, I know," I said, wary. "I took lessons in middle school." Three years of them, weekly, with practice in between. And I still couldn't sight-read, or play like that.

"It's funny, they always got a piano at places like this. They got two at the shelter." She was right, I realized, though I'd barely noticed them, and had never seen them played. "Maybe they'll have one at rehab."

She slid from the bench back to her chair, nonchalant, but I couldn't be quite as blasé about her virtuosity as she was. Even if she'd had informal lessons, it didn't explain how she got so good, how she'd stayed so good without practice. The music just seemed to come naturally to her—as natural as quoting the *Tao Te Ching*, as natural as applying physics to the problem of how to sneak a cigarette. I already knew the kid was a prodigy, that she could read a book in a day and discuss it with you the next; I'd noted her vocabulary, I'd read her poems. I'd seen her discussing her meds with the nurses—"Is that the vancomycin? Am I through with the nafcillin?" Now, watching her sight-read "The Rose" off the rack of a psych ward piano, it was like all six sides of the Rubik's Cube clicked into place.

I turned to her, sheer wonderment all over my face. "You're a savant, aren't you?"

Sam drew back and wrinkled her forehead at me. "I don't play *that* good."

I shook my head, brushing her off. "You're a fucking savant. You're a supergenius. You're like Good Will Hunting, or somebody. You have an eidetic memory, don't you."

Anybody else would have had to ask what *eidetic* meant. "What are you talking about?" she asked, uneasy.

I had not stopped staring at her, my mouth hanging open. She fidgeted a little under my gaze.

"You're kind of freaking me out," she said.

Well, vice versa, Einstein. "I'm sorry." I shook my head again, trying to dispel the weird feeling I had, a combination of jealousy and possessiveness. Maybe she was smarter than me, but she was still my discovery. I eyed her covetously, and she looked nervously back at me. "I'm just . . . impressed."

"Anyway," she said, breaking eye contact. "I think it's almost eight o'clock."

The nurse who'd unlocked the ward for us came into the lounge and made the announcement—"Visiting hours are over in five minutes, please say your good-byes." I rose slowly from the piano bench, loath to leave Sam again.

"It was great seeing you," I told her. "Despite the circumstances."

She rose and hovered next to me. The chiseled line between her eyes was back, deep as ever. "You too."

"And you know, the circumstances are only going to get better from here."

She exhaled and put on a brave face. "I know."

I reached out for a hug, and she reached down to receive it—a loose clasp, brief but satisfying. I slung my bag over my shoulder.

"Hey, Janice?" I turned, and Sam bit her lip. "Can I ask . . . would you give me your phone number? I wouldn't use it unless it was an emergency. Just in case I get moved again, or something. I want you to know how to find me."

"Oh! Uh . . ." Twelve thoughts at once: *Yes! No. Bad idea, not kosher; then again, none of this is. Say yes, you want to, and she needs you—you're her mentor. But not twenty-four hours a day. It's too much; you're going to regret it when the phone starts to ring. But at least you won't lose her again.* "Sure."

She reached into her cargo pants and pulled out the notebook, the one I'd given her two months ago. The tan cardboard back was soft with wear, like a teddy bear.

"I read what you wrote all the time," she said, and flipped to the back page. She passed me the book, and I scrawled my cell number under my name, adding a smiley face with a ponytail.

"Thanks," she said, smiling at it.

"You're welcome."

The other visitors started to trickle out; the agitated man was taking his leave, agitatedly. I turned to follow, and Sam stopped me.

"And, one other thing—do you think, tomorrow, could you maybe bring me something to read? It's so boring in here, I just . . ."

Tomorrow. Another internal argument started to brew. The holidays were over; I had work to do. I couldn't afford to get back into the habit of visiting her every day. Then again, it hadn't been every day—we'd just missed two weeks.

"Sure thing," I decided. "See you tomorrow."

Of course, tomorrow turned into every day. Every day after work, I ran over to the psych ward to sit with Samantha until visiting hours were over; then I'd run home, burst through my front door, and greedily suck down a joint. Bill tried gently suggesting that I take a break—"Babe, you're running yourself ragged again; please don't overdo it."

"I won't," I swore. It was just temporary, anyway. Soon Sam would go to rehab, and I wouldn't have to visit every day. But today she needed me. She was in crisis; it was even more severe than usual.

She'd called me the night before from the patients' pay phone. She wouldn't say what had happened at first, but then she broke down and spilled it.

"This guy, one of the patients, he came into my room, and he started . . . trying stuff with me."

"Oh my god." I'd clenched the phone in my hand until the veins popped. "What the fuck is going on at that place? Who the hell—did you tell the staff?"

"No! No, Janice, please don't say anything. They'd just make a big deal out of it, and I don't want to talk about it. I just want to get out of here as soon as I can. Please."

"Okay," I'd agreed, unwilling. But it definitely put a jog in my step as I wended my way to see her.

The nurse let the visitors onto the floor, and there was Sam, right by the pay phone, waiting for me, her face pale. I hugged her, briefly, and pulled back to look into her eyes. They were wide, red, and haunted.

"How are you?" I asked, though the answer was apparent—she

was terrible. Why did things like this always happen to her? she asked me. She must have invited them. She must have deserved it. She collapsed into a seat next to me, let me put my arm around her. We'd just been talking the day before about the time she was raped in Boston, and the subsequent abortion she'd had; she'd asked the same thing yesterday, too. Why did this always happen to her?

"Please let me tell the staff," I asked. "It won't make trouble for you, and they should know what happened so they can isolate the guy."

"No," she insisted. "It'll make it worse. Please, I got enough to deal with. Just let it go."

It had been a brutal few days—she'd been coming face-to-face with old nightmares, things she'd managed to blot out with heroin and meth and whatever else was handy. Now sober, she was having flashbacks, night terrors, panic attacks; even with the meds, she was a wreck. From the time I got off the elevator every day to the time the nurse escorted me away, Sam stuck to my side, begging me for some kind of answer, some kind of relief. How was she supposed to live with all this? When was this going to get better?

Rehab, I told her. Rehab was going to help her out so much, and then, a year from now, when she graduated . . . "How about this," I blurted. "When you graduate from rehab, I'll take you to Disney World."

She gaped at me, astonished. "Are you kidding me?"

Are you kidding *me?* I asked myself. *What the hell are you promising her? Man overboard! Man overboard!*

"I'm totally serious," I replied. "Let's make a bargain, and shake on it. If you go to rehab and stay sober for a whole year, next winter I will take you to Disney World."

"For real?" Sam looked awestruck, almost frightened, as the idea dawned on her—I really *was* serious. Me and her, we'd go to Disney World, just like Ashley and her family; we'd ride all the rides and eat all the candy and buy matching souvenir T-shirts. "I . . . I always wanted to go there, when I was a kid."

When she was a kid, she was beaten with an electrical cord. When she was a kid, she had to steal her own food or starve. When she was a kid, her parents took them all to Thailand for a few months, so they could make money off the kids while the heat cooled in the States. She could still speak the language, though she didn't much care to. Samantha had never been a kid, but I would fix that.

"It's a deal, then." I extended my hand. "Shake."

Sam shook my hand, still wary, despite her widening grin. "This is, like, legally binding, right? You're really serious?"

"Certifiably," I promised.

"Oh *man*, I am *totally* going to stay totally sober from now on," she vowed. She straightened her posture, and her face was shining with reverence. "I'm not even gonna huff the air freshener I got stashed in my room anymore."

I walked home that evening, high off the contact with her happiness. I'd done it; I'd given her something to look forward to, some tangible reward for staying alive and fighting. When I came in that night she'd been terminally despondent; when I left, she was grinning ear to ear. I'd worry about how to tell everyone later—Bill, my family— *Oh, by the way, I'm taking my little homeless junkie to Disney World.* Right now, I wanted to enjoy my success.

Bill was already home when I walked in.

"How was she tonight?" he asked, fixing himself a few fingers of scotch as I lit my post-hospital joint.

I kept my eyes averted and my voice noncommittal. "A little better, I think."

"That's good." He was noncommittal in return. "Have they told her when she's getting out?"

"Well, she told me probably by next week, but when I ran into Jodi at the shelter the other night, she said it might take longer."

"Huh," said Bill, his upper lip thin and tight. His upper lip always tightens when he's upset; it's what makes him no good at poker.

I said, "She won't be there too much longer, I hope."

"I hope not. It's been really tough."

I turned away from him, sucked on the joint. What was tough— me not being home in time to make dinner every night? Was it so hard for him, listening to the secondhand stories, the stories I barely hinted at, sparing him the worst of the details? What about the fact that I was nobly caring for one of society's most abject castoffs? I took another whopping hit and held it, stern-faced. I was sorry if Bill was feeling neglected, but *he* didn't have it tough.

I blew out the smoke in a long, thin line over my shoulder, away from him. "It *is* really tough," I said, short. "She's had an unbelievably tough life."

"I'm not saying I don't believe it."

I looked over at him again. He met my gaze, tight-lipped. "What are you saying?"

"I don't know. Just, every time something happens with her, it's like, you're running out the door."

I gave him a frosty smile. "That's what you do in an emergency."

"She has a lot of emergencies. I mean, she calls last night, and you're foaming at the mouth—"

"I wasn't *foaming at the mouth*," I fumed. "I was *worried*. That's what happens when you care about someone."

Bill looked down at his glass, swirled it. His voice got softer. "You really do care about her."

"Well . . . yeah." It probably wasn't meant to be an accusation—he sounded more resigned than anything. Like he'd caught me in bed with the mailman, and now he wanted to know, *So, you love this mailman guy, huh.* I felt stung with guilt. "I mean, not like I care about you, Shmoo." I laughed a little. "I don't want to have sex with her."

He didn't laugh. "That's good."

I frowned, turning away again. Of course, the thing with Sam wasn't sexual. But it was almost romantic, the way I thought about her constantly, talked about her all the time. If she were a man of my age, with her same wit and intellect, I'd probably fall in love with that man the way I did with Sam. And where would that leave Bill? I felt a moment of fear for our relationship, that I could be so easily swayed by someone else. It had happened before, with other boyfriends—I'd met someone new, and I'd moved on. But Sam wasn't a man, and

I loved Bill first and foremost, and there was no question about it in my mind. I was sad that there was a question in his.

I'm sorry, I wanted to say, but he spoke first.

"I would just hate to find out that she's . . . playing you, somehow."

My mood flipped again. Was he fucking kidding me? Nobody could *play* me; I knew the game too well. Who was at the shelter week after week; who knew these girls from the inside and out? *Me.* And besides me, there was Jodi, Sam's other biggest fan—with twenty years of experience under her belt; nobody was *playing* Jodi. I smirked at Bill's civilian ignorance.

"How in the world could she be playing me? What's she playing me for, a notebook? Some cookies? She hasn't asked me for a single cent, and I haven't offered her one." *Not one cent, just a week in Disney World.* I barreled past the thought. "All I'm giving her is my time, and my caring. What's she playing me for, hugs? She's a homeless junkie, Bill, I'm just trying to do the right thing here, and I don't understand why everybody is fighting me on this!"

"Nobody's fighting you!" he said, exasperated.

"Then why are we fighting?" I yelled.

"I don't know!"

He put his scotch down too hard on the table, put his head in his hand. This was making him miserable. *I* was making him miserable. I stubbed out the joint and moved over to sit next to him.

"I'm sorry, babe. I know I've been distracted a lot, and I have been spending a lot of time with Sam. And I know I've said this before, but she will be going to rehab soon. She should be ready to get out of the psych ward any day, and they're going to send her straight upstate, and then things will settle down. I promise. But I can't just abandon her, now that I've made the commitment. I just want her to get to rehab, that's all I want."

Bill nodded at his lap. "I know."

"I mean, you're right, I'm right back where I was over the holidays; I'm totally stressed out and overtaxed—"

He cut me short. "I know."

I didn't know what else to say. It scared me when Bill pulled away like this—that was supposed to be *my* prerogative. I put my arms around him, and he wrapped one arm around me.

"I love you," I tried.

"I love you, too," he said. It sounded more like, *I would pay you to shut up and leave me alone.*

For the first time in three years, we went to bed unhappy.

Sam was two days away from going to rehab when she smashed the mirror in her room and was committed to the psych ward for another week.

I arrived at the ward at the start of visiting hours, bearing a Mountain Dew and a Kit Kat bar, excited to update our Disney countdown— only 367 days to go!—when I saw her in the hallway, stripped of her street clothes and clad only in a hospital gown and slippers. She looked bleached again, her expression ghostly. There was a series of fresh cuts on her newly healed hand.

"What happened?" I asked, swooping to her side. We sat right down in the lounge, and she began.

Well, everything had been really hard, she said. Even with the meds, she was still completely depressed. And the ward wasn't helping her; it was making it worse.

"Which is why you have to get to rehab as soon as you can," I interrupted. "This place isn't doing you any good."

"I know," she said. "I just . . . the stuff we've been talking about the past couple days . . ."

What we'd been talking about: Sam blamed herself for the death of a friend, murdered in a drug deal. She blamed herself for turning a girl on to meth; within eight months, the girl was dead. She had a lot on her conscience, she told me, hinting that there were things I'd rather not know.

It's like child soldiers in the Congo, I'd told her. They're children. Nobody blames them for what they were forced to do to survive.

She'd told me more about her younger sister, Eileen, the one who'd tried to kill herself and failed, wound up comatose and then in a group home. Eileen had joined Sam on the streets for a few weeks two years ago; it hadn't worked out, so she'd gone back to living with friends. Then she found out she was HIV-positive. Then she tried to kill herself.

"So all of this has just been on my mind, so much, you know? And I can't stop thinking about it. About how shitty my life has been, and how I deserve it, and how nothing is ever going to change what happened, or who I am. I mean, even if I go to rehab, I'm still going to be the same person, with the same past—what's rehab going to do for me? It's just going to change the outside. Inside I'm still going to be a worthless piece of shit."

So she looked at herself in the mirror, and she saw her reflection smirking back at her. "And it was like nothing had changed." Sam shook her head, ground her fist into her palm. All the work she had done over the past few months, all the relationships she'd tried to build—she'd thought she'd made progress, but she still had that look on her face. Like she was damaged and proud of it, and it was never going to change.

"So I punched the mirror. I didn't think it would break! I mean, what kind of psych ward is this? They shouldn't have mirrors that break! That's not my fault, and now they're punishing me!"

I wasn't going to be drawn into the no-fault conversation now. "So what happened after you broke the mirror?"

Nothing, she said. Nobody even came to investigate the sound. She sat there looking at a shard of mirror, wondering whether or not to cut her own throat, until finally one of the orderlies came in and saw the broken glass.

"See, that proves I'm not going to kill myself. I totally had the chance, and I didn't take it!"

Now her chin was up, defiant; she looked almost pleased with herself. I narrowed my eyes. Sam knew exactly what she was doing. She knew what was going to happen if she punched that mirror; she was going to get to stay at St. Victor's, where the creeps and molesters were at least the ones you knew, where the orderlies sneaked her cigarettes, where Janice was available every single day. Goddamn it, I'd been so blind, so completely counterproductive. Sam was afraid to move on to rehab, and I'd been enabling her to stay.

"So now what?" I said, to myself as much as to Sam.

She shrugged. "I don't know. They said I have to stay another week or so before I can go upstate, which is bullshit. I want to get out of here." Her usual complaint, delivered with the usual doe eyes.

They weren't working on me today. "Then you shouldn't have punched a mirror," I exhaled through clenched teeth. "Didn't you just get over an infected hand from punching a wall? And you almost died from that infection—do you want another one? Jesus, Sam, you could have been at rehab two months ago; I thought that's what you wanted. Is that even what you want?"

Her face crumpled and she hung her head. "Please don't be mad at me, Janice." Her voice was small, almost a whisper. Tears slid from her eyes. "I'm sorry. I'm really sorry."

I exhaled again and put my hand on her back, feeling a pang of guilt. It was unfair to berate her for being self-destructive, when that was all she'd ever known how to be. I was angry at myself, not her. "I'm not mad. I'm just worried about you."

She nodded, head still hung, tears still sliding. "I know. I'm sorry. I want to go to rehab, I do. I'm gonna. It's just been so hard."

"I know. I know." I rubbed her back with my flat palm. "It's okay."

"And . . . and I know it's not fair to you, you've gotta come see me all the time, you shouldn't have to deal with this shit, I wish you—"

I cut her off. "I *want* to come see you. We've established that. Remember? You tried to get rid of me, and it didn't work. Don't worry about me. I'm not mad; I'm still going to be here. I'm just worried about you."

She nodded again, to herself. Shook with suppressed sobs, dripping tears. I continued to rub her back.

"I really do want to get better," she said, small-voiced. "I just don't know if it'll ever happen."

"I know."

I moved my hand to her shoulder, pulled her toward me so her head was leaning almost on top of mine, her side pressed against me. We sat this way in silence for a minute or two.

If she didn't get to rehab soon—if I'd helped to fuck this up for her—I'd be punching my reflection, too.

Absurdly, through all of this, I continued to have a life: working, hanging around with Bill and the cats, seeing my friends and my family.

"So how's your little homeless girl doing?" they'd ask me.

Twenty minutes later: ". . . So for now, she's still in the psych ward, waiting for rehab. But how are *you*?"

And I continued to volunteer, going directly from the psych ward after a quick session with Sam to the shelter, where I'd found my little butch friend, Mel, in the cafeteria having a hushed discussion with four other girls—Lola the suicidal pregnant girl, Lola's girlfriend Vivian, and two girls I didn't recognize.

"They say we're all getting discharged, all of us who went to PA."

They'd allowed me to sit at their table, so I took the liberty of joining the conversation. "Who's getting discharged?"

"All of us," moaned Mel. "That's what Andreas told me. He said since we were gone for three days, they shouldn't have even taken us back, and he was going to get us discharged."

Andreas was a counselor on the boys' floor, rumored to be a real hard-ass prick. Sam told me she thought he was on drugs, probably coke and pills—*You can kind of smell it on him,* she said, and if anyone had a nose for drugs, it was Sam. "Andreas can't discharge you," I said. "He's not on your floor. And why would he want to, anyway?"

"Because we were gone. But it wasn't our fault!"

Oh, of course not. "What happened?"

"We ran away to join a Jesus cult," said Lola, waving it off like this happened all the time. "Like, eight of us was hanging out and these people was talking to us about their place in Pennsylvania, and they made it sound really good, so we went with them, and then all of a sudden we're in this van, and we're praying at three in the morning—"

"Yeah," Mel interjected. "We were there on this cult farm for a few days, and then the cops came, and it turns out the cops were watching the cult people, and the FBI and everything, so I don't know what happened after that, but they brought us back here. But now they say they're gonna discharge us early."

What the fuck? I had to hear more about this one. "Wait, wait, wait, you're going to have to slow down." But they couldn't, they were too busy trying to figure out the ramifications for themselves.

"Well, they can't discharge me, I'm MHP. I'm *supposed* to do crazy shit." Lola made a *nyah nyah* face. MHP stood for mental health program; it was a special designation within the shelter for girls who were planning to get public assistance for being crazy. Lola's nickname at the shelter was "Lola Lola Bipola."

I let Mel and Lola and Vivian hash it out and went to see if I could catch Jodi before she took off for the night. She was just locking the door of her office behind her as I approached.

"How you doin'?" She gave me her arch smile. "How's our little friend today?"

I smiled in reply. "Well, she's not great—of course you heard she punched her mirror?"

Jodi rolled her eyes. "Oh, I heard. I'm in touch with the hospital every day about that kid, and she's not even officially a resident anymore. You know she blew her spot in rehab again with this mirror thing—now this place is saying they won't take her, and I gotta find her *another* program. She's gonna be the death of me."

I shuddered from the chill that hit me—no, Sam hadn't mentioned that she'd blown her spot in rehab. I thought she was leaving as soon as she was discharged from the psych ward. Now there'd be another delay, another string of days or weeks I'd be spending by her side, soaking up the aftereffects of her miserable childhood. "The rehab won't take her?"

"Nope. They're just a rehab; they can't take you if you're mentally ill. A little suicidal ideation, okay, but now they're balking at the mirror thing, saying maybe she's really a threat to herself or others. So I have to find her a place that takes MICA patients—mentally ill, chemically addicted. But I think we got a thirty-day program that might have room sometime this month. We'll see."

"Oh, wow." I slumped, resting my butt on the arm of the green chair outside her office. "I didn't know that. I thought she was still going to rehab in a week."

Jodi looked sympathetic. "Well, she may be, but only for a month. And then, I don't know. Maybe we can get the place upstate to take her, if she stays stable and doesn't pull any more stunts."

"Oh, wow."

"I know. She's a lot to deal with." She cocked her head and one eyebrow. "I talk to her every day. She tells me you come visit her all the time."

"Well, I've been . . ." I flushed and tried to cover, but I couldn't. It was true, and so what if it was? "Yeah," I admitted.

The eyebrow got higher. "She told me about Disney World."

Damn you, Sam. The Disney World deal was not supposed to be something that everybody knew about. It kind of didn't sound so good, when Jodi said it out loud. It kind of sounded like I was a child molester. I braced myself for it—*I think you should cool it with Sam.* "Okay," I said.

Jodi held my eyes. "And I think it's a good thing that you're doing for her. You've been very dedicated, and that means a lot to a kid like her. You know, she's going to need a lot of help if she's ever going to lead any kind of normal life, and if you feel like you can provide some of that to her, I think she's very lucky." She reached out and patted my arm—*Good girl.* "Listen, I gotta get out of here. My own kid is probably starving. Good to see you, though. I'll let you know what's happening, when I know."

She walked away, and I composed myself on the arm of her waiting chair. Good news, bad news. The good news was, Jodi approved of me. She told me I could take Sam to Disney World. She didn't tell me to hand over my volunteer ID and get the hell out of the building before she called the cops. The bad news was, Sam might not make it to rehab before I lost my mind completely.

Oh! Speaking of which. I jumped up to see if I could catch Jodi, but she was gone.

Hey, Jodi, what happened with that cult thing?

I finally got the story from Ashley, and I brought it home to Bill like a bouquet of flowers—*Look what I got for you!*

"Whoa," he said, rapt, as I described the scene—the girls packing their bags in a frenzy to go off with the cultists, the counselors and security guards begging them to stay; then the gaggle of kids all filing back into the shelter again with their heads hung, accompanied by the police, requesting readmission. "That's it?"

"Yep." I spread my hands like a blackjack dealer. "Pretty crazy, huh?"

"That's a chart topper," he mused. "That's up there with the best of Samantha Dunleavy."

"Right?" I didn't linger on the subject of Sam—it had ceased to be a sore one between us, but I was definitely prattling on about her less than before, especially tonight. *So, how's the kid today? Well, she's never getting to rehab.* I just smiled and passed the salad dressing. "And how was your day, Shmoo?"

Internally, however, the subject was so sore it was blistered. The idea chafed at me constantly—maybe our relationship wasn't helping Sam after all. Maybe it wasn't helping anybody. I'd been so sure I was doing the right thing, running to the psych ward every day, whether or not I was actually in the mood to hear about the worst of human depravity and try to mitigate its aftermath. Now Sam had sabotaged her spot in rehab, and I was part of the reason why. I couldn't avoid it anymore. I really had to take a break—for her sake, if not my own.

I was at my desk the next day when my cell phone buzzed, displaying the number of the psych ward pay phone.

Voice mail, I instructed myself, but a shriller voice prevailed—*Emergency!*

I picked it up. "Hello?"

"Hey Janice, it's Sam." Her voice was a little rushed, with an undertone of panic; she tried to cover by sounding upbeat. "I just wanted to let you know, I found out they're sending me to that thirty-day rehab in Larchmont on Wednesday."

"That's great!" I felt a huge rush of relief—*so she'd make it to rehab after all!*—then a stab of separation anxiety. Wednesday was only two days away. Well, obviously I couldn't take a break from her *now*. I had to see her before she left; we had plans to make. She'd have to give me a list of things she needed, like for summer camp; I'd have to give her my address, so she could write. Maybe I could even escort her to rehab—the social worker at the hospital had come over to our couch during visiting hours the other night, introduced herself, said she appreciated my commitment to Sam. *If there's anything I can do to help Sam . . .* , I'd told her. *There might be*, she'd said.

"Anyway," I continued, "I can't wait to hear all about it. I'll see you tonight as soon as visiting hours start. I think it's six to eight tonight, right?"

"Yep. See you then."

I put my phone away, smiling. I'd pore over my bookshelves later, see if there was anything I hadn't loaned her already that she might like to read. I'd ask her if she wanted something special to eat for our going-away party. She'd shown me a list of things she wanted to do before going away. *Fly a kite* was one. *Go to the dog run. Learn how to yo-yo.* Maybe I'd get her a yo-yo.

An hour later, my phone rang again. Sam again.

"Hello again," I answered, amused.

There was no hiding the panic in her voice now. "Janice, they're saying you can't see me anymore, they're saying you can't come visit. Why are they doing this to me? I can't believe it. I'm gonna—"

"What?" I jumped out of my chair, almost tripped and fell over. "What do you mean? Who said that?"

"Nadine, at the shelter," she cried. "And her boss, Kathy. And the hospital. The social worker just told me."

"The one I met the other night? Why?"

"I don't know! They said you were coming too much; they think there's something wrong with it. Janice, why are they doing this?"

Oh, this was bad. I'd been visiting her every day, I'd brought her presents, given her my phone number, promised her a trip. I winced—she'd recently asked me for a Polaroid of myself, and I'd given her one. Oh, this looked very, very bad. I folded my arm against my chest, tried to breathe deeply. "Sam, I don't know why they're doing this, but I'm going to call Nadine and find out, and then I'll call you right back."

"Okay. But don't ask for me, ask for . . . Britta, she'll come get me. Janice, I'm really . . . I'm really freaking out."

Yeah, so was I. But I had to stay calm, and so did she. Nothing had happened yet; this could all be a misunderstanding. "It's going to be okay. I'll call you back when I hear from Nadine. Just hang in there, and don't punch anything."

"Okay," she whimpered, "but—"

Damn it, Sam. I didn't have time to babysit her—I had to do damage control. "I'm serious! Stay calm, or they're going to think something fishy is going on. If you throw a shit fit, they're going to say our relationship is bad for you. So you have to *cool off*. I will fix this, and I will come see you. Okay?"

I was surprised by the firmness in my voice, how sure and capable I sounded. I would fix this, because I was the adult. For once, crisis was bringing out the best in me, instead of the worst. "Okay," she said, more convinced this time.

"I will call you as soon as I talk to Nadine. Now, go show them that you're calm and compliant. All right?"

I hung up and tried to take my own advice for once. I had to calm down and stop hyperventilating before I called Nadine in a lather and made it all sound worse than it was. *Everything's okay*, I told myself, channeling Bill's reassuring voice. There had been a misunderstanding, but everything was going to be okay.

I dialed the shelter and asked for Nadine. She picked up right away. "Older Females."

"Hi, Nadine, it's Janice." I kept my voice light and friendly.

Her voice was neither. "Juh*neece*. I was just going to call you."

"Okay. Is everything all right?"

"No." *Uh-oh.* "It's not a good idea for you to visit Samantha right now. I told you, she's too disturbed, and she's got to get to rehab this time—"

"I agree," I interjected, still trying for calm, a fake smile plastered on my face as I paced the living room. "Look, I'm fine with not visiting, I just wanted to make sure—"

Nadine blew air through her teeth, frustrated. "I told you, Juh-*neece*, if you visit her, you go off the record, not as a volunteer. The social worker said you told her you were Sam's caseworker."

"I never said I was her caseworker!" I caught myself yelling and modified my tone. "I never said that. She asked me how Sam and I met, and I said the shelter, but I never said I was her caseworker."

Nadine did not play any he-say she-say. "Well, I don't know who said what to who, but everything is too confused right now. You need to step away. The hospital is telling me you were trying to escort her to rehab. That's not your job! And now Samantha says she doesn't want to go unless *you* take her. Because she thinks if you take her, she can get away with something. And I'm not going to let that happen."

I breathed deeply and tried again. "Nadine, I understand there's been confusion, and I'm sorry if I added to it in any way, but I never said I was her caseworker, and I wasn't trying to escort her to rehab. The social worker said maybe it might help, but obviously it wouldn't, and I—"

"But I told you, don't be so involved with her, and then I hear you're visiting her every day. And now I don't know who's telling me the truth, or what's going on, but I am telling you, you cannot see her anymore. When she comes back here from rehab, you can see each other on Wednesday nights. But no more visits now. Samantha is trying to manipulate the situation, and pit everybody against each other, and it's working. No more."

"Okay." At least she mentioned Wednesdays. She wasn't canning me, not yet, anyway. "I understand. But I still think there was some miscommunication—"

"Juh*neece!*" Nadine's voice rose sharply, and I cringed. "You understand what I'm telling you. I don't have time for this. Samantha is not our only resident. I have too much to do. You don't visit her anymore until she goes to rehab. That's it."

"All right." *But I'm innocent!* I wanted to say. *It's not fair!* Okay, so I'd visited a lot—I thought that made me a *concerned citizen,* not a criminal. I clenched my teeth in frustration; she wouldn't let me clear my name. "I'm sorry for the confusion, Nadine, I appreciate—"

"I will see you on Wednesday," she said, and hung up.

I put the phone down, reeling. What the fuck was this, now? What could have happened since yesterday to ring Nadine's alarm? What had Sam told them? What did that dingbat social worker say? I called the pay phone at the psych ward, where it took a chain of three residents to get Sam on the line.

"Hello?" she said, meek.

"Hey there. So listen. I spoke to Nadine, and she's serious. I can't visit. They said I was passing myself off as a counselor, and that I shouldn't have offered to escort you to rehab, and that's why they—"

She broke in, whining. "But I want you to escort me! Why won't they let you visit me? I'm all freaked out here, and they're trying to take away my only support! What am I supposed to do? I'm gonna—"

"Sam." My firm, capable voice was back, I noticed; I was the adult again. "Listen to me. I'm right here, okay? I'm not going anywhere. I can't come see you, but I can call you, and you can call me. Okay? Nobody's taking away your support. They're not ending our friendship. They can't do that."

"But it's not fair! You weren't doing anything wrong! Why are they doing this to me?" I could hear her quick breath, feel her heart racing like it was my own.

"You've got to keep it together," I warned. "Remember what I said before? Be cool, or they will suspect foul play. And I'm in enough trouble here — I don't know who told them I was supposed to be your caseworker, but they're ready to fire me as a volunteer, okay?"

"I never told them you were my caseworker! I just said you were like a counselor to me! And now they won't let you come because I said that? That's totally . . ."

I closed my eyes and tried to summon my strength. So she'd told them I was her "counselor." No wonder the social worker had been so impressed by my visits; no wonder she'd mentioned me escorting Sam to rehab. She thought I was a social worker.

Samantha is trying to manipulate the situation, Nadine had said. *And it's working*.

"Sam, there's nothing we can do about it today. The only thing we can do is not make the situation worse. You've got to calm down and accept this. I want to visit you just as much as you want me to. But I will see you as soon as I can, when you get to rehab. If you do something crazy right now, you'll have to stay in the psych ward, and they won't let me visit you at all. Is that what you want?"

"No." She was meek again, her voice frail and sorrowful. "I'm sorry. I'm sorry I got you in trouble."

"You didn't get me in trouble." I'd gotten myself into it. "Just let's both try to stay out of trouble in the future, okay? I'll call you tomorrow, and I'll ask for Britta, and if you need to call me, you know you can, anytime — just, be discreet about it, okay? We'll play along for a day, and then you're going to Larchmont, and life will change very much for the better."

"I know. I just wish . . . it would mean so much if I could see you."

Yeah, it would. To see her, and to give her a hug good-bye. To tell her one more time, face-to-face, before she went away, how proud I was of her, and how grateful I was to be in her life. I didn't even know if she'd actually make it to rehab, or if she'd ditch her escort and run; I didn't know if she'd stay once she got there. As always, every time I let her out of my sight, I risked never seeing her again.

"I will see you as soon as I can," I promised. "You know I will."

• ■ •

I wasn't looking forward to going to the shelter that Wednesday. I wanted more than anything to blow it off, to say to Nadine, "You know, I come here every week at my own expense for no reason except the kindness of my heart and soul, but I don't have to." And "If you don't like the way I volunteer, maybe I shouldn't volunteer at all." I mean, Nadine had basically called me a liar, told me I was out of line, and hung up on me. Why? Because I had shown an above-average level of commitment to a young person who needed it? I mean, rules aside, I wasn't a detriment to Sam. I didn't see how it hurt the other girls if I visited Sam at the psych ward. This was bullshit; they acted like I needed them more than they needed me. And to impugn my character, to insinuate that I'd been *improper* in any way — that was practically slander.

Still, I had to go. I couldn't quit volunteering over Sam; that would be proving them right. I had to take my own advice again, hold my head up and show them that I was a team player. My bead bag seemed extra heavy and odious as I dragged it down the block toward the shelter, and my feet didn't want to take me there. The only consolation was the memory of the message from Sam that morning — "I'm here in Larchmont. It looks all right. Here's the number, you can call between six and eight every night. If it's busy, just keep trying. Thanks for everything, Janice. Hope I'll see you soon."

If Sam could go to someplace she didn't want to go, so could I. I marched my unwilling ass through the shelter doors, up the stairs, and straight to Nadine's door. I wasn't going to skulk around and avoid her; if I couldn't clear my name, at least I wanted to know where I stood.

She waved me right in. "Juh*neece*. Sit down. I want to talk to you."

"Okay, great." I sat and gave her my obedient look.

She appraised me, not unkindly, and her face relaxed. "So, what happened on Monday — it was the hospital's mistake. The social worker called me, she said you never claimed to be the caseworker, it was Samantha. She said to tell you she was sorry for the confusion."

Well, hallelujah. I broke into a smile. "I'm glad to hear that."

So was Nadine, obviously. "But you know why she was confused —

because Samantha made it sound like you were the caseworker, and she saw you there all the time. . . ."

"I know." I shook my head, laughed at myself. "I guess I overdid it a little bit."

Nadine looked at me, pointed. *Yeah, you did.* "And so did Samantha. She overdid it a lot."

"I guess she did."

She shook her head, like, *You don't even know.* "She had everybody here in an uproar the past two days. Nothing else got done. Jodi was calling my boss, and my boss was calling the hospital, and Samantha was calling everybody, trying to get us all confused—she was running the show. You know, she's very smart."

"Oh, I know," I said.

"And she's very good at getting what she wants. That's how she survived those years she was on the streets. She knows how to read people, and how to get them to do what she wants. When I told you to be careful with her, I wasn't just talking about her. Some of these girls will take over everything, if you let them."

I looked back at the last ten weeks—how quickly I'd gone from not knowing this girl at all to signing on as her full-time advocate for life. "I know."

Nadine smiled at me, head tipped in warning. "The rules are to protect the volunteers and staff, too."

I smiled back. "I'm starting to figure that out."

I realized, looking at Nadine now, how young her face was. I'd always thought of her as my elder, but tonight it dawned on me that she was probably my age, maybe even a year or two younger—thirty-three or thirty-four, at most. And here she ruled this floor like the prime minister, like she was Golda Meir, motherly political leader to forty or fifty severely troubled teenage girls. My prodigious respect for her grew tenfold.

"Good." She rose from her chair, and I did the same. She came around to my side of the desk and put her hand on my shoulder for a second. "Look, Juh*neece*, I know you meant well. I know that. I see how you are with the girls. You're good for them. They look forward to seeing you every week, and it's not just for the beads. They know you used to be a resident, and they see you as somebody that they could be one day. That's very important for them."

"Oh, pfff," I sputtered, tongue-tied with pride.

"I notice you've been here for almost a year now. Not many people make it that long." One corner of her smile twisted upward. "I didn't know how long you were going to last, when you started. You surprised me."

I surprised myself sometimes. "I'm just glad everything worked out."

And it had. Sam was at rehab, at long last, and I was back in Nadine's good graces. What a blessed place to be.

I waved and shut Nadine's door behind me, headed into the lounge to see my girls. It was time to string some beads.

Chapter Six

Rehabilitation

So Samantha was ensconced at rehab, and I was in a state of jubilation. I *had* helped her, after all; I'd seen her through the most precarious phase of her recovery. I'd put my arm around her while she cried, witnessed her pain, tried to absolve her of her shame. I'd shown her what real love looked like. I might have actually helped to save somebody's life—what greater purpose on earth could there be? And now I was free to stretch out in the king-sized bed of my life, and luxuriate in the lush comfort of it all. I could meet friends for drinks in the evening instead of running to the psych ward for visiting hours, or I could come home and read in the easy chair. I could see my brother, Jake, on a visit from college in Boston, and make leisurely dinners with Bill.

"Nothing new with Sam," I reported happily to everyone. "She's still away at rehab."

I didn't even have to miss her, because I spoke to her every night, sometime between 6 and 8 P.M., even if it meant standing outside of a restaurant with my finger in my ear, yelling, "Just keep going, babe! Twenty-six more days!" into the phone. She'd had some trouble adjusting to rehab at first—three days into her stay, she was vowing to break out of the locked ward and run away—to "elope," in the institutional parlance. She swore that rehab wasn't working—she wanted to use drugs more than ever. But her new counselor, Maria, convinced her to give it another twenty-four hours and then decide whether to stay or to go.

"Maybe this isn't working right now," Maria told her. "But the other thing you were doing wasn't working, either."

I was hearing a lot about Maria now, as Sam entered her second week of all-day meetings, workshops, and therapy sessions. Maria was young, only twenty-five, an ex-junkie and a practicing Catholic, now ministering to other addicts, some twice her age, while going for an advanced degree. "She sounds amazing," I said, that familiar jealousy rising in my throat, but I swallowed it—what was good for Sam was good for Janice. "I'm so glad you and she found each other. Didn't I tell you how great rehab would be?"

In fact, I was overjoyed that Sam was in such good hands and off of mine. I sang in the kitchen while making dinner, buoyed by the evening's phone call: "Today we had art therapy; I did these really cool pastels, I can't wait to show you when you visit." Bill and I spent uninterrupted weekends at home, walking down to Chinatown for dim sum, having dinner with other couples. I didn't have to run out to any hospitals. Nobody was calling to say they'd nearly been molested or had punched something inanimate. I went to the shelter on Wednesdays, smiled brightly and waved at Nadine when I saw her, and she waved back.

By the second week of rehab, I'd gone from speaking to Sam every night to speaking to her every other night. Soon she'd be allowed to have a visitor; I could come up on Sunday and spend two hours with her on the ward. It would be good to see her—our phone conversations had grown a little strained lately.

"So, how are you today?" I'd ask.

"Good. I got to play basketball after lunch."

"That sounds fun."

"It was."

(Awkward pause.)

Well, she was standing in a hallway in rehab—she wasn't going to spend half an hour going through her private innermost feelings, the way she used to. Sometimes she said, "I was really down today," or "Maria and I have been talking about my mom," but most of it was pretty prosaic—a joke she'd heard or a prank she'd pulled ("So I held my breath until I passed out, and they were like, oh my god, she has epilepsy!"). I tried to take it as a good sign—things were stable in her life right now, she could focus on the day-to-day. Play basketball, tell a joke, be a kid. She was doing the hard work with Maria.

Still, I was starting to wonder if she was slipping away from me a little. "I think she loves Maria more than me," I complained to Bill.

"Impossible," he judged. "Who is this Maria-come-lately, anyway?"

"Well, you know, I think she sounds great, she sounds perfect— she's young, she's really dedicated, and she's an ex-junkie, so they have that in common." *Damn it,* I thought, *why didn't I ever do any heroin? God knows I did enough of everything else.* "Anyway, the more support Sam has, the better. I mean, now she's got Jodi, *and* me, *and* Maria—she's in great shape."

I thought I might meet Maria on visiting day, but Sam told me she'd be off duty that weekend. "I hate it when she's not around," Sam confessed. "Me and her have grown real close, and then stuff comes up and I want to share it with her, and she's not here."

You can always call me, I wanted to say, but she couldn't. She could only receive calls, and only between six and eight, and only after I'd dialed and dialed and dialed for a half hour, waiting for someone else to get off the line. "I wish I could meet her," I said.

"Yeah," she said, wistful. There was another one of those awkward pauses.

"So, is there anything I can bring when I come see you? Books or magazines or anything?"

"Nope. Just bring yourself."

Her perky voice, almost rushed. Probably couldn't wait to hang up and go smoke a cigarette before evening free time was over. Kids—they outgrew you so fast.

"Will do," I said, letting her go. "I'll see you then."

I had my notebook on my lap on the train to Larchmont, but I was nervous and the train was shaking, so I didn't write; I just stared out the window, thinking. This was the same train I used to take to visit my mom and Jake when they were living in Westchester, back when I was in my twenties, before my mother and I dropped out of touch. She was still living nearby; if I stayed on the train for another few stops, I could go visit her instead of Sam. I hadn't visited my mother in years.

I got off the train at Larchmont and followed the directions to the rehab hospital I'd printed off the Internet. I'd been advised to show up a little bit before 2 P.M.—visitors had to sit through a presentation about 12-step recovery before they were allowed to see patients. I surveyed the other visitors as they arrived in the waiting room: a thirty-something man holding a squirming three-year-old girl on his lap; a couple in their sixties, who looked like they'd been through this before. Two women, Central American maybe, a mother and a daughter, holding hands. I wondered what I looked like to the others, pacing around in my down coat and hooded sweatshirt. Probably like I was going to see my boyfriend and slip him some cocaine with my tongue.

By 2 P.M., we were a motley crowd of twenty or so visitors, escorted by a facilitator into a meeting room with a big-screen TV on a cart. We signed in at a table bearing stacks of literature about addiction, 12-step recovery, and codependence. *Are you a marijuana addict?* asked one leaflet. I didn't bother to take one. I already knew the answer.

I chose a plastic chair and turned my attention to the facilitator, a woman in her fifties with a weary, seen-it-all look on her face. She stood at the front of the room and began her spiel. "You're here because you love somebody who's an addict. It's a hard thing to do, and sometimes you find you can't do it anymore. Here are some things you should know about addiction and recovery so you can understand what your loved one is going through, and so you can help yourself through this process."

She turned on the TV and started to play an Al-Anon video. The salient points of the video were:

- If you're involved with an addict, there's probably something a little addictive about your personality, too.
- You might want to look into that.
- Also, you might think you're helping the addict to get better, but you're probably not.
- In fact, you're probably *enabling* the addict.
- Relationships with addicts = generally unhealthy.
- The addict might have to leave the relationship with you in order to get healthy.
- That might not be such a bad thing for you, either.

Right. I looked around the room at all the other people, to whom this applied. Not me, of course — the only thing I'd *enabled* Sam to do was get to rehab. So could I see her, already?

We formed a line behind the facilitator and were ushered one by one through the double doors to the ward. I took two steps inside, and there was Sam, all six feet of her, leaning against the wall with one shoulder, hands in her pockets, grinning.

"Hey there!" I said, and went in for the hug. She hugged me back, reaching down to embrace me, then broke away.

"Hey," she said. She sounded out of breath, nervous maybe. "It's great to see you."

"You too!" She was pinker than she'd ever been, her eyes clear and wide, ten more pounds on her than when I'd seen her last, three weeks ago. No scowl of self-hatred like the one she'd seen in the psych ward mirror. "You look like you're doing just great."

"I'm getting fat." She laughed. "I keep eating and eating. It's, like, the closest I can get to a sedative." She extended her arm toward the patients' lounge. "Want to go sit?"

I sat across from her at a table for two and draped my coat over the back of my chair. "So."

"So." She smiled, fixing me with that hungry, penetrating look of hers. "Here we are."

There we were. Heady, to be in her company again, to feel that intense vitality she radiated. "So, how is this place?"

She widened her eyes, serious. "It's really good. Remember how I always said the shelter was the nicest place I'd ever lived? This place is even better. They keep us busy all day long, which is good—I mean, sometimes I hate it, but I always know, okay, just get through this one part and then something better will happen. You know? Like, I'll talk to Maria, or I'll go play basketball, or I'll write in the notebook you gave me. And I just give it another day. And it works— I been totally sober since I left the psych ward, not even air freshener or anything, completely sober. And no street drugs since detox. I mean, this is the first time I wake up in the morning and using isn't the first thing I think about. I still want to use, but I want to *not* use more than I want to use, you know?"

I beamed at her. This was exactly what I'd hoped she'd say—*You were right, Janice, you promised me that things would get better if I went to rehab, and they did.* "That's great. That's so awesome. I'm so glad to hear it. See? You worked so hard to get here, and you've worked so hard since you've been here, and it's really paid off."

"Yeah, I know. I mean, when I think about how much I didn't want to come here, and now I only have ten more days, and I don't want to leave. I mean, I don't want to stay here forever, but right now, this is where I need to be. And I don't know what's going to happen when I get out of here—I don't want to go back to the shelter, there's too much temptation there. I need someplace where I can't get away with *anything*, like this place. Like a halfway house or something."

My brow furrowed before I could catch it. They weren't really going to send her back to the shelter, were they? I'd thought the plan was to find her a nice yearlong version of this place, someplace strict and rigorous and long-term, and transfer her there directly. Someplace where we could talk on the phone, and I could come see her once every few weeks on visiting day, and somebody else would be taking care of her daily emotional needs. I couldn't do it; I shouldn't have even tried, and I wasn't game to try again. The past few weeks away from her had shown me how much I'd needed a break, how ill-equipped I was to minister to someone full-time. I might have been jealous of Sam's counselor Maria, but I didn't envy her.

"Will this place help you find a halfway house?"

"Well, Maria's working on it, and so's Jodi—I've spoken to her a few times. I'll probably have to go back to the shelter for a little while, probably a week or two, and then they should be able to get me into another program." She frowned. "It sucks, though. This is the first time I been sober this long since . . . since I can remember, barely. Since I was a kid. When I leave, I'll have thirty days sober. I don't want to mess that up."

"We'll all be there to help you," I promised.

She wanted to show me her drawings, so she ran to her room while I waited, trying to eavesdrop on the conversations around me: "So I had to get rid of the credit cards." "You're telling me they only give you decaf here?"

Sam sat down again and unrolled the sheaf of smudged pages: a desert sunset, reds and pinks and purples and blues, hand-blended and thumbprinted, with a black cactus in the foreground. A self-portrait of Sam on a skateboard, jumping off the loading dock at the shelter. The head of a wolflike dog, snarling, on the same page as a handgun. A self-portrait of Sam sitting against a tombstone, her arms folded over her head, with a thought bubble: a razor dripping blood.

She watched me linger over this last one and cringed, apologetic. "It's still real hard sometimes."

She moved her drawings aside, and we gossiped about the shelter. I told her the latest stories about the new crop of girls, all of her old contemporaries long gone by now, and she had gossip for me: Jodi was leaving the shelter for another agency. "But you can't say anything," she warned me. "She's not leaving until the end of the month."

"Wow. Did she say why she's leaving?"

"Nope, she said she couldn't talk about it. But Nadine's quitting, too; she already announced it."

"Really?" How did Sam, in Larchmont, hear about things that I didn't hear about from ten feet away? Something big must have been happening at the shelter, if they were losing their senior staff like that. "That sucks. That's really bad news."

Sam shrugged. "Not for me. Because Jodi told me she was gonna stay in touch like always, and she could give me her cell phone number now, since I'm not gonna be her client anymore. And Nadine was a bitch! She wouldn't let you come visit me at the psych ward!"

I thought about Nadine, working vigilantly as Sam went to the hospital, to detox, to the psych ward—even when Sam wasn't technically a resident, Nadine was on her case. I thought about her standing at her desk behind her stack of folders, phone on one shoulder; how she had to walk quickly wherever she went, or the girls stacked up behind her like a conga line. Her hand on my arm, *You surprised me.* "I'm going to miss Nadine."

Two hours passed like minutes, with only a few of those awkward pauses—the rest of the time it was all jabber jabber jabber. Books this, and TV that, and the activities the residents kept busy with all day. Everything was good.

"Eleven months and ten days until Disney World," she reminded me.

"Keep it up," I replied, smiling. "I can't wait."

Soon enough, it was time to go. "I guess I'll see you in ten days or so," she said, as we reluctantly made our way toward the door. "That Wednesday, at the shelter."

"Yeah, that'll be great."

"And we can hang out a bunch before I go wherever they're sending me, 'cause I won't be on full restriction anymore. I'll be able to do whatever I want, as long as I'm back by curfew. We could even go to a museum or something. The Museum of Modern Art is free on Fridays."

I blanched inside at the idea of Sam loose in the city, her long days free until she could get to another program. Dangerous, for both of us.

I would have to enforce some kind of moderation on myself, or I'd be back to spending every day after work with her, and she'd never make it to the halfway house. "Great," I said. "We'll definitely hang out."

We stopped in the hallway by the door, watching couples hug good-bye—"Come home soon, Papi." "Okay, tell Elena I miss her"—until we were the last ones there. Sam turned to me, the old *visiting hours are over* anxiety flashing across her face for a second.

"Thanks for coming, Janice. You're the greatest friend, seriously. You've done so much for me."

I cleared my throat, looked at my sneakers, tears in my eyes. "And you've done so much for me."

We hugged, then broke away, then reached out and hugged again, laughing. "Okay."

I pushed open the door, then turned around.

"I . . ." I knew what I wanted to say, but I couldn't quite say it. "I've got a lot of love for you, kid."

She smiled and nodded, like she knew what I meant. Then she waved, and I walked out the door.

And so the countdown began: ten, nine, eight, seven days until she'd be home. I stuck to my routine: running in the morning, work all day, dinners with Bill. I went to the shelter on Wednesday and heard that Mel had been discharged for fighting.

Alas, poor Mel—I knew her, Horatio.

Jodi was missing, too, taking her unused vacation days before leaving the shelter for good. Sam said that Jodi had found her a decent halfway house, but there'd be a few weeks' wait until they had an open bed. And I didn't see Nadine, though I knocked on her office door. No answer; she wasn't there. It was one of the few times I'd been there, day or night, that Nadine wasn't around.

So I strung beads with the new crew, Fatima and Jenny and Marisol, and a white girl from Texas named Karen who would not shut the hell up the entire time—"So I told him, I got *too* many men tryin'a spend time with me, I am *not* waiting around for your sorry ass, I don't care *what* you got in your pocket, 'cause I don't *need* your dick and I can get my *own* yayo. . . ." The other girls shot one another looks, especially when Karen started a new bracelet in yellow and black, the colors of the Latin Queens. "'Cause I used to be down with the Latin Queens back home, we always used to get high and party—"

"Ain't no 'used to' in the Latin Queens," corrected Marisol, whose own black-and-yellow bracelet read MARI WANNA SMOKE. She put down the earrings she was working on and gave Karen a direct look. "Once you down, you either down, or you dead."

Karen pursed her lips, dropped her eyes, shrugged it off. "Well, back in Texas, the way they do things there . . ."

Marisol raised an eyebrow at Fatima. Fatima rolled her eyes. I hoped Karen would be smart enough to drop the subject, maybe add some other colors to her bumblebee bracelet, before somebody decided it was time to school her in remedial gang studies.

Fortunately, Karen dropped it, and the night passed without incident. "How'd it go?" asked Bill, kissing me hello as I came in the door.

"Fine, I guess." I let my bag slide off my arm with a thud. "Nothing interesting. Mel's gone, the boxer, discharged for fighting. I guess that was apropos."

"Sorry to hear it. We liked Mel."

"Yeah." But not enough, apparently, to go chasing after her, the way I chased Samantha. I wondered, who was looking after Mel? If she wound up in a psych ward or a detox, if she needed hand surgery and the wound got infected, there wasn't anybody there for her. Or for any of them. Okay, Marisol might have her Latin Queens, at least, two or three other scowling girls with giant white T-shirts and skinny, overdrawn eyebrows, to sit around in the emergency room with her. But Fatima, Jenny, Karen the white girl—they'd be on their own.

I was feeling depressed about volunteering again, feeling like it was all futile, like whatever few drops of caring I managed to add to the bucket all ran out the hole in the bottom. I'd devoted myself to Sam nearly full-time, and she was still barely afloat, buoyed only by the good graces of Jodi and Maria and the rehab program. Support like that, and her head was just above water. What chance did the rest of these girls have, with no support at all?

I'd just hit my first anniversary of volunteering. Maybe it was time to stop. I'd already impressed Nadine with how long I'd stayed; I'd impressed myself. Hell, even Nadine was leaving. I could hardly be blamed for doing the same. It was just too much sadness, too much frustration. Too much of the same thing—falling in love with a girl, then losing her, again and again.

But I wasn't going to stop volunteering now that Sam was coming back. I called her at rehab three days before her departure date—it had been a few days since we'd spoken. "She's not here right now," one of her fellow patients informed me, and I felt like I'd been punched in the stomach. *Where the fuck is she, then? Don't tell me she took off. . . .*

I heard the story the next night, after a frantic twenty minutes of dialing and redialing. She'd been unable to come to the phone last night because she'd been struggling with the security guards. "They wouldn't let me leave! And I was like, 'You can't keep me here, it's voluntary, I know my rights, you can't detain me against my will!'"

Samantha Dunleavy, judicial expert. I felt like smacking myself in the forehead. But at least she was all right, I told myself; at least she didn't manage to run away—this time, anyway. "Why were you trying to get out? I thought you didn't want to leave."

I could picture her chin jutting out; her proud, defiant face, the same face she made after she broke that mirror, the smile that was almost a sneer. "I didn't. But I gotta leave anyway, so I wanted to do it on my terms."

Right. I softened. How hard must it have been to accept safety and comfort from other people for the first time in your life, and then to feel like you were losing it. I remembered how one of the doctors at the shelter told Jodi she thought maybe Sam had let her hand get infected after her wrist surgery so she could stay at the shelter for a while before she had to move on. It didn't seem too far-fetched, and who could begrudge her?

"It must suck," I empathized, "to have to leave Larchmont. Especially to leave Maria."

Sam's voice lightened at the sound of Maria's name. "Yeah. Maria's the one who got me to stay last night. She made me come into her office to talk"—here she dropped her voice and cupped her hand over the phone—"and she told me she would stay in touch with me after I leave here, but only if I stayed the full thirty days." Her voice went back to light and chirpy. "So I thought about it, and I said okay."

Ah, Maria. I sighed, both relieved and resigned. "That's so great. That's so great of Maria, and that's so great of you. I can't tell you how happy that makes me, that you stayed."

"Me too," she agreed. "And, Janice, I can't wait to see you again, and Jodi, too. You guys have been so supportive of me—I knew I'd be letting you down, too, if I didn't stay, so . . . that also helped me to do the right thing."

Well, I was just glad to be one half of the backup reason. "You did it, kid. And I can't wait to see you on Wednesday, too. You can make a key chain for Maria!"

Chapter Seven

Spring

Now it was March, and like the crocuses pushing through the dirt in the sidewalk flower beds, the redhead on my corner was back. I observed her that Wednesday night, on my way to the subway uptown, sitting on the sidewalk under some scaffolding with a guy her age, furiously counting her change and scratching her face. I'd seen the guy before; I recognized the long hair and the scabs; he, too, was a neighborhood regular. I'd usually see him sitting on his backpack a few blocks away reading a book. He rarely bothered to panhandle—the guys don't make nearly as much money as the girls do. But they're still useful, as part of a team; they can provide protection, security, companionship. They can go cop the drugs.

I walked past the two of them to the train, my heart ramping up like it did on my morning run. It was Samantha Day, at long last; she was back at the shelter. I'd gotten the message from Jodi that morning: "The eagle has landed." Jodi would be leaving the shelter at the end of the week; Sam would be staying almost through the end of the month. Then she was due to depart for a yearlong halfway-house program in Brooklyn on March 28—three days before her twentieth birthday on April 1.

Nadine was already gone. As was always the case, I didn't get to say good-bye.

At least Ashley the counselor was still there—I spotted her right away as I entered the cafeteria, swiveling my head and looking for Sam, who seemed to be absent. "How's it going?" I asked.

She gave me the usual answer.

"Crazy," she said, cheerful as ever. "There's a ton of new intakes, and they still haven't found a replacement for Nadine. But our friend Samantha's back from rehab, did you hear?"

"I did." I smiled. "Is she around?"

"Somewhere. I think she had some re-intake stuff to take care of. She should be down here any minute."

But I had to wait until I was upstairs and unpacked before Sam appeared, casually loping into the lounge with a grin on her face. "Hey, beads, cool."

"Hey there!" She looked fantastic, and not just because I was so happy to see her—she really looked great. Happy, healthy, confident—just as good as she'd looked at rehab, if not better. I burst into a grin of my own. I wanted to spring up out of my seat and embrace her, but that would have been impolitic. Instead, she leaned down, and I gave her half a hug from my chair. "How the hell are you?"

She pulled up an empty chair and scooted it in between me and Fatima, ignoring Fatima's dirty look. "I'm good! I'm actually kind of glad to be back here. I got to see Jodi, and she told me all about this halfway house I'm going to at the end of the month, so I'm psyched about that. Plus I decided to go for my GED, and I signed up for a free class I can take, so that's good."

The rest of the girls eyed us sideways as we spent the next fifteen minutes chattering away—"And I already spoke to Maria to tell her I got back okay, and I think she's gonna come down here on her day off and maybe we'll go to the movies or something. . . ." Occasionally someone would pass me an earring to hook—"Miss!"—and grab my attention for a second or two, then it was right back to the Sam and Janice show. "Great, that sounds great. You're going to blow right through the GED. You could probably take it tomorrow and kick its ass."

Bead Lady was definitely playing favorites. "Look at you two," said Fatima finally. "Like lovebirds."

Sam drew back, spread her hands on the table, and looked at them, the pink weal on the right one. I tried to shoot her a warning look—*No punching, Sam.*

"Lovebirds?" I laughed. "This is my little sister! We go way back, me and her. Friends for a long time."

"Oh." Fatima still looked suspicious. "You sure is good friends."

Sam pushed her chair back slowly, flashed me a little smile. "Well, I gotta unpack the rest of my shit and everything."

"Okay," I chirped, trying to hide my disappointment. I'd known that seeing her at the shelter wasn't going to be like our old, private visits, but I'd hoped for a grander reunion than this.

She rose and turned toward me, adding quietly, "Then later, I'm gonna go get some Dunkin' Donuts down the block."

I met her eyes and smiled. *Gotcha. I'll meet you there as soon as I'm done cleaning up.* It would leave us only a half hour before she had to come back for curfew, but it was better than nothing. "Sounds good."

She gave me that pressed-lip smile and walked away.

Fatima scooted her chair closer to mine again. "I'ma get my GED, too," she announced. "Soon as I get my Section 8."

An hour and a half later, I walked into Dunkin' Donuts to see Sam grinning from a back table. She jumped up when she saw me, and we hugged tightly, my head tucked under her chin like I was the kid. "I don't know why," she said, still grinning as she released me. "I just had a real craving for donuts."

I laughed, stealing a look out the window facing the street. Nadine was gone, but her boss, Kathy, was still around, and after the big psych ward kerfuffle, I didn't really want anybody seeing me and Sam together off campus. "Funny, I felt like a donut, too."

She indicated the counter with her arm. "Well, since we bumped into each other, *shall* we eat donuts together?"

"On me," I insisted, following her to the counter. "You want coffee or something, too?"

Once seated with our donuts, she got me with those big brown eyes, her gaze steadier than I'd ever seen it. She sat up straight in the chair, head high, smile wide—she hardly looked like the girl from the psych ward anymore, the one with the pallor and the scowl and that battle-scarred look. Now she looked like a regular teenager, a college kid knocking off after a part-time shift at the video store, on her way back to the dorms to study for midterms. Like my brother, or one of his friends.

"You look terrific," I told her sincerely. "You look . . . peaceful."

She accepted the compliment with a nod. "Thanks. I feel real good. I mean, I don't want to get cocky, because that's when I'm most likely to mess up. But for the first time, I really feel good about myself and my life and my prospects. I mean, if you told me in October, when I was laying on that sidewalk, that by March I'da made it through rehab, I'da been clean for over a month, that I'd have people like you and Jodi and Maria in my life . . ." She shook her head.

"It's pretty incredible," I agreed. I tried to imagine the redhead, four months from now, sitting clear-eyed and upright at a donut shop, telling me how grateful she was that her life had changed. "And you know, it only gets better from here."

She bobbed her head, chewed and swallowed. "That's what I'm hoping. I mean, I know I gotta be careful while I'm here, because this is, like, the hardest part, probably. Once I'm at the halfway house, then I'll be more secure. But still, right now I'm kind of psyched to have some freedom, you know? And to get to spend time with you, and Maria. 'Cause once I go to the halfway house, I'm not gonna be allowed to have any contact for the first few months or so, and I'm gonna have to earn privileges to go outside and stuff."

She was right, I realized—this was our window of opportunity. Whatever plans for moderation I'd made with myself might have to be revised, in light of the time frame. Besides, this was the most crucial juncture; this was when she was most likely to use. "Well then, we'd better enjoy this time while we can."

We finished our donuts and picked at the crumbs, talking about her plans for the next three and a half weeks. She couldn't really job-hunt, since she'd be going to a facility where she wouldn't be allowed off the premises for the next thirty to sixty days. The GED thing, though, that would be a productive use of her time, and she was going to try to make at least one 12-step meeting a day, and check in with Maria or Jodi or me by phone. "And of course on Wednesday, the Bead Lady comes—I always make sure to be there for that."

I mirrored her smile. "Of course. And maybe Friday we can go to MoMA. You want to meet outside at five-thirty?"

"It's a date," she agreed.

It was almost curfew time, so we bussed our table and put on our coats. "You go first," she suggested, standing back from the door. "I'll wait a minute, then leave."

Secret Agent Sam—nothing she loved more than a scheme. Not that it wasn't a good idea. I hugged her good-bye and yelled, "Great running into you!" as I pushed through the door. I could hear her laughing as it swung shut.

Moderation—I could manage that. We only went to MoMA twice, which was moderate, and we only went twice because the first time she'd scared the shit out of me, hadn't shown up, left me waiting for an hour before she realized she was standing in front of the Metropol-itan Museum instead. My cell phone rang, a stranger's number— she'd borrowed someone's phone on the street to make the emergency call. "Janice, I'm so sorry, I screwed it up, I'll be right down!" But by the time she got there, sweating with exertion and apology, the mu-seum was almost ready to close.

"That's okay," I said, wholly relieved just to know where she was again. And I couldn't help but notice that she'd arrived on a well-worn skateboard. "Where'd you get that?"

"Oh!" She looked at it like she'd forgotten about it, looked up at me and grinned. "Uh, somebody gave it to me."

The next Friday we had more luck; she was only twenty minutes late, and we managed to see a few galleries. "My art is usually more, like, traditional," she judged, "but I think I *appreciate* modern art more, you know?"

"It leaves a lot of room for interaction," I agreed.

I couldn't get over how thrilling it was, to be walking around the museum discussing art with her, my very own homeless girl, just a more fucked-up version of the homeless girl I'd been in my youth, when I'd have died from gratitude if someone had taken *me* to a museum. I basked in the aptness of her comments, in my apt replies, in the picture we presented—the brilliant street kid and the selfless volunteer, enriching each other through art. It was like one of the scenes in the movie I'd imagined, the one that ended with me and Sam laughing in the sunshine as she threw her mortarboard in the air. And just as I was looking around for a witness to all this altruism, there he was: Edward, a dear friend of mine and Bill's.

"Edward!" I leapt through the crowd like a gazelle and seized him by the arm. "How wonderful to see you. How've you been? You look great! This is my friend Samantha; Samantha, this is our friend Edward."

"Of course!" Edward's eyebrows rose as they shook hands—here she was, the famous Sam, whom he'd heard so much about. "A pleasure to meet you."

"Nice to meet *you*," she replied politely.

Edward and I chatted for a minute—"How's your latest play?" "Coming along, thanks." "We'll have to have dinner with Bill sometime soon." "Oh, absolutely!" And the whole time I'm making eyes at him, like, *Isn't she great? Isn't she something? Look at us, Edward, we're at the museum!*

Soon Edward went his own way, and Sam and I stayed until the museum closed, wandering through the throngs of people, talking about the other patrons as much as the artwork ("Look at the guy over there—his haircut looks like it could cut glass"). We followed the dregs of the visitors out through the front door, and I started walking her back toward the shelter.

She said she'd been enjoying her freedom—"Not *too* much," I interjected hopefully, and she laughed. No, she'd been good. Which I knew. I could see it in her eyes, in her skin, in her posture. She'd just been hanging out, studying for her GED, going to the Virgin Megastore and listening to CDs, walking dogs around the Union Square dog run for money. Skateboarding.

"Ten months and two weeks until Disney World," she reminded me.

"Oh, I know."

I hopped on the subway a few blocks short of the shelter. At the top of the stairs she hugged me; "I'll call you tomorrow," she promised. Then I got myself home, where Bill was waiting, Friday-night take-out menus in hand.

"I know where you've been," he said, kissing me hello.

"Well, yeah," I scoffed. "Because I told you where I was going to be."

He shrugged. "Well, that. And also, Edward called. He says he ran into you and Sam at MoMA. She's 'quite something,' he said."

I laughed, *hah*. "That she is. You should have heard her riff on pointillism and methamphetamines." I switched into her hey-dude voice. " 'See now, that's the perfect thing to do when you're tweaking, paint a hundred million little dots like that.' "

"Seurat as a speed freak." He smiled. "I like it."

We ordered dinner and arranged ourselves on the couch together, me with my customary joint in hand, fogging myself up as usual. "It's funny," mused Bill. "Hearing about her from Edward—I almost felt possessive of her, like I should have met her first. It's like I know her, and I've never met her." He frowned a little, pondering. "Edward says she's really tall and really butch."

"Well, *I* told you that," I protested. "I described her to you a bunch of times. The kind of messed-up teeth, the brown hair—"

He nodded, *right, right*. "I know, but now I feel like she really exists. She's not just a product of your fevered imagination, or a cover story for one of your many affairs." He was kidding but with a serious look on his face. "She's real. She's a part of our lives. I've heard all about her. Now I'm curious to meet her."

Huh. I'd always meant for them to meet, and Sam had mentioned it, too—"I want to meet Bill sometime. He sounds like a really good guy." I'd thought about introducing them long ago, but the psych ward didn't seem like the right circumstances, nor did visiting day at rehab. Now that she was back at the shelter, it might be time—though the prospect was a little worrisome. Sam was still emotionally vulnerable, and I didn't want her to feel threatened by my relationship with Bill. When we were together, she needed all of my attention; she shouldn't have had to compete with anyone. Nor should Bill have to play second fiddle to Sam. But if she was going to continue to play such an important role in my life, if I was serious about my commitment to her, then she was going to have to meet my partner. And he would have to decide for himself whether he was committed, too.

"Sam's heard all about you, too. I think she'd love to meet you."

"Excellent." He looked satisfied. "We'll arrange that soon, then."

In the meantime, Sam and I spoke almost every day, saw each other at the bead table on Wednesdays, made after-work dates to go browsing bookstores and novelty shops. She told me about her 12-step groups and GED classes, about riding her skateboard off the handrails in Union Square, and again, it was like watching the montage I'd dreamed of: images of happy Sam, running around the city, clasping hands with her fellow recovering addicts in a sober circle, whooping with joy as she soared on her wheels.

I blew off work one afternoon, and we went for lunch at a Vietnamese restaurant in Chinatown. Sam was in great spirits—she'd conned me into ditching work, and she'd seen Maria just a few days earlier. Maria had driven down from Larchmont with a kite for Sam, and they'd flown it in Central Park. "I brought my kite with me today, in case you want to try it. It's not so windy today, but maybe it could work." Everything else was going really well, too: she was ready to take her GED next week; she'd get her results before her transfer to the halfway house in Brooklyn. "I'm going to be a *high school graduate*," she said, savoring the words.

Great, great, great. I could hardly stop smiling enough to stuff the food in my face.

"And the writing's going real well," she told me. "I feel inspired a lot, even when things are down—like, even when I feel depressed, or whatever, I write about it, and it feels better. I had to get another note-book, 'cause I filled up the one you gave me—I been writing a lot of poems. I want to get them all together in a bunch so I can show you."

"I can't wait to see them, whenever you're ready."

She nodded, eyes wide. "And I was even thinking . . . maybe you and me could write a book together."

"That sounds great." I beamed. More fodder for my montage: the idea of Sam pacing as I scribbled, of meeting at coffee shops to com-pare chapters, of a book with our names on it, a picture of us at Dis-ney World on the back flap. "What should we write about?"

"Well, I was thinking about this kid I met at the shelter, the first time I was there, last fall. I can't remember his name, but he was from the Sudan, and he'd come over with some aid agency when he was, like, thirteen—they rescued him from the war or something— but then it wasn't working out with his foster family, so he split."

"Wow." I'd just read about a bunch of kids like that, Sudanese refugees who'd come to the United States, in one of the papers.

"Yeah, and he was telling me this one time about how he ran away, and how he was on the streets, eating garbage and stuff, and he was like, 'Oh my god, this is so much better than where I came from.' 'Cause where he came from, there wasn't even any garbage to eat. Where he came from, they made you kill your own parents and then join the army." She stopped and shook her head. "And I was like, I thought *I* had it rough."

Um, I thought, *you did.*

By the end of the meal, we'd drafted a plan for a cooperative novel, something about a Sudanese kid and the volunteer who helped teach him English, and were trying to think of a title—"How about *Everyone Suffers?*" she suggested, and I wrote it down in my notebook. This was one of my favorite things to do, coming up with creative projects; why weren't all my friendships this much fun? So many of my girlfriends just wanted to talk about boys, or diets, or one another. We never planned novels, or debated Nietzsche; it was never like it was with Sam.

After lunch, we got some green-tea ice cream and walked southwest toward Hudson River Park. Sam told me about the kid she'd seen on her way to GED class, panhandling outside a McDonald's. The kid looked like he was twelve, wearing nothing but a ratty T-shirt and zipped jeans in all the March bluster. She'd wanted to stop, but she had nothing in her pocket. "And I keep thinking about that kid," she said. "I can't stop. I really wanted to do something for him, help him out or something. It's like, he kind of reminds me of how I was at that age. Like, if I could help him, it would almost make up for what I went through, you know?"

"Yeah," I said. "I do know."

It was a beautiful afternoon, bright and sunny, if not quite windy enough for the small bat-shaped kite, but Sam dug it out of her knapsack and assembled the struts, and we tried it anyway. "Okay, hold it up, now *run!*" The kite trailed behind us, skidded and bumped against the grass. "Wait, try it this way!" "I think you have to run faster!" Eventually we gave up, but not before we'd exhausted ourselves from sprinting and laughing.

"What about those swings over there?" Sam pointed to the empty swings nearby.

"Yeah!" We threw down our stuff and sat on neighboring swings, started pumping our legs until we were soaring, almost synchronous for a second, then I was flying after her, watching the sun glow red through her mop of dark hair one minute, feeling the rush of air as she swung the other way behind me. *Whoosh, whoosh.*

A group of high-schoolers on a field trip, maybe ten kids and one teacher, passed by, one of the kids pointing up at the soles of our feet as we scraped them against the clouds.

"Swings!" he yelled, and within seconds the kids had all dropped their bags and dived for the empty ones. "Woo-hoo!"

We laughed, left the swings to the high-schoolers, and continued our walk through the park, then up through Tribeca and SoHo toward my apartment—just ambling, no destination in mind. It was getting to be late afternoon, and I had a few e-mails to send before the end of the business day.

"I'm going to have to take off soon," I said with regret.

"I'll walk you home," she offered.

Yeah . . . no. Sam had never been to our place—I'd never invited her. It felt like a bad idea, for a number of reasons. I mean, it wasn't like she and I had played exactly by the shelter's rules for volunteers, but this was a very big, obvious no-no, inviting one of the girls to your apartment. If anybody found out about it, and wanted to misinterpret it the way they misinterpreted things at the psych ward, I'd be in big trouble. Furthermore, yikes. I knew Sam wasn't going to steal anything from me, but . . . yikes. To invite a homeless junkie into your home—an ex-homeless ex-junkie, even—just didn't seem like a sound domestic policy. Even if nothing were to happen today, I had to think about later, down the line. I had to think about what would happen if she relapsed, if she eloped from her halfway house, about all the years to come when she was going to need things. I really wasn't going to want her showing up on my doorstep.

"Well, actually," I lied, guilty, "I've got to stop at a friend's house— I'm helping her with this proposal she's working on, so . . ."

"Oh." I couldn't see Sam's face to tell if she'd bought it or not. "That's cool."

We parted ways on the corner by the subway—she'd continue uptown, and I'd walk east to my imaginary friend's house.

"I had a great time," I said truthfully. "I had so much fun today."

"Me too." She stretched her arms over her head, exultant, and yawned. "Hope it goes well at your friend's house."

"Thanks. Hope it goes well up at the shelter. Say hi to everybody for me."

"I will. See you Wednesday."

We hugged, as we always did when meeting and parting these days. "Be good," I warned her. Then I waited until she'd walked away, and started for home.

• ■ •

"Bead Lady!"

It was the last Wednesday before Sam went to her halfway house, and I was walking into the cafeteria at the shelter when I heard the call and stopped short, delighted. It was the triumphant return of Mel, the boxer who'd escaped from the Jesus cult.

"Mel!" We clasped hands, pulled in toward each other, and bumped shoulders. "Great to see you. How you been?"

I looked over her head to see Sam, sitting with a book at another table. She gave me a quick flick of the wrist—*I'm over here, when you're done.*

"I'm a'ight," said Mel, trying to sound positive. "I'm back here, so . . ."

Right. Not exactly a sign of progress, being back at the shelter; then again, she'd probably been worse off since she left. "Well, it's good to see you," I said, moving away. "We're stringing beads after dinner, if you want to join us."

Sam put down her book as I sat across from her. "Got something to show you," she said, by way of greeting.

"Oh yeah?"

She rifled through her backpack, forehead creased with concentration, and came up with it. An official-looking piece of paper with a stamp on it, and her name in a calligraphic font—*Samantha Eliza Dunleavy.*

My eyes widened as she passed it to me for inspection. "Your GED. Oh my god. That's so awesome. Dude, that's so awesome." I passed it back to her, holding it reverently.

"It was easy," she protested. "Next I want to take the SATs. I was thinking maybe when I get out of the halfway house I could go to the New School for college—that's near your house, right?"

Sam at the New School, a year and a few months sober, working toward her degree. What I wouldn't give to see it come true. "Yep. I think that's a great idea. And if there's any way I could help you with

the applications, or the financial-aid forms—I could write you a rec-
ommendation, whatever you need."

"Thanks, Janice." She ducked to put her diploma away, and I saw
the flash of a proud smile. She straightened up again and met my eyes.
"You know, I was thinking about when I was in St. Victor's the other
day, and I was thinking, like, as much as it sucked, the whole hand
thing, the surgery and the infection and everything, it feels like it must
have happened for a reason. You know? Like being in the hospital was
almost a good thing. Because that's how we got to know each other."

"It was *not* a good thing," I said, mock-scolding, though I'd come
close to thinking the same thing a few times. "You were already stuck
with me, whether you knew it or not. And we'll have no more hospitals in the future."

She put up her hands in surrender. "No argument here."

We trudged up the stairs to Older Females, and she told me she'd
seen the kid again, the McDonald's kid, panhandling in the same
ratty T-shirt as the week before. "But I talked to him this time. 'Cause
I had these McDonald's coupons from Maria, and so I went up to
him, and I said, 'You want something to eat?' "

"Really?"

"Yep. And I bought him, like, a whole bunch of stuff, and he was
eating real fast, like he was super-hungry. And I was trying to get him
to tell me, like, where he lived and stuff, but he was being real evasive, you know? So I was telling him about this place here, how I was
on the streets and I came here, and how good it was and shit."

"Oh, good, that's good." I started unpacking the beads on the
table, and girls started claiming the chairs, grabbing the colors they
wanted to use.

Sam perched on the corner of the table next to me. She was so excited about this kid, the animated look on her face so earnest, almost
maternal. "Yeah, I was telling him, you know, I didn't have a place
when I was your age, and this place is cool, they're not gonna fuck
with you or anything, they just help you out. I was like, 'I'm going
back there right now, you could come with me.' And he was thinking
about it, I could tell, but he wouldn't come with me right then."

"Wow, but that's great, that you reached out like that." I wanted to devote myself to this conversation, but everyone was pressing me for strings and earring posts. "Okay, hang on one second, I'm still getting organized here."

"So I told him I'd be back there on Thursday, 'cause I wanted to go back to GED school and find out about SAT class, for when I get out of the halfway house. And I said, if I saw him again, we could go to McDonald's and talk some more. And maybe he's thinking about it, you know?"

"That would be great, Sam. If you were able to help this kid . . ."

"I know."

I handed out the various materials requested—"Bead Lady, let me get a string this long? Miss, you got sparkly ones this color?"—and Sam straightened up and turned.

"I think I'm gonna go write in my notebook," she said, giving me the eyebrow. *See you next Monday, right?* Monday would be her last night before the halfway house, and we were planning a good-bye-for-now dinner.

I nodded in reply, and she walked out of the lounge. Then I turned to Mel, making her umpteenth rainbow bracelet in the seat to my left.

"So, Mel, what's new with you?"

The next evening I was at home, waiting for Bill to get in, when my cell phone rang with a number I didn't recognize.

"Hello?"

"Hey, it's me." Sam. Outside at a pay phone, panting like she'd been sprinting. "I'm . . . something bad happened."

I was already on my feet. "What happened? Are you okay? Where are you?"

"Union Square. I'm mostly okay, I just . . . can I come over? I really need to see you right now, if—"

"I'll meet you," I said, jamming my feet into sneakers. "In front of the bookstore. Five minutes. Don't go anywhere!"

I was flying out the door, down the staircase, pulling my coat on as I hurried to the bookstore. There she was, looking like she'd been smacked in the face with a brick. An actual brick. Her cheek and lip were badly bruised, just starting to turn blue; her left eye swelled with the makings of a shiner.

"Hey." She hobbled toward me, pressing her hand to one side of her rib cage.

"Holy shit," I said, panic and rage rising in my chest. "Holy shit. What the hell just happened?"

"Where can we go?" she pleaded. "Can we—"

"Did you get into a fight? Do you need to go to the emergency room? What happened?"

She shook her head, stiff, her freaked-out eyes the size of pinwheels. "I got beat up. But I'm all right. No hospitals, I don't want to mess up my bed at the halfway house. I just gotta . . . sit down somewhere. . . ."

"The diner down the block," I instructed, and we set off. "Tell me what happened."

It was the kid, she said. She went back to GED school that afternoon, and there he was, in front of the McDonald's. They talked some more, and he said he'd been thinking about it; he was ready to come with her to the shelter. "He said he just had to go get his bag, and so I go with him around the corner, figuring he's got it stashed in some hiding place."

We entered the diner, and the host looked askance at us—me, the slumming yuppie, with this giant black-eyed, beat-up street kid in tow. We slid into a booth and accepted menus; I ordered something to make the waiter go away. "So then what?"

Her voice quavered as she continued. "So he goes into this brownstone, and into this apartment, and there's this guy there, like, in his forties, with some Russian accent, and he's like, 'Where the fuck have you been? Where's the money? Where the fuck do you think you're going? I told you what was gonna happen if you tried to leave!' And he starts smacking the shit out of the kid."

"Oh my god." I clenched my fists under the table—I'd call the police as soon as she told me the rest.

"Yeah, but the kid manages to break away and run past me, and he's out the door. And then the guy's coming after *me*, like, *Who the fuck are you? I should kill you!* And he grabs my throat, starts punching me, and I'm fighting him—he hit me a couple of times, thank god he didn't have a weapon or anything—but I was scared, he was choking me—Janice, I was so scared. I used to fight all the time, but I haven't been in a fight in months, and I was fighting him, but he was kicking me—"

"Oh my god."

She dropped her volume and leaned in, urgent. "So I stabbed him. I had this pen in my pocket, and I just pulled it out and put it right in his neck, right·here." She pointed to the soft hollow at the base of her throat, bruised with thumbprints from this guy choking her, like, *half an hour ago.* "And he fell, and then I ran out the door." Her face was sheet white, her eyes practically shaking in their sockets, her voice high and tiny. "Janice, what if I killed him?"

I couldn't even consider this; it wasn't a possibility. "We're calling nine-one-one," I decided. "Are you sure you're all right? You don't need a hospital?"

She shook her head, emphatic. "No, I'm all right. I don't think my ribs are broke, I'm just . . . I'm scared to call the cops, I'm afraid what I did to this guy. . . ."

"I'll call. It'll be anonymous. There's a pay phone outside. I'll say I heard a fight. Where was it?" She didn't answer. "You've gotta tell me, there's a kid out there, Sam—"

"And I tried to help him, and this is what I got!" She pointed to her battered face, streaked with grime, contorted with pain and fear. She was nearly hyperventilating; one of us had to calm down. I slowed my own breathing, tried to get a grip on reality.

"I know. I know. I'm so sorry this happened, Sam, I know everything was going so well." Everything was going so fucking well, damn it! Less than a week until she went to the halfway house! And she had to go stab a pimp in the neck with a pen? Jesus! "And it's going to be okay. I promise. It's going to be okay. The police will handle this, neither of us will be involved, and everything will be okay, all right?"

Reluctantly, she gave me the name of the block, right near the Atlantic Avenue subway station in Brooklyn, and I put a twenty on the table so the waiter wouldn't think I'd skipped out. "I'll be right back."

Standing at the pay phone, shivering without my coat, I lifted the receiver off the hook, then put it down again. Suddenly I could picture myself three weeks from then, sitting in an interrogation room in a police station, listening to a tape of my own voice making this 911 call, then pleading with them—"Officers, her name is Samantha Dunleavy, and you can find her at this halfway house. But you can't arrest her; please, she told me it was self-defense!"

Instead of calling 911, I called Information and got the non-emergency number for the correct precinct. "Hi. I was just calling because I saw a homeless boy in front of the McDonald's, twelve or thirteen years old, I've seen him there a few times, and about half an hour ago, I saw him go into a building just off Atlantic and Boerum, and it sounded like there was a fight. I wasn't sure if it was an emergency, but I was hoping someone could maybe check to see if the boy's all right."

The operator asked me to describe the boy and double-checked the information. "Do you want to give your name?" she asked.

"Well, I just wanted to report it, I don't know if—"

"All right." I could tell that my call would not be ranked high on the priority list. Fine with me; at least I'd made it. I had to do something about the situation, but if the cops wanted to do nothing, that was their prerogative. "Thank you for your call, ma'am."

My civic duty fulfilled, I gulped a few deep breaths of cold air, trying to restore some kind of homeostasis, and went back inside. Sam was staring at her water glass like she was in a posttraumatic trance. God, this was bad news; this was a huge setback. Which is what you got, with recovering addicts.

I slid back into my seat. "It's all right," I reassured her with a confident smile. "I called the nonemergency number, and I doubt they're even checking on it, but I told them to look out for the boy, so hopefully . . ."

My voice trailed off as I looked at her mournful face, the tears welling in her giant eyes. How often this must have happened in her past; how often she'd worn that choker of bruises, been kicked in the ribs. And this was supposed to be her future, where shit like this didn't happen anymore; I'd promised her that this part of her life would be better.

"So what do we do now?" I asked. "Besides calm down, and thank god that you're all right."

She stared at the water glass like she could make it catch fire with her mind. "I know what I *want* to do," she answered. "Get high."

Yeah, she and I both. I was supposed to be sitting on my couch with a joint in my hand right about now, listening to Bill tell me about his day, not sitting here dealing with the aftermath of a pimp fight. "Well, you're not going to do that. You've got to get back to the shelter in time for curfew, and you've got to hang in there for the next few days until you can get to the halfway house. Okay? You're not going to blow everything for a fight you had with some scumbag."

"I know, I know." She shook her head again, transfixed by her glass. Then she tore herself away and looked up at me. "But how am I supposed to deal with this? I mean, I'm real freaked out, Janice, I don't know—"

Again I was surprised by the voice that came out of me: firm, calm, and decisive. "Sam, you're going to be all right. This is a terrible thing that happened, but it's over, and you're all right, and everything is going to be okay. You got into a fight. It happens all the time at the shelter. It was a serious fight, but you're okay now, and you've just got to move on from here and make sure that nothing like this ever happens again."

"But it wasn't my fault!" she protested, eyes pleading. "I was trying to help someone!"

I exhaled slowly. "Sam, I know. And I know I encouraged you here, but maybe it's too early for you to be trying to help anybody but yourself. Okay? Now you've got to chalk this up to a bad fight that could have happened to anybody, and you've just got to concentrate on what's ahead."

It took another ten or fifteen minutes of me reasoning with her, trying to keep my voice calm and my breathing slow, like whispering to a drunk. "Sam, you're okay. I know you're freaked out. But there's nothing you can do now. Everything's taken care of. Everything is going to be fine. This isn't even the worst thing you've been through in your life, and you made it through before, so you're going to make it through now. No, Sam, you didn't kill the guy. Because you didn't, that's how I know. Sam, you've got to calm down."

She was just starting to show signs of cooperating when my cell phone buzzed. *Home,* said the display. "Hang on," I said to Sam, then, into the phone, "Hey, babe, I'll be home in a few. Minor Sam emergency, but everything's okay. . . . No, she's all right, she says hi. I'll be home soon. . . . Okay, love you, too. See you."

She looked at me with those pleading eyes. "Please don't go yet," she asked, voice rising again. "I'm really . . ."

"I know." I was really *dot dot dot,* too. I sagged against the back of the booth. I couldn't take much more of this; I had to get home and turn on the TV and pretend for an hour or two that this wasn't happening—that Sam hadn't just been beaten up by a pimp, that people didn't prostitute children, that everything was basically okay in the world. "We'll sit for a few minutes, and then I'll put you on the train."

She started hyperventilating again. "But I'm not ready to go back there! What are they gonna say when they see me looking like this? What happens if they wanna kick me out?"

My parental, authoritative voice was starting to fray around the edges, frustration creeping in. "You got into a fight, Sam. It happens all the time. As long as you didn't fight anybody there, they can't kick you out. And listen, you remember the psych ward, when you broke the mirror? You can't do anything like that right now. You've got to hold it together. You understand? This sucks, but I will be here for you over the next few days, and you know you can always call Maria and Jodi, too. So that's the plan, all right? You go back to the shelter, you tell them someone tried to steal your skateboard, and you know it was wrong but you got into a fight and you're not going to get into any more fights, ever. And if you need anything at all, you call one of us."

Eventually, I convinced her to listen to me, and I walked her, limping and mewling, to the subway. "You sure you don't need a hospital?" I asked, and she shook her head again. "Okay. But call me, and tell me you got back to the shelter all right, okay?"

"Okay." She nodded, her battered face bobbling on top of her bruise-circled neck. "I'm sorry, Janice, I didn't mean to cause all this trouble. I wish—"

I cut her off. "I know you didn't. It's okay. Everything's going to be okay." I gave her an almost convincing smile. "Get back safe, and I'll talk to you in a few, all right?"

Stumbling down the block toward home, I felt light-headed with relief, almost exhilarated, like after a good cry. Another crisis averted, for now; another train saved from plunging off the tracks by Super Janice. The cops would clean up whatever collateral damage had been done. I could put away my cape and pretend to be a normal citizen again.

"What happened?" asked Bill when I got home. He gathered me in his arms for a gratefully accepted hug.

"She's okay," I assured him. "She got into a street fight, and she got banged up, but no broken bones. She was just feeling freaked out by it, like she wanted to get high, so she called me. Her sponsor." I tried laughing. "Anyway, she's on her way back uptown to the shelter, and I think we're missing *Survivor*. What do you want for dinner?"

"Jeez, hon, I hope she's all right." Bill frowned and asked more questions, but I brushed it off and he let it go. We made a chef's salad for dinner and flicked on the TV. And just as I was starting to enjoy the spectacle of a bunch of well-fed Americans ripping one another's hair out for a hot dog, the phone rang. Sam.

"I'm here," she said, the comforting din of the shelter in the background. "I'm okay. Thanks, Janice."

The shelter put Sam on full house restriction for the next few days, much to my relief, until she could get to the halfway house. She railed against the injustice—"Someone tries to take my skateboard, and I get put on restriction?"—but at least none of the plans had been compromised, and she was still set to transfer to Brooklyn at the end of the month. And while she could call me every day, sometimes more than once, she was stuck indoors again, so I knew she'd be safe from bodily harm—imposing or receiving it.

"But we're still gonna have a good-bye dinner on my last night," she insisted over the phone. "I gotta leave for a doctor's appointment that afternoon, and then I'm not going back until curfew. What are they gonna do to me, punish me? I'm leaving in the morning!"

There was no talking her out of it—she'd made up her mind. "I'm gonna see Maria for coffee after the doctor, and then you for dinner. My treat. I still have some money from dog walking."

I couldn't deny her, though I knew I shouldn't be encouraging her to bend any rules; I couldn't deny myself. Not seeing her for four or five days was a nice break for me, but not being able to see or talk to her for over a month was going to suck. I'd grown awfully attached to near-daily doses of Samantha. "All right," I caved. "Where are we going to go?"

She wanted to meet me in Union Square, by the dog run, and then she wanted to go for Thai food at a place on Seventh Avenue. *Why Thai?* I wondered, walking over to the park that evening to meet her. I would've thought it would bring back less than pleasant memories of the time she spent there as a kid.

"Hey, there!" She was hanging over the fence of the dog run, looking at all the excited dogs running around and sniffing one another. Her face still bore the faint marks of last week's fight, but the bruises had shrunk and turned to brown, and she was smiling. She turned from the fence and we embraced gently, sparing her sore ribs. "How're you doing?"

"I'm doing real good," she said. "How are you?"

Well, if she was good, then I was good. And she seemed good, loping along next to me on our way to the restaurant. As shitty as the restriction had been, she'd dealt with it, and she hadn't let it sidetrack her from her halfway house—she'd kept her cool, for once, and she was proud of herself. And she'd just seen Maria, on a special trip down from Larchmont to say good-bye to her favorite girl. "She bought me this T-shirt," bragged Sam, pointing at the brand-new Yankees logo across her flat chest.

"Awesome," I decreed.

She was bubbly throughout the evening, greeting the hostess at the restaurant in Thai, bantering with the waitress as she ordered for the two of us.

"What did you just say?" I asked, after the waitress looked at me and laughed.

She smirked. "I told her to be ready with a lot of water, in case it's too spicy for you."

Over our food (very spicy—I ate slowly and drank plenty of water), we discussed the next few months. Jodi had explained the program in depth to Sam—"I can call to let you and Jodi and Maria know I made it there okay, but then I can't call for thirty days. And then it's only if I earn privileges."

Frustrating, that they'd cut off her backing like that. I knew patients couldn't get phone calls from friends, but Sam's calls would be coming from social workers, drug counselors, volunteer mentors. We were her professional support team; they shouldn't box us out. "But at least you can write. We can write letters, right?"

"Yeah, I'm pretty sure. And they have a family day, where you can get visitors, but I think that's not until, like, May."

I tried not to look stricken. May was two months away. Well, all right. I remembered how peaceful and fulfilled and well rested I felt when Sam was at rehab; it would be like that again, just a little lonelier, without her phone calls. "I'm sure you know I'll be there. And I'll write to you all the time."

"I'll write, too. And I'll start working on our novel." She grinned at me. "And only, like, ten months until Disney World."

"That's right." I smiled. Then I was hit by a troublesome thought. "Wait—by then, you'll have enough privileges to go, right?"

She laughed. "By then, if I don't, I'm eloping."

We talked about the usual: books, science fiction, physics—this is when I started to lose the plot a little bit. "Wait, so the photon does what?" "It's like, it disappears, and when it comes back, it's aged faster than time could elapse." "Oh." We talked about her brother again, about the last time they saw each other in Chicago, a year earlier.

"He was on leave for a few days, and I went to go visit him, and we went out to this Greek restaurant, and it was real uncomfortable. Like, he's wearing his navy uniform, and I could tell he was ashamed of me 'cause I was still a junkie, and I was all mad at him, like, 'Don't think you're better than me, you used to do this shit all the time.' And we were gonna spend the whole weekend together, but then he said right after dinner he had to go, and I was pissed, 'cause we used to be best friends, you know? I mean, all throughout when we were kids, it was the two of us, and we'd protect my sister. We had a real close relationship. Plus I'd hitchhiked all the way from Colorado to see him. So I was like, fuck you and fuck the navy, and I don't ever want to see you again, and he was like, that's good because I don't want to see you, either. And that's been it. For over a year." She pondered it. "But now I think I get it. 'Cause, it's hard to be sober, and especially if you're gonna be around a junkie. I mean, I've been mad at him for that for a long time, but now I think I understand why he couldn't be around me."

We finished our meal, and she insisted on paying, pulling a crumpled wad of fives and ones from her pocket. "I can't wait to get out of the halfway house," she said. "I decided while I'm going to college to be a vet, I'm gonna take care of people's dogs for a living. You know how much people pay for a walk?" She shook her head, mystified at the yuppie lifestyle, and I laughed.

We hit the street, headed toward the subway she'd take uptown, and she slowed a little as we approached the station. "Can I ask you something?"

"Anything," I replied.

"Can I . . . come over and meet Bill?"

She peeked sideways at me, biting her lip. There was such vulnerability in her voice. I didn't want to say no to her, but I couldn't comfortably say yes, especially not without asking Bill first. I knew she'd never steal from me, or hurt the cats, but she was so unpredictable, so volatile and prone to disaster—I could easily imagine her deciding, once she was at our place, that she didn't want to go back to the shelter for the night, that she wanted to crash on our sofa instead; the next morning she could well decide she didn't want to go to the halfway house. Once we let her into the apartment, we might never get her out. "I'd love for you to come over and meet Bill," I said, thinking fast. "But he's not home yet. And I don't think it's a good idea tonight. It's just . . . the place reeks of weed, there's ashtrays full of roaches everywhere you sit . . . it's definitely not the place for someone in recovery."

"Oh." I cringed at the sadness of the syllable, hearing the arguments in her head—*But I don't care about weed, I'm not going to smoke any of it, I'm going to the halfway house tomorrow.* "I understand."

"Seriously," I babbled. "I do want you to come over. As soon as you get privileges to go off-site, I want you to come visit me. I just . . . I wasn't thinking, or I'd have cleaned up tonight."

"That's cool." Her disappointment was palpable, even as she kept her tone light. "We'll do it some other time."

"Absolutely." I cleared my guilty throat and changed the subject. "So, what do you want for your birthday? It's only a few days away, right?"

"Tickets to Disney World." She laughed. "For ten months from now."

We stopped at the subway station and stood chatting for a few minutes more. "All right," I said, checking the time. "Time for you to head uptown."

"Okay." She reached out for another hug, wincing a little at the pressure. "Bye, Janice."

Not good-bye. See you soon. I felt the tears collecting in my eyes, tried to blink them away before she could see. There was nothing to be sad about; this was a wonderful day. Sam had survived—she'd survived the hospital, she'd survived the psych ward, she'd survived rehab, and she'd survived everything since. Tomorrow she was going to a halfway house. She was halfway home.

Chapter Eight

Second Verse

So Sam was gone again — boo-hoo, hooray. Again, I felt the anxious peace of her absence, the same mix of relief, and the guilt over that relief, that I felt when she went to rehab. One day I wrote in my notebook, *Wish I could give her a call*; the next day I wrote, *Thank god she's off my hands — what the hell was I thinking?* And really, what the hell *had* I been thinking, getting mixed up with this kid who couldn't go three weeks without attracting some kind of near-fatal tragedy? I replayed the events of the past four months and shuddered; I felt like I was walking down the street and just missed being hit by a car. I mean, the story had ended well, for now — she was safe from danger, and I was safe from fucking things up — but the ending could have been much different; it still could be.

At least now that she was gone, I could breathe easily again; I could step back and review the past few months, look at them critically. Try to figure out how one visit to see this girl in the hospital had turned into a lifelong commitment to save her from the ravages of her abusive past. This always seemed to happen to me with people; I had a long-standing habit of adopting stray neurotics as friends, trying to fix them·

up, and then resenting them when I couldn't. Now here I was, doing it again. I hadn't meant to sign up for permanent duty with Sam. I'd never wanted this kind of responsibility; still, I'd made promises, and now I couldn't renege. And I didn't want to renege; I wanted to succeed. I wanted to help save Sam's life. I just wanted it to be easier.

Which it was, now that she was in someone else's care for a while. Bill came home at night and asked, "Any news?" And I got to tell him, "No." Really, that's all I wanted—no news.

And then I felt guilty again. I missed her. I worried about her. I wondered how she was doing, whether they were taking good care of her. I sent her a package for her twentieth birthday—an SAT-prep workbook, a Disney World guidebook, a stuffed monster, a custom-mixed CD from Bill—and got gloomy when she didn't reply. I called Jodi, just to catch up; she was happy at her new job at another agency for kids, and unruffled by Sam's absence. "She's where she needs to be," said Jodi. "We'll hear from her soon enough."

Indeed, not two weeks had passed when the phone rang at two in the morning, startling me from a deep sleep. I was on my feet in the kitchen and answering before I even knew it. "Hello?"

A woman's voice, loud confusion in the background: "Hello, is this Miss Erobum? This is Bushwick Hospital, you're the emergency contact for a Samantha Dunleavy? I wanted to let you know, she was admitted to the Intensive Care Unit; she was unable to breathe and we had to intubate her."

I was disoriented, confused. Was this a bad dream, or was this actually happening? The tile floor was cold under my feet—it must have been real. "Oh my god," I heard myself say. "What happened?"

"Her chart says she collapsed and was unresponsive, then she was brought here by ambulance about an hour ago. But now she's getting some air, she seems to be stable."

"When can I see her?" I turned to see Bill standing behind me in his boxers and bed head, deep lines of concern on his face. *Sam*, I mouthed. He nodded, still frowning.

"Visiting hours for the ICU are ten A.M. to noon. We'll let you know if anything else happens before then."

"Thank you." I hung up and turned to Bill. "She couldn't breathe, and she collapsed, and now she's in Intensive Care, and they said she's stable. That's all I know."

"Oh, babe." He held out his arms, and I went to hug him, still dazed from being jolted out of sleep. "Listen, she's stable. Come back to bed, and you'll see her in the morning."

"Right." We shuffled back to the bedroom and lay down again. I did not sleep. I dozed, one eye on the clock, until the sun came up, and then I got up and did a little work on the computer. A few hours later Bill got up, looking extra tired.

"Any news?" he asked.

"No," I said, glum. "But I'm going to shower and get over to the hospital as soon as visiting hours start. I'll call you when I know something."

I took the subway to the hospital, where I got my pass and went up to the ICU. There she was, alone in a room with a huge window facing the ward, hooked up to what looked like a robot army of machines. Her eyes were open but heavy, and her skin was the color of parchment. There were two thin tubes up her nose. She tried to smile when she saw me, busting into the room like a fireman and rushing to her side, but it was too much effort. "Hey," she managed to croak. "Thanks for coming."

"Of course." I petted her head, and she leaned against me. "Are you okay? What happened?"

It took a while, but she croaked out the story for me—she'd blacked out from lack of oxygen, due to advanced pneumonia. She'd cracked a rib in that fight she'd had and hadn't known it; the rib had punctured a lung, which had become infected. "I knew it hurt," she admitted. "But I thought it was healing."

"Guess not." Goddamn it, I should have taken her to the hospital the night she had that fight; I shouldn't have let her talk me out of it. But she'd seemed fine at our good-bye dinner, and she'd just seen a doctor that day—they must have missed it, too. "So they're treating the pneumonia, and the rib, I hope. Did they find anything else?"

"No." She shook her head and swallowed miserably. "I mean, my kidneys are still all fucked up, and my lungs were already shot to begin with, but other than that . . ." She turned her head abruptly as a young woman with dark, curly hair swept into the room.

"*There* she is," said the woman, swooping around the side of the bed and planting a smooch on Sam's cheek. A *smooch!* "How are you? What happened? They called me at two in the morning; I'm just glad I had the day off today."

Maria. Who else could it be? "Oh!" she exclaimed, noticing me. "You must be Janice. I've heard so much about you; it's nice to finally meet you!"

"You too." I smiled and shook her hand. And then we both tried to say the same thing at the same time—"Lousy circumstances, though." "But this isn't how I was hoping it would happen!"—and laughed.

Maria sat down in the extra chair, and Sam brought her up to date on the progression of the ailment, pausing here and there to huff on her nose tubes. I studied Maria, the new girl on duty, finally here in the flesh. She was very cute and instantly likeable, animated and charismatic and sharp, and I could see how Sam lit up around her, glowing even as she lay in yet another hospital bed suffering from six things at once. "And *how* did you get a broken rib?" asked Maria, arms folded and eyebrows raised.

"I don't know," Sam wheezed. "Skateboarding, I think."

Maria looked drolly over at me, then back at Sam. "Well, I think you need to be a little bit more careful when you skateboard!"

Sam dipped her head like a cartoon scamp—*Aw, shucks, I didn't mean it, it was an accident!*—and sneaked a look at me. I wasn't going to say anything she didn't want me to say.

The three of us talked about the halfway house, which Sam hated. "There's no therapy there, not even twelve-step meetings until I'm off orientation. (*Huff*.) I'm in the house all day and night. It's just babysitting for adults. (*Huff*.) It's just as bad as the psych ward, except more boring. I miss rehab. I wish I was still in Larchmont." She and Maria looked at each other fondly—*Remember Larchmont? How great that was?*—and I started to feel a little extraneous.

"So listen," I began. Since it had been determined that Sam was all right, since the doctors had averted the crisis and they were treating the symptoms, maybe I'd head out and get back to work, leave Sam and Maria alone for a while. Maria had come all the way from Larchmont on her day off, and I was only a few subway stops away. I was sure I'd have plenty of occasion to visit over the next few days. "I'll come back tomorrow," I promised, over their objections. "And I'll call to check in on you later."

Maria and I shook hands again, and she looked right into my eyes. I could see the strength, the determination, and the goodness in hers. I wondered if she could see the joint I'd already smoked that morning in mine. She smiled widely at me. "So good to meet you," she said again.

"And you." I came around to the foot of Sam's bed and grabbed her foot, our old good-bye hug. "You, on the other hand . . . we've got to stop meeting like this."

"Yeah," she croaked, her lopsided grin starting to spread. "But at least we didn't have to wait until the end of May to see each other."

"No, we didn't." I waggled the foot. "Pretty devious, how we got around that, huh?"

And so we were back to another two weeks of near-daily visits. *On my way to the hospital*, I wrote in my notebook, the rocking of the subway jostling the pen as I scribbled. *Again*. Sam's pneumonia started to get better within a few days, and she was moved out of Intensive Care, but the healing was slow—her kidneys were strained, and they had to take it easy on the antibiotics, so she kept spiking high fevers, her organs inflamed. "And they don't want to give me pain meds," she reported, between noisy, labored breaths. She put one hand on her ribs, a deep frown on her face. "Which is good, I guess. I don't want to have to quit opiates again."

I couldn't believe how sick she was, again, for the second time in a few months; I wanted to ask a doctor what was going on, but the doctors made their rounds before visiting hours, and the nurses didn't have much information for me. "She's doing better than yesterday," they'd say, or "The fever's really high today." That was it. No conclusive statements like "The tests show she's recuperating," or "She should be out by next week." Half the time, Sam was sleeping when I entered her room, or groggy; she tried to take me through the specifics of what the doctors had told her, but most of what she reported amounted to "They don't really know yet."

On her more cogent days, the suffering was worse. It wasn't just the physical pain, the chills and fevers and nausea; it was the nightmares, the flashbacks. They'd been pronounced ever since she got sober, but since she'd been at the halfway house, where she had no psychological support, she'd been waking up screaming and sweating, and the hospital was not much better. I walked into her room one day and awakened her, and she sat upright so fast she almost ripped out her IV, her face a grimacing mask of terror.

It took ten minutes to calm her down. She'd been having a dream about being back in Colorado, about her father making her watch while he beat her brother until he puked. Worse than being beaten herself, she said. I held her hand, and she squeezed it, exhausted tears streaming down the sides of her face. We stayed like that on and off for an hour and a half, then I went home and cried until I could barely breathe.

Sometimes, between visits, I'd get calls from the hospital phone. She needed to talk things over with me, for instance, did I think God would punish her for things she did when she was on the streets? What about karma? She'd done terrible, unforgivable things; was that why bad things kept happening to her? I assured her over and over that she'd done nothing to deserve this, that she'd just done what she had to in order to survive. "And you've got to keep surviving," I said, squeezing my free hand into a fist of solidarity, the nails digging into my palm. "You're not allowed to quit now."

Other calls were lighter: she was thinking about me, and she wanted to let me know how important I was to her. She'd been writing in her notebook, and she had this plot for a story. She was reading the Disney guidebook, and she thought early December might be a better time to go than January. "It gets real crowded around the holidays," she cautioned.

"I'll keep that in mind," I replied.

I couldn't wait for her to get better, and not only because I cared about her; I couldn't wait for her to get out of the hospital and back to the halfway house, where they'd limit her contact with the outside world, so I could get a break from all this again. *Why?* I berated myself; *so I can mope around and write about her in my notebook, without being distracted by the real thing?* For three weeks I'd been wishing she could have contact, I'd cursed her program for shutting me out; now I was anxiously awaiting the day when they put her back on ice, in suspended animation, and I got to run around with my feel-good fantasies of her, my kites and my swings and my ice cream.

In the meantime, I went to the hospital in the evenings after work. Ran into Maria again, chatted as a threesome with her and Sam for a few minutes until she left for an overnight shift at Larchmont. Just missed Jodi on another night, stealing some time from her own kid to visit this one. Sat and watched *Law & Order* on the TV Sam had finagled. Now when I came into her room and she was sleeping, I just pulled out my book and read, grateful for the reprieve. Then she woke up and got upset. "You shoulda woke me! I didn't know you were here!"

"You're supposed to be resting." I smiled, sliding my book back into my bag. "That's why you're here, remember?"

On my way to the hospital one evening, I decided to stop at the donut shop—what the hell. Sam's appetite had started to return; she could use a couple of powdered jelly donuts, and so could I. Pre-dinner donuts weren't officially sanctioned on my self-imposed diet, but she was my excuse. I had to eat donuts with Sam. She couldn't be expected to go through that alone.

As I rode the elevator to her floor I could hear my stomach growling, like it was going to snatch the bag right from my hand and stuff the whole thing inside itself, without help from the rest of my body. I strode quickly to her room and stopped short. Empty.

This time I didn't panic. Much. She must have been discharged; I'd just speak to a nurse and get that confirmed. Yes, said the woman at the nurses' station; she'd been sent back to the halfway house that afternoon. I checked my stupid, lazy, cell phone, and there it was, an hours-old message from Sam saying she was on her way back to purgatory.

So, good. Sam was recuperated and out of the woods; she was back behind the walls of the halfway house. And I had time to run to the grocery store before Bill got home. We'd have a healthy, home-cooked meal for a change—a stir-fry, maybe, with tofu and vegetables. Then after dinner we could sit on the couch and talk about anything but Samantha.

I ate all three donuts on the subway home. Thank you, Sam.

April 25, 2005

Janice,
Thanks for visiting me so much when I was in the hospital.
I thought maybe this place would count those two weeks
towards my orientation and I'd be closer to level one, but no
such luck. So I still can't call or get visits, but at least I can
write. I even got my hands on an old typewriter so my hand
won't hurt so bad when I write. Enclosed are some of my
latest ideas for stories, please pick the one you like best and
circle it. Also enclosed is some random stuff I wrote, so let
me know what you think about that, too. It was miserable
being so sick but your visits made me feel better, and the
docs are keeping an eye on me as an outpatient, so next time
we hang out it won't be in a hospital (I hope). Can't wait to
visit when I get to level 1. You're a great friend, Janice.
    Peace,
    Sam

Now that she was back at the halfway house, Sam was writing again. I got two letters in one week, each with various story premises, poems, and autobiographical jottings enclosed. The next week a small package arrived, with her telltale spiky handwriting; it was a wooden frame with the word FRIENDS on it. She had illustrated a quote from the *Tao Te Ching*—"While we value things for their tangibles, it is the intangibles that make them useful." I put it on the bookshelf, next to the picture of me and my brother.

I came home one evening after catching a drink with a girlfriend to find Bill already home, changed out of his work clothes and watching the news as he fired up the stove for dinner. He gave me a big hello kiss and a message. "Hey, babe. Sam called about a half hour ago."

"She did?" I raised my eyebrows—she wasn't supposed to have phone privileges yet. I pulled my cell phone out of my pocket: no messages. "Are you sure it was her?"

"Yep." He nodded, pleased. "Knew it was her as soon as she asked for you. I said, 'She's not home right now, but is this Sam?' And she goes, 'Yeah, is this Bill?'" He did a goofy, spot-on imitation of her voice, and I smiled. "And we talked for a minute—she thanked me for the CD I made her, and I told her I was looking forward to meeting her, and she just said she'd try you some other time. And that was it." He nodded again, like he understood something now. "It was funny, hearing her voice. She was so *polite*."

I wanted to revel with him, but I was perturbed by the unscheduled call, and to the home phone, no less. "You're sure that was it? Everything was okay? Was her voice normal? Did she sound like she was in the hospital?"

"Oh, yeah," he reassured me. "Her voice was fine; she sounded fine. Actually, it sounded like she was outside somewhere."

"But she wasn't panicky or anything."

"Not at all. I told her she could call your cell phone if it was important, but she said it wasn't."

I chewed my bottom lip, frustrated. "Well, I guess there's no way to know what she wanted, unless she calls back. Anyway, thanks for fielding that one."

"No problem. I was happy to get to talk to her, finally. I can't wait to meet her at this point." He looked bemused, like he was recalling the high points of their conversation. "Where's that accent from?"

"All over," I said. "Hell and back."

There were no more phone calls from Samantha that night,

though I got one from Jodi the next day: "Sam got permission to go to the doctor for a follow-up yesterday, and she skipped her halfway house for a few hours. She called me from a pay phone and told me she was leaving there, and she wanted to come over to my place—it took me twenty minutes over the phone to convince her to go back."

"Oh my god." So that was the call Bill intercepted. What if I'd been home to receive it—*Janice, I skipped my halfway house—can I come over?* I would have tried to talk her into going back, too, but I didn't know if she would have listened to me. I could feel the wind from another near miss with disaster. "So she went back? That's amazing, Jodi. Thank god for you."

"Well, it wasn't easy. I understand her frustration with the program—there's no psychological support, and it's not the best place for her. I still wish she'd been able to go upstate, where she'd be getting some real therapy. But this is what she's got for now, and she's got to follow through with it and get whatever she can out of it. And we'll still be able to visit her on family day—at least she didn't lose that—so put it on your calendar—two Saturdays from now."

"Okay. Great. Thanks for letting me know."

Jodi heard my dispirited tone and tried to reassure me. "Don't worry, she's all right again. Everything's okay, for now. We'll all muddle through this somehow."

I hung up, put my hand to my forehead, started rubbing my temples. Bill hovered behind me. "What's the latest?" he asked.

"She tried to take off from her halfway house. That's when she called here. But she didn't get me, so Jodi talked her back in."

"Huh," he said, reflecting. So he'd been talking to a fugitive; we'd narrowly avoided harboring her. "The fun never stops, does it."

"The joys of parenting," I muttered.

Well, at least I could relax a little now; I knew I wouldn't be hearing from Sam again any time soon. She'd be stuck on orientation level for a while, following her great escape attempt—no contact other than letters for another thirty days, and the staff would be keeping a much closer eye on her from now on. Her health was being monitored; there'd be no more surprise hospitalizations, we hoped.

I tried to calm down, trust that she was being looked after, and enjoy the quiet.

Refreshing, really, when I could live my own life, uninterrupted by emergency phone calls or hospital visits. I went to the shelter on Wednesdays, came home and told Bill about the girls I'd met—a four-foot, baby-faced charmer with a thick lisp whom everyone called Mini-Me; a natural comedian called Philly ("Like the blunt," she clarified, "not the city"), who had me crying laughing with her stories about her neighborhood bodega. I worked uninterrupted all day, wrote voraciously in my notebook, started planning ahead to Bill's thirtieth birthday, six weeks away. Maybe we'd go to the beach for the weekend, or out to a fancy dinner with my dad and stepmom. It had to be something really special, after all the support he'd given me this year.

I was at my desk working when I thought of it: I'd ask Bill to marry me. I sat up straight in my chair, the screen swimming before my eyes—of course, it was perfect. I'd propose to Bill. If anybody had asked me what I wanted for *my* birthday, I'd have said, "A ring." I had little doubt that Bill felt the same way. We'd talked about getting married a few times; after attending a friend's wedding last year, we'd noted all the things we would have done differently (i.e., better), should we ever theoretically decide to have a wedding of our own. But neither of us had mentioned it in a while, probably because we were still so high from moving in together just seven months earlier.

I should do it, I thought, my excitement growing as I pretended to debate the idea in my head, though by this point there was no debate: I was going to propose to Bill. I was already thinking ahead to how I'd use his old class ring to find the right size, how I'd wait until the perfect moment on his birthday, how thrilled he would be, how he'd look into my eyes and say *yes*, or so I fervently hoped. Thinking ahead to the wedding, to the marriage—how lucky and secure and invincible I'd feel, knowing that Bill was my partner for life. He'd probably have to take some shit for it at his job—"*She* proposed to *you*, Scurry?"—but Bill was man enough to take it, to enjoy it, even. He'd accepted my last proposal, to move in with me; I could only hope he'd accept this one, too.

The more I thought about it over the next few days, the more I became sure that this was my most brilliant idea ever. My only problem was keeping such a brilliant idea to myself and not sharing it with Bill, or my folks, or other mutual friends, who might let it slip to him. He came home from work at night, kissing me and unbuttoning his cuffs, and I thought, *Marry me.* He reached out from his side of the sofa while we were watching TV, put his hand in my hair, and kissed the side of my face. I opened my eyes in the morning and he was there, stretching to hit the alarm, scratching the lazy cats under the chin as they awoke with us. "Good morning, Shmoo."

Six weeks started to seem like a long time to wait to propose. After years of resisting growing up and settling down, I felt now like it was the smartest possible thing to do, and I wanted to do it right away. I'd already grown up so much this year—I'd gotten over my fear of commitment and asked Bill to move in with me; I'd taken on caring for Sam. Now I wanted to start my family, already.

The next Saturday, visiting day, was sunny and humid, and I stopped at the bodega down the block from Sam's halfway house to buy some extra bottles of soda to bring with me. A few pit bulls and their owners growled as I passed; the flags of several Caribbean countries were displayed in windows. We were in *el barrio*, where the girls at the shelter lived before the shelter. My first apartment, when I was eighteen, was in a neighborhood like this.

I rang the bell at the halfway house, and a young man with a pitted face and a too-big white button-down shirt greeted me and escorted me to the backyard, where I spotted Sam sitting with Jodi at a table. There was a kid next to them—Jodi's ten-year-old son, Evan, whom I'd heard about but never met. Sam looked hilarious; they'd obviously insisted that she try to tame her mop of hair somehow, and they'd gotten her to tuck her shirt into some donated dress pants. She looked like Alfalfa, from *The Little Rascals*. But her face was rosy, and she was smiling—bashfully, almost. "Hey, Janice." We hugged. "Good to see you."

It was good to see her, too—always better when she wasn't in a hospital, when it had been weeks between visits instead of hours.

When the feelings of fondness won out over the feelings of obligation, as they did now, as I looked at her forelock of hair struggle against whatever gel she'd applied to it. Six months now, we'd been friends, though we'd been separated for the past few weeks; as with Bill, I couldn't imagine life without her anymore. "Good to see you, too."

I said hi to Jodi and was introduced to Evan. "Nice to meet you." Took a look around me. "So, this is it, huh?"

"Yep." Sam raised her eyebrows. "You see what I'm talking about?"

I did. This place was as bad as the psych ward, if not worse. The other residents milling around the penned-in backyard looked busted as hell; several would have appeared most at home behind a shopping cart full of cans. Tattooed necks, pitted skin, bent backs, scarred and swollen lips—this was a tough bunch. Most of them were court-mandated; they didn't want to be here; and would be back to using as soon as they were let out the door. "Wow," I said, contemplating Sam spending another ten months at this place.

Maria couldn't make it, said Sam. She had to work up in Larchmont. So it was just Sam, Jodi, and I catching up on things, while Jodi's son played a handheld video game. Sam ran down her list of grievances with the program; Jodi and I agreed but encouraged her to stay. "In the meantime, I'll keep looking for a new place," promised Jodi, still counseling, even while off duty.

Sam told us how she'd been spending her time—reading, studying for the SAT. Scrubbing things with toothbrushes, when she did something like cursed or showed insolence. "It's real therapeutic," she said, rolling her eyes.

I told them how different the shelter was these days, with no one overseeing the girls' floor and nobody replacing Jodi. "They need people like you and Nadine," I told her. "We all do."

At one point Sam went to the bathroom, leaving me alone with Jodi and Evan. "This place may not be great," I said, "but thank god you talked her into coming back here. I don't know what I would have done, if it was me."

"You would have done the right thing," Jodi assured me. "It wasn't easy, though. Part of me wants her out of this place, too. The only time she can talk to us is when she's in the hospital? That's no good. And they're not doing a thing for her. But like I said, I can look around while she's here, maybe we can find her something better. For now, this is what she's got to deal with."

Sam rejoined us. "Talking about me?"

"Who else?" asked Jodi.

We chatted some more, and I told them my upcoming good news. "So, I'm going to propose to my boyfriend, Bill."

Sam's eyes flew open. "No way! That's so great! Congratulations!" Jodi echoed her. I flushed with excitement, saying it out loud like that—carrying around the good news and not being able to share it had been killing me. "Bill's so awesome," Sam told Jodi. "He made me this CD, and he put in these real funny liner notes. I spoke to him the day I called you."

"Yeah, that day." Jodi looked pointedly at Sam. "We're not going to have any repeats of that."

"I know," Sam groused, rolling her eyes. "Trust me, I know."

Watching her face now, I could tell that she did know. She knew this horrible place was her only chance at staying sober; that's why she chose to come back. She knew better than anybody how few alternatives she had, and in case she forgot, Jodi reminded her—she wasn't crashing with one of us, not even for a night, not ever. Sam had thought of everything she could to get out of here; she'd told me she'd even fantasized about getting high, just so she could get sent back to Larchmont, until Maria told her she wouldn't be taken back like that. But now something about her had shifted—she sat up straighter and more still, and she looked farther into the distance. Like she'd accepted her time here as something else she'd survive, another sacrifice she'd make to save her own life.

"I should give you the grand tour," she said abruptly. "And I want you to meet my roommate, Valentina, the one I told you about. She's a tranny; her birth name's Jesus. Me and her get along real well."

"Cool." Jodi and Evan and I got up and followed her into the building, a standard-issue five-story Brooklyn limestone. Like the shelter, it was covered throughout the common areas with construction-paper signs bearing inscrutable motivational slogans (*Life become your dream*) and memos about the possession of cigarette lighters (forbidden, in case anyone thought they could keep one hidden). The TV room was a near replica of the shelter's—the couch with the frayed arms; the sour, permanent smell of potato chips and feet. We peeked into the office—same whiteboard, same desks covered in manila folders. Upstairs, the residents' rooms were closed. Sam stopped and knocked on her door.

"Valentina." *Knock, knock.* "Valentina."

"Mmmmph," came the muffled reply.

Sam cracked the door, looked in. "Hey, my friends are here. Can I show them our room?"

We craned our necks to look around her, and I saw Valentina, lying curled up on the bed with her back to us. I caught a glimpse of the drawings on the wall—Sam's work. I wanted to go look at it. "Sleeping," grumbled Valentina.

"Sorry." Sam closed the door behind us, dropped her voice. "She's real sensitive today, 'cause she doesn't have any visitors."

"That's a shame," I said, casting a look back at the door. "I'm so sorry to hear it."

"Yeah, the only family she has is, like, a bunch of tranny hookers. Her real family in Puerto Rico disowned her when she came out as a kid, and she had to trick her way to Miami to be with her trans mom." Sam grinned. "Me and her have a bunch of fun together. The other day we were daring each other to pull the fire alarm at the top of the stairs, and we kept pushing each other away from it, so we invented a new game, King of the Stairs. It's like King of the Hill, but with stairs."

We pressed on with our tour, Jodi chastising Sam for courting grievous bodily injury, me looking back at the door one more time. Sam had me and Jodi and Maria looking after her, but nobody had shown up for Valentina today. Poor girl. I wanted to go back, sit down on the bed next to her, and rub her back in circles. Instead I followed after Sam, who pointed out the fire alarm in question. "I said I'd give her five bucks if she pulled it. That would be so funny."

When we got back downstairs, the entirely unsociable staff was starting to indicate that it was almost time for us to move along. "So, when do we get to talk to you again?" I asked Sam.

She jammed her hands into her pockets, anxiety in her voice. We were leaving, and she'd be here for the next eternity, playing Scrabble with missing pieces with a bunch of bench-dwelling transients. "When I get off orientation. Hopefully by the middle of June. And I'll write more letters in the meantime. I been writing all the time, since there's nothing else to do."

I reached out, and she bent down to hug me. "I can't wait to read it," I said.

Jodi and Sam hugged, and Evan shook Sam's hand good-bye. Another poignant farewell, marred only by the leering toothless guy trying to get hugs from us, too.

"Good-bye!" he called, arms open as he followed us, now fleeing down the front stoop. "Good-bye!"

Two weeks passed in silence—no letters, though I sent a few, enclosing another CD from Bill. I worked peacefully and productively all day long, no phone calls from Sam to field; I beamed at the FRIENDS frame on my bookshelf. I went to the shelter on Wednesdays—things were in chaos there. With budget cuts, staff reductions, and space consolidation, the girls were stacked up like cordwood, piling one on top of the other on their way into the lounge, desperate for attention. "Miss, I'm hungry! I'm pregnant! I need my medication! They won't let me ride the elevator! This bitch stole something out my room! *You* is who I'm calling a bitch, bitch!"

"Ladies, ladies." You can only say that so many times. It's not *abracadabra*, it's not going to do anything magic if you keep repeating it. "Ladies, I know it sucks right now, but try not to get thrown out of here, because it's a lot better than the alternatives." They should have seen where Sam was living. She couldn't even go outside.

The simple gold band I'd bought for Bill shone like a beacon when I dared to wrest it from its hiding place and peek inside its box, where it was nestled next to a matching ring for me. He'd been hinting around about things he wanted for his birthday, various clothing items and obscure Japanese movies on DVD, and I pretended to take note, thinking, *Too bad, you'll have to get it yourself.* But as the day grew closer, my palms grew clammier. He was going to like his birthday present, right? He wasn't going to say no, was he?

I was at my computer one night after dinner, poking around online, when the phone rang. Sam.

"Hey there!" My voice rose in undisguised pleasure at the sound of hers. "I was just thinking about you! Are you off orientation now?"

"Not quite, but almost." She sounded a little guarded, less animated than usual—maybe she was sick again. "I been doing real good, though. I haven't had any setbacks or anything, so it should be soon."

"Oh! So this is just a bonus call, then." I rose from my seat and started pacing. She was still at the halfway house, I hoped; she wasn't calling from Grand Central station or anything.

"Kind of. They gave me special permission to call you, 'cause . . ." She paused for a second, and her voice grew even more hesitant. "Now I don't know how to say it over the phone."

"What? Say what?"

"Uh, well . . ." She sounded like she was about to change the subject. "Do you think you'd rather get important news in writing, or by phone?"

I'd rather you stop stalling, I thought, *and tell me what you called to tell me.* "By phone. Why, what's up?"

She took a deep breath. "I . . . I tested positive for HIV."

Wham. The news hit me like a crowbar. "Okay," I said, steadying my voice. "That sucks, but we can deal with it."

She didn't say anything. I just heard her breathing, so I continued, as calmly as I could.

"I know a few people living with HIV, and they have to take a lot of meds, but they're doing all right. Some of them have been totally fine for years, even decades. So you're going to be all right, okay?"

Bill came into the room, face grave. He looked at me—*Tell me I didn't just overhear* . . . I nodded, tears in my eyes. He sat down heavily in the nearest chair, shaking his head.

"Yeah," said Sam, resigned. "It sucks, though. It's like, I didn't have enough to deal with."

I tried to stay firm. "Look, it sucks, but it's good that they caught it. Now they can treat it." Again, no reply. "How'd they find out? You got tested, I guess."

She sighed. "The pulmonologist, he's the one who said it. He said, 'You keep getting real sick, you know, and maybe you should take another HIV test.' 'Cause I tested negative back in November, when I first came into the shelter; I knew that was one of the first things I had to do when I came in, 'cause of everything I'd been doing. I mean, this isn't really a surprise, considering my background." She approximated a chuckle, *huh*. "I was more surprised when the November test came back negative. I was like, 'Are you sure?' "

I kneeled down, put my forehead to the floor like I was praying toward Mecca, and picked it up again, reeling. I had to get it together and not make this worse, had to tell myself that AIDS was not a death sentence anymore. I couldn't think of the people I'd known who'd died. I had to remember the ones who were living.

"Well, if you tested negative as recently as November, then they caught it right at the outset, which is great." Unless that was a false negative. I'd heard about those, but I wasn't going to mention that possibility to Sam. "Did they tell you your T cell count and viral load?"

"I'll find out soon." Another heavy sigh. "I'm still . . . dealing with it. They just told me yesterday."

"Oh, babe. I'm so sorry. This isn't what you need right now. I know it complicates things for you. But I'm not kidding, I promise you, you're going to get the best possible care, and we're all going to get through this with you, okay? This doesn't change anything. You're going to live a good long time."

Bill was shading his eyes with his hand, his mouth drawn down in an exaggerated frown. I was still on my knees. Sam sounded like she was spacing out again, staring at a wall or something, her voice distant and flat. "That's . . . I hope so."

"You will." I struggled to my feet, struggled to keep my voice upbeat. "I promise. And I wouldn't promise unless I was sure."

She sighed again. "I know. I . . . wait a minute." She put her hand over the phone, had a brief discussion with someone, and when she came back her voice had quickened. "Hey, they say I have to go now. But I'll write to you as soon as I hear more from the doctors."

I balled my fist in frustration—they couldn't give her another two minutes to talk to me right now? This phone call was impeding her recovery from drugs? "T cell and viral load," I stressed. "Let me know, okay? And listen, hang in there. This isn't going to change anything. You have to stay strong, and stick with the program, and you're going to go to college and become a vet, and do all those things you want to do, okay?"

"Okay. Thanks, Janice."

"Thanks for letting me know."

I hung up the phone and sank back to my knees, then crumpled all the way down until I was lying on my back on the floor, staring at the ceiling. "Uuuggghhh," I groaned.

"Oh, babe." Bill shook his head. He looked as devastated as I felt. "I'm so sorry."

I groaned again, trying to expunge the sick feeling from my gut, trying to talk sense to myself the way I did with Sam. *Okay, it's bad news,* I instructed myself, *but not fatal.* I couldn't start thinking of her as sick, couldn't picture her dying, but hadn't I been doing that since the day we met, practically? All those days in St. Victor's, the times she went missing, the phone call at 2 A.M.—in truth, I'd grown used to picturing her dead. She'd been on the verge of death for as long as I'd known her. It was a miracle she'd made it this far.

Bill attempted a smile for me. "You sounded great, though; you sounded totally positive. You didn't sound fazed at all. I'm sure that's just what she needed to hear."

"Thanks." Trust Bill to find the bright side in all of this—*Well, at least* you *were awesome.* And ridiculous as it was, it actually perked me up a little, made me snap to attention. I rolled onto one side. "And you know, I wasn't lying; she can live a long time, if she takes care of herself. This doesn't have to inhibit her at all." Except for the nine thousand pills she'd have to take, and all their side effects. And how was she going to afford them? I'd have to go online and start researching treatment. Hopefully the halfway house was looking at the various aid options. Jodi would probably know; Maria might, too. "I mean, it does suck, but it's not a huge surprise, really. This is probably the best we could have hoped for, that they'd catch it and treat it fast."

"I guess this explains why she's gotten so sick so often."

"Right." I thought back to the hand infection, how fast it had become sepsis, how the doctor at the shelter thought Sam might have sabotaged it so she could stay at the shelter, the first safe place she'd ever known. Wrong diagnosis, Doc. Try, "the first stirrings of an autoimmune disorder."

"So what happens from here? We wait to find out the numbers?"

I rolled back flat on the floor. "That's all we can do," I said to the ceiling. Wait. There was nothing else to be done. I couldn't help Sam in any way—I couldn't handle her health care, or her social services; I couldn't even hold her hand over the phone while she dealt with this. I couldn't do anything, fix anything, call anybody, pay for anything. The only thing I could control about the situation was my own reaction.

Unsurprisingly, I had a hard time falling asleep that night. I lay in bed cursing god, or disappearing photons, or whatever force had conspired to do this to Samantha, whoever or whatever had decided to make her life a cruel joke, starting twenty years ago, on April Fool's Day, 1985. After one of the worst childhoods imaginable, against tremendous odds, she'd been busting her ass to try to live a decent life—checking into a lockdown detox, persevering through hospitals and psych wards and rehabs, sticking it out in this degraded snake pit of a halfway house—and just as she's six months sober, what happens? I'd start to doze off and dream that someone was telling me it was a mistake. I saw her empty hospital room, the flat slab of the bed; relived the 2 A.M. phone call. I was wide awake again.

This wasn't a dream. This wasn't a mistake. This wasn't the movie I'd imagined, where Janice was a hero and everything worked out okay in the end. This wasn't in the papers or something I read online—"Homeless Kids Face Higher Incidence of HIV Infection, Duh." This was reality. This was the redhead on the corner, and the scabs on her face were looking more and more like lesions. This was Sam.

This was what I had signed up for. This was what I was going to see through.

Chapter Nine

Elopement

Two weeks later, and there'd been no further word from Sam. No follow-up call, no letters—but *no news is good news*, I tried to tell myself. I'd have to settle for no news for now; it was better than most of the news I'd gotten from Sam in the past. Besides, I had news of my own to make.

It was Bill's thirtieth birthday, and he'd swapped days with a co-worker so he could have the day off. We woke up late, took a long run together, and went to an opening-day afternoon showing of *Batman Begins*. We ate popcorn and candy for lunch, then strolled toward the park in the sunshine. "What do you want to do now?" he asked.

Propose, I thought, my heartbeat quickening. Today was the day, and now was the time. I had to get him home and spring the ring on him. "I don't know," I said, trying to sound casual. "Maybe head home?"

We were on our way home when Bill got a call from work—some bullshit Mac problem—they wanted him to come in and fix something. He snapped his phone shut, grumbling. "You're not going down there, are you?" I asked, anxious.

"I don't want to, but apparently they can't do a goddamn thing without me."

"Well, call them back and tell them you can't." My voice rose in frustration. We didn't have a lot of time before the dinner plans we'd made with my dad and stepmom, and now Bill was in a shitty mood, and how was I going to ask him to marry me if he was all cranky and snappish, as I was now, too? We bickered—yes, we actually bickered on the day of our engagement—but then his phone rang again, and the problem had been solved, and by the time we got home, he was putting his arms around me and turning me to face him.

"This is why our relationship is so important," he said. "Because there's all the bullshit and stress we both have to deal with, and then there's you and me. And as stressed out as we get, I know you're always on my side, and you know I'm always on yours."

I looked past his glasses into his green-brown eyes, and my pulse raced again. "Funny you should mention that." I took a few steps to the cabinet I'd been using as a hiding place and pulled out the velvet box.

"What's this?" he asked, making greedy hands. "My present?" A *pair of cuff links,* he thought, or so he told me later.

"This . . . I . . ." I flipped open the box to reveal the matching rings. I had this cute little speech prepared—*Honey, we're so crazy about each other, I think we should be committed*—but it flew out of my head. "H . . . honey," I stammered, mouth dry. "I love you, and I want us to be together. Always."

"Oh. Oh wow." Bill gaped at the rings, the idea dawning on him. "Is this . . . Are you asking me . . ."

By now I was crying too much to speak, so I nodded, laughing and crying as he rushed in to grab me, holding me so tight, kissing my face, and crying himself. "Oh, honey. Oh my god."

"So . . . yes?" I asked, over his shoulder.

He drew back and looked at me like I was crazy, brilliant, possibly dangerous, totally irresistible. "YES," he said.

We ran to the bedroom and cemented the deal.

Once we were showered and dressed for dinner, Bill called his family with the news; I called my brother. Bill called his best friends; I called mine. I heard him on the other side of the room, laughing.

"I wasn't expecting it, either!" I grinned over at him, cupping one ear. "I'll tell him you said so!" We took a picture of ourselves together and e-mailed it to the rest of our friends—subject line: *Committed!* Then we took a cab uptown and met my father and stepmother at a restaurant in Midtown.

"What's different about us?" we demanded, holding up our ringed fingers.

My stepmother's hands flew to her mouth, and my father looked like he might *plotz* from joy. "You're engaged!"

And so we were. We spent the next week making lists, checking the calendar, planning locations and menus, listing our invitees. "Samantha," said Bill, like, *of course*.

I put my hands in the prayer position. "*If* she can get permission to come. She's got to get off orientation, first. And there'll be alcohol there; they might not let her come without a chaperone. Or at all. But I'll write her and ask her, honey. That would be so awesome, if she could make it."

Everything made its way onto a list. We ran around town looking for venues, and I danced in front of him on the sidewalk, gesturing to where I thought we'd stand, where our families could be, how the whole production would *flow*.

"So you think we can do this by September? That only gives us three months. We'll have to book the place as soon as possible, get the invites out in the next two or three weeks . . . plus the food, the dress. . . ."

"Are you thinking you might like to invite your mom?" Bill asked delicately.

Huh. Funny enough, the last time I'd seen my mom was six years earlier at her own wedding, to a guy I'd met only once before. Nice enough guy; nice enough affair. I sat at a table with my then-boyfriend and my brother and his girlfriend, kept my profile low. Toward the end of the event, my mother and I chatted alone for the length of one of her cigarettes, then I left, and we went back to exchanging greeting cards. "I've been to three of her weddings," I said. "I guess I should invite her to one of mine."

I left her a message that night. "Hi, Mom. Just wanted to let you know that Bill and I got engaged, and I'll be sending you an invitation to the wedding as soon as we have the date. Just wanted to share the good news. Hope all's well with you. Bye."

So the wedding plans took shape, with the help of my dad and stepmom. We booked the banquet room at a nearby hotel, designed the invites, and set up an appointment with a baker to sit around and taste a variety of cakes. I tried not to go too Bridezilla on anybody, tried not to talk too much about my dress or the flowers or the menu, tried to just live my life as usual—running in the morning, working, going to the shelter on Wednesdays. Except now I had something extra nice to think about, and a pretty ring to wear.

I mailed an invitation to Sam's halfway house, with a note attached, addressed to whomever it concerned: *I hope you'll consider letting Samantha attend this event; if there's any way I can facilitate that, please let me know. Thank you sincerely, Janice Erlbaum.* Drummed my fingers waiting for a reply. My mother had not replied to her invitation, either. But other friends and family were responding right and left; it was shaping up to be a very special day for us. "You two certainly are a happy couple," marveled the baker, almost suspiciously, as she walked us to the elevator of her loft and bade us good-bye. "Most people aren't nearly as relaxed and cheerful as you two."

Well, most people weren't marrying Bill (or getting domestically partnered to him—we'd decided to save legal marriage until all of our friends were granted the same right). I felt like I'd just met him again, this adorable, funny, generous, patient guy who rubbed my shoulders at night, cleared the table after dinner, told me, "I'm happy to deal with the programs, Shmoo, if you want to take care of the flowers." I still couldn't believe I'd wound up with someone so even-tempered, so attentive, so unlike anyone I'd ever dated before. After six or seven months of being blinded by Sam, I was rubbing my eyes and blinking in amazement at the brilliant man I'd conned into becoming my partner.

While I was making wedding arrangements, I took the opportunity to call the Disney reservation line and inquire about a week's vacation in early December ("the best possible time to go," according to Sam and her guidebook). She'd only be eleven months sober by then, but now that we knew her diagnosis, I felt like it was okay to let the extra month slide. Depending on her T cell count and viral load, I thought, time might be of the essence.

"And how many will be in your party?" asked the reservation agent.

I had to ask Bill before I could answer. When I'd originally conceived the trip, in that flash of desperate inspiration, I'd thought it would just be me and Sam. Now, five months later, I was an engaged woman. If I was unofficially adopting Sam, I wasn't doing it alone. Bill had made it clear that he wanted to be my partner in every way, including my relationship with Sam. Which was typically wonderful of him but also made me nervous. I didn't know what I'd do if they didn't get along, if Sam was jealous of Bill, or vice versa. Maybe she'd feel like I did, all those times as a kid, when my mom would invite some guy along on one of our weekend jaunts, and he'd ruin the whole thing, and then she'd wind up marrying him. *Sam, meet your new stepfather, Bill.*

Except Bill wasn't just *some guy*. Maybe Sam hoped it would just be me and her on this trip, but she'd soon see that she was better off with the twofer. Bill made my life better; he'd do the same for her. And Sam would enrich Bill's life in return.

I pitched Bill the Disney scheme as though it had just occurred to me. "I was thinking, since Sam got her diagnosis, I'd really like to do something for her around the holidays. She'll be about a year sober by then, and I think it'll give her some extra incentive to hang in there through this difficult period. Maybe we could take her to Disney World for a long weekend or something."

Bill was an easier sell than I'd thought. Aesthete that he was, I expected him to scoff at Disney, but he surprised me. "I think that's a great idea, babe. You pick the dates, and I'll arrange for the time off."

"You'd want to come with us?"

"Sure," he avowed. "I mean, I'm sure it's cheesy, but I've never been, and you've made it sound kind of fun. Especially with you and Sam."

"That's great." I beamed. "I'll book the rooms this weekend."

So this was how the rest of the year was shaping up: Get married, take weeklong honeymoon in Bermuda, go to Disney World with Sam. It was almost too much to look forward to, too much to plan, too much to think about when I lay down to sleep at night. Too much good fortune, and too much guilt—spending too much money, when everybody else had none. When I went to the shelter on a Wednesday night, and girls were arguing over a four-pack of SnackWells, pushing one another hard enough to nearly get themselves discharged. When people were dying in Iraq, in Darfur, in an AIDS hospice a few blocks away.

I squeezed my eyes shut and turned over. *I'm doing my best.* And turned over again. *No, I can't accept it.* But most of all, what I couldn't accept was my own happy, privileged life.

July 11, 2005

Janice,

Thanks for your letters. I'm sorry I've been so lame about writing back. I think about you all the time and stuff I wish we could talk about. And I'm really happy that you and Bill got engaged. I know I barely talked to him, but he's a great guy. I can't wait for the wedding in September, and you can put me down as a guest for sure, because I'm moving out of this dump this weekend! They don't know yet, only me and my roommate Valentina know. Me and her have been saving up and we have enough to live on for a few months, so I'll have time to get a job. We're bouncing on Sunday as soon as we get our allowance and we already talked to this lady who's renting us a room. So everything is set up, and I'll call you as soon as we break out. I can't wait to talk to you in person but for now here's the info you asked for: T cells = 145, viral load = 275,000, multiple opportunistic infections, multi-drug-resistant strain. So the doc says it looks like full-blown AIDS, not just HIV. But I'm still doing really well for right now,

I feel good and happy and motivated. Every day I wake up grateful for what I have and I look forward to what's coming (school, work, spending time with friends, Disney World). Believe it or not, life is really good, and like you used to tell me, it's only going to get better from here. Well I better go but I'll talk to you real soon.

Until then, peace.

Sam

I read and reread the letter, trying to figure out what to do. *She's going to elope from her program,* I told myself. *What's to figure out?* I remembered when she almost skipped out on the halfway house last time, how grateful I was that Jodi had talked her into going back. I had to be the responsible one now. I had to call the program, call Jodi, call Maria, call everybody, and tell them what Sam was planning. She could not be allowed to run.

But . . . the numbers. *T cells = 145, viral load = 275,000, multiple opportunistic infections, multi-drug-resistant strain. So the doc says it looks like full-blown AIDS.*

The numbers were bad. They were beyond bad. Five minutes of web searching confirmed it: she was toast. There were not enough meds in the world to keep her alive for more than a year, if that. It was a minor miracle that she was standing upright.

I called my friend Jay, who had volunteered for God's Love We Deliver. He tried to buck me up. "You know, sometimes people on my route who looked like they were seriously dying would surprise me and rebound for a few months. People can live long past their doctors' prognosis, you never know."

Right. In which case, she might live to see twenty-one. "Thanks," I said.

"I'm sorry," he said.

I decided to sleep on the news of Sam's escape plot, call Jodi in the morning, let her decide whether or not we should tell the halfway house what was going on (which would win her yet another thirty days with no contact), or if we should somehow try to appeal directly to Sam (how, when we weren't allowed to call and speak to her?). I could afford to think about it overnight—it was only Thursday, and Sam said they weren't planning to bolt until Sunday.

I was at my desk the next afternoon when my cell phone rang. "Hello?"

"Hey, it's *me*." Sam. She was overjoyed, her voice brash and excited; I could hear her mile-wide grin, along with the traffic in the background, the music from a passing radio. *Shit*. I'd blown it. They'd already eloped.

"Hey! Where are you?"

"We're in *Union Square*," she said with relish. "I'm so psyched to be *outside*. Can you come meet us?"

I was already rising from my chair, stuffing my feet into my sneakers. "I'll be there in ten minutes. By the dog run."

"Great. Thanks, Janice."

I dashed off, calling to leave a message for Jodi as I jogged toward the park. "Hey, it's Janice. Sam and her roommate just eloped from their program. I'm going to meet them in Union Square and try to talk them into going back. Please call me if you get a chance." I rehearsed my pitch in my head—*Listen, you guys have to go back. You need the support right now. Jodi's looking for a new place, but in the meantime . . .*

I arrived at the park, saw Sam sitting on a duffel bag under a tree near the dog run. She was positively pink and glowing, cheeks flushed with excitement and stretched into a huge grin. "Hey!" She rose to embrace me, and I noted her outfit with an internal smile—same old black cargo pants, now worn with new spiked leather wrist cuffs, a T-shirt featuring a smiley face with a bullet hole in its forehead, and a homemade choker with the anarchy symbol on it. No more hair gel and dress pants; Sam was on the loose. "Janice, this is my friend Valentina."

I turned around and got my first good look at Valentina. She was almost as tall as Sam, with long, flowing brown hair and an elegant, feline face. Budding breasts pushed against the fabric of her T-shirt, and muscled, hairy calves peeked out from under her basketball shorts. "Hello," she said, in the dulcet tones of a teenage girl.

"So nice to meet you," I said.

We sat on the grass for an impromptu conference. What were they planning? I asked. "I thought you two were going to wait until Sunday; I was hoping to reach you before then and see if I could convince you to stay."

Sam shook her head, defiant. "No way. I already called Jodi and left her a message. We're not going back. And they told us when we discharged ourselves, they wouldn't take us back even if we wanted them to. But we saved up some money, and we got a plan—Valentina already arranged to get her government check directly, so we'll have that every month, and I'm going to apply for benefits, too, while I'm looking for a job. But right now, she's going to the bank, then we're going up to the Bronx to meet this woman who has a couple of rooms for rent. We already spoke to her this morning; she said come up as soon as you get the cash. So we should have a place by tonight."

She smiled smugly—everything taken care of—and again, she made me want to smack my forehead. What kind of harebrained scheme was that? *This is New York*, I wanted to tell her; *you can't find a place to live in an afternoon.* "Are you sure you're going to have a place by tonight? Because I don't want you guys spending the night without a place to stay."

Valentina pouted a little at the "you guys" epithet. "Naw, we're good," said Sam. "We already spoke to this lady, now we just gotta get her the money." She turned to Valentina. "You want to go do that, and I'll wait here with the bags?"

Her partner in crime nodded. "Be back in an hour," she promised, slipping away. She had to go to her home branch in Brooklyn to withdraw directly, Sam explained; she had no bank card because they charged fees. In the meantime, though, Sam and I could catch up.

"So." She looked so happy and triumphant; I didn't want to plunge her straight into despair—*So how's that advanced case of AIDS treating you?*—but it seemed the most salient topic of conversation. "How are you feeling?"

"I'm . . . all right," she admitted. "I mean, it's definitely been hard to deal with. I was real depressed for the past few weeks, but I think part of it was the halfway house, and the way they were treating me. 'Cause once they found out my diagnosis, it was like, everybody was real weird around me, and that was bumming me out. The staff didn't do a real good job of keeping my privacy."

Neither did I, I realized, sheepish. I'd already told Bill and my brother and a few friends; if I hadn't been sure it would alarm my dad and stepmom, I would have told them, too. "That sucks," I said. "You'd think they'd be more sensitive; I'm sure they deal with HIV-positive residents all the time."

She wrinkled her nose, looked skeptically at me. "That place was the pits. They don't do shit for you but give you a bed and some food. I'm so glad to be out of there, Janice—you know I never complained about the shelter, or rehab even, but this place. . . ." She shook her head, and I knew there was no way she was going back.

"And how are you feeling physically? You've been okay since the pneumonia, right?"

She waved her hand, *so-so.* "Mostly. I had a couple of bad fevers, and my lungs aren't so great—I gotta keep using the inhaler they gave me. And the doctors are worried about my kidneys again. I can't take a lot of the sulfa drugs because of them. But they worked out a meds plan for me, and I got everything with me." She patted the duffel under her butt. "Plus I'm gonna keep following up with them at the hospital. I'm doing what I gotta to stay healthy."

"Good." I smiled, looking into her eyes. There was so much more I wanted to ask—chiefly, *Did they give you a prognosis?* Or, more bluntly, *So how long do they give you?* "It's good to see you," I said instead.

"You too," she agreed, real gratitude in her voice. "It's *real* good to see you. You been an awesome friend to me, Janice; without you, I wouldn't have gotten through all of this."

I tried to brush it off. "Oh, you made it far enough before you met me, and you've got Maria and Jodi, too."

"I know." She looked down at the grass, face serious, picked up her head again. "Sometimes I can't even believe how lucky I am."

There she was: the lucky girl with the losing numbers. My heart officially broke. "I feel lucky, too," I said.

What do I do now? I wondered, as Sam detailed more of their plans—the list of calls she and Valentina had made to various employment agencies, all the interviews they'd set up for next week. I couldn't spend the day walking around with them, looking for these elusive rooms for rent; I had to get back to work. But as always, if I didn't sit directly on top of her, I risked losing her completely.

"Listen," I said. "You're not going to be able to get a job or an apartment unless you have a phone number where people can call you back. Let's go across the street and get you one of those no-contract phones—then at least I'll know how to reach you."

"Oh, great, that would be so great." She was instantly on her feet, struggling with her huge duffel and grabbing her skateboard while I hoisted Valentina's bags. We crossed the street to the Virgin Megastore, and I bought a phone with twenty hours of talk time. Then we made our way back to our original spot. "Thank you so much, Janice. I'm totally going to pay you back."

"No worries," I told her. "But I'm going to have to get back to work soon, and I'm trusting that you and Valentina have really thought this through. You're saying you have a place lined up, you just have to get the money?"

"Yep. Spoke to the lady right before I spoke to you. It's all good." She grinned, resuming her cross-legged seat on top of her duffel, pulling her Converse-clad feet toward her.

I frowned, ever the killjoy. "Well, I don't know. You haven't seen the place. It might not work out. You're sure it's not a scam, right?"

She shook her head impatiently. "We got it from the newspaper! Rooms for rent! Same day! We spoke to her!"

I put my hands up in surrender. "Okay, just give me a call every few hours, all right? And if you haven't signed an agreement and got a key in your hand by five P.M., let me know, okay? I'm not letting the two of you spend the night outside—worst-case scenario, we get you a hotel room overnight."

"All right. But we're not gonna need it." She was already fiddling with the phone, listening to the available ring tones. "This is so cool of you. It's really gonna help us out a lot, like, for jobs."

"I'm glad." I entered her new number into my phone: *Sam*. "But you better use it to call me. And Jodi and Maria, too."

"All right. Thanks, Janice—thanks a lot."

She gave me a hug good-bye, and I trotted back home to my desk, where I kept checking my phone for unannounced messages. No call by five, no call at six. I called Sam's new number, smiling at the outgoing message she'd recorded since lunchtime: her voice, over some loud death metal, politely asking callers to leave their name and number at the beep. "It's me," I said. "I hope everything's okay. Call me when you're in your new place, or if there's been any kind of problem. Talk to you soon, I hope."

But it wasn't until Bill got home, around eight o'clock, that my phone finally rang, interrupting my latest Sam update. "That's her," I said, and picked up. "Hello?"

"Hey, Janice." She sounded frustrated, dejected. "We had a problem. Can you come meet us in the park?"

Of course I could. I'd already discussed the matter with Jodi, briefly, between her many appointments. "Look, they're not going back," she'd said, "and the halfway house won't take them back anyway. I don't know what they've got planned from here, but I hope it's good. If you want to try to help them find a room for rent, that'd be great of you, but I wouldn't give them any money. I think this is a premature step for Sam to take, but I don't blame her, considering the news we just got. Let me know how it goes."

So I had my mandate—help Sam and Valentina find a room for rent; don't give them money. I said good-bye to Sam, hung up, turned to Bill with a grimace. "I think I've got to get them a hotel room for the night. You want to come meet them?"

"Hell yeah," he said—if I was in this, then so was he. He rubbed his hands together, excited; he was finally meeting Samantha. "Let's go."

It was a muggy summer Friday night, and Union Square was packed with musicians, political protestors, tourists, skateboarders, college kids, and various street urchins. Sam and Valentina were sitting under the same tree by the dog run, looking significantly more bedraggled than when I'd seen them earlier. "Hey!" they hailed us, Sam's eyes lighting up when she recognized Bill with me. "Oh, hey! You're Bill!"

"And you're Sam!" They shook hands enthusiastically, and Bill met Valentina, then we huddled for another conference. There was a problem at the bank that morning—the welfare check that was supposed to be directly deposited to Valentina's account had been sent to the halfway house instead, and the house hadn't received it yet. "They should get it tomorrow," Sam asserted. "Then alls we gotta do is go get it, and cash it." Meanwhile, they'd called the broker who was supposed to show them the rooms; she wouldn't make an appointment with them until they had cash in hand. "But we can meet her tomorrow, right after we get the money."

I told you, I wanted to say, but Sam said it first, shaking her head at the ground. "You told me something could happen, but we planned so hard, I thought for sure it would all work out."

I reached up and put my hand on her shoulder. "Well, I'm glad you called me. Let's get you someplace overnight, for now, and we'll figure it out from there."

I pointed the four of us toward St. Marks Place, to the hotel on the corner of Third Avenue. Sometimes kids used to scrape up a few bucks and crash there, back in my day; it wasn't a flophouse anymore, but it still looked cheap. Sam and Bill took up the rear, starting an amicable chat about the anarchy symbol around her neck—"I'm more of a nihilist these days, actually," she clarified.

"I guess nihilists don't have a logo," said Bill.

I took the opportunity to try to get to know Valentina, who was humming to herself as she carried her oversized purple handbag and a giant plastic tote from Chinatown. "So Sam tells me you've been going to school at night?"

She cast her brown eyes down and to the side, like a geisha, and smiled faintly. "Katharine Gibbs School," she said in her breathy voice. "Business management."

"Wow, cool. Is that your interest, or is this a career move?"

"I want to open a spa, for ladies," she said, still looking sidelong. "For health and beauty."

"That sounds great." I smiled at her. I could hear Bill and Sam behind me, chatting away like old friends—"Of course, the German outlook is always going to be the grimmest." "Well, the Scandinavians, they're not the most fun-loving bunch." The foot traffic in the East Village was thick, the energy Friday-night high, as our improbable foursome wended its way through the familiar streets. I knew this was an emergency in progress, but it was going so well, it almost felt like a party.

We got to the hotel, and I proffered my credit card to the clerk behind the Plexiglas barrier as Sam and Valentina huddled behind me with Bill. "One room, for two people, overnight please." The clerk looked around me to see the three of them—a clean-cut guy in rectangular glasses with two grubby, luggage-toting street rats. He looked at me, at my credit card, and back at them. "The room's just for the two girls," I clarified. "My nieces, from out of town."

American Express approved of me, even if the clerk was still unsure. He slid a key and a receipt through the slot. "Checkout is at eleven," he said.

We helped them get their bags to the room, Valentina and Sam thanking me with every step. "We're gonna get a place tomorrow, Janice, I swear it, and we'll totally pay you back."

"I know you will," I said, smiling. Sam unlocked the door to reveal a small, cruddy room with two twin beds and a TV. "But this is home sweet home, for tonight."

They threw their luggage on the floor and started investigating the room. "Ooh, there's a tub," cooed Valentina, shucking her beat-up sneakers. "I'm going to take a bath."

Sam sniffed her pits. "I could probably use one, too."

"All right," I said. We'd leave them to their bathing, but I told them I wanted them to stay in the room, not go running around the streets or anything. They had a long day of apartment hunting ahead of them, and I didn't want to have to worry about where they were. And they had to promise to call me in the morning before they checked out, and let me know what the plans were. They swore they'd stay put for the night, bathe, watch TV, and fall asleep, so Bill and I accepted another round of *Thank yous* and *You're so awesomes* and headed home.

I felt like skipping down the sidewalk, elated by my crisis-management skills and by Bill's burgeoning friendship with Sam. "Wow," he said, walking briskly beside me. "She really is unbelievable. Where does she get all that philosophy stuff from?"

"The public library," I gloated. Sure, all parents bragged about their kids, but the one I'd picked out for us really was the most special.

"Wow." He'd caught it, I could tell; he'd gotten the Sam bug. He had the same excited flush as I did—the flush of discovery, of success. "She seems like she's in good shape, too, considering."

So she did, now that he mentioned it—she looked better than I'd ever seen her. "I think she's happy to be out of that place."

We got home, and the first thing I did was call their hotel room. Valentina answered, sounding sleepy. *Not drug sleepy*, I told myself. *Just tired.* She put Sam on the phone. "Hey."

"Just wanted to make sure you aren't getting into any trouble."

It had been twenty minutes since we left them. "We're all right," she protested. "We're just watching cable. Don't worry about us. We'll call you in the morning."

"All right." I let her go.

Still, I called the hotel first thing the next morning, after an anxious night spent wondering if I'd just enabled a huge binge for them. Maybe they left the room after my call, went out pickpocketing or shoplifting or tricking for money, got a bunch of drugs, and ingested them in the hotel room I'd paid for. How better to celebrate your elopement from a halfway house?

"They checked out already," said the clerk. "Not too long ago."

Fuck. "Thanks." I dialed Sam's new phone. "Hey, it's me. I thought you guys were going to call me. Let me know what's up."

Bill monitored the phones while I ran and showered; then, while he did the same, I puttered around, cleaning the house. Noon came and I called again. "Me again. Listen, just let me know where you are."

We made brunch, and Bill had to leave for a Saturday-afternoon shift at the paper. I wasn't going to sit by the phone all day; I took my cell phone and followed him out of the apartment with the grocery cart, intent on doing some chores. "Don't forget, we have to approve the wedding programs today."

"Seven o'clock," he confirmed, kissing me good-bye in front of the subway stop. "I'll meet you at the printers."

I crossed the park to the grocery store, grateful for the roaring blast of air-conditioning that hit me upon entry. It was another beastly, roasting July day—not the day to be carrying all of your worldly possessions on a three-borough quest for a residence. I started combing the store aisles for staples, remembered a gallon of low-fat milk for Bill. And stopped still, laughing.

There they were in the dairy aisle, Sam and Valentina, carrying a bag of hamburger buns and a pack of sliced baloney. Valentina was eating a donut from the bakery display. They both stopped with their mouths open when they saw me. "Well, *hello*, ladies," I said, gleeful. "So good to see you again."

"We were gonna call you," protested Sam, brow lined with sincerity, the corners of her mouth edged with powdered sugar. "We just wanted to wait until everything was worked out."

I pointed at their baloney, still smiling. "Having some lunch in the meantime?"

"Well . . ." She grunted a little in frustration. "See, here's what happened."

I put up my hand: *Enough.* "Why don't we go to my house for lunch, and we'll discuss the situation."

Sam's already wide eyes got wider. *My house?* Here she expected me to chastise her, and I was offering them this bonus instead. Valentina's eyes widened, too. "Do you have air-conditioning?" she asked.

"Plenty," I assured her as we breezed through the rest of the aisles and headed to the checkout. Valentina reached out for a jar of mayonnaise, but I stopped her. "We have that, too."

They insisted upon paying for their own groceries, not including the donuts they'd eaten. Valentina, I noted, had a supermarket bonus card. She counted change out of her coin purse like an old lady: "Sixty-three, sixty-four, sixty-five . . ."

We pushed the cart back across the park, Sam trotting at my side. "So the problem is, the check didn't come today, and it's not gonna come till Monday now. And we're screwed. We found a place that'll rent to us, but we don't have enough to put down the deposit."

"I see." I indicated my building—*in here*—and noted the look they exchanged. I was acutely aware of how ritzy the place must have looked to Sam and Valentina, and how unritzy they must have looked to the doorman. *Nothing to see here, just my nieces from out of town.*

"This place is fancy," noted Sam in the elevator.

"It's not too shabby," I agreed. I stopped and sorted through my keys at the door. "Here we are."

All three cats peered up at us, the three humans, entering and then stopping in the doorway. "Holy shit," said Sam, awed. "Look at your place."

I pushed the cart toward the kitchen, flipped on the air conditioner, and started unloading groceries. "Well, put your stuff down, come on in. Bathroom's in the hall, if you need it."

They took a few tentative steps into the living room. "Holy shit," said Sam again.

"It's very lovely," whispered Valentina.

I smiled, lips tight. It *is* lovely, far lovelier than I deserve, I'm sure, which has caused me no end of guilt, especially when faced with Valentina and Sam gawking like it was the Sistine Chapel. "Thank you," I said. I stopped myself from saying, *Make yourselves at home.*

They looked around for a minute, then Sam flopped down in the easy chair and Valentina perched on the couch. They ripped into the baloney and buns I placed on the coffee table before them. "Man, it's comfortable here," Sam enthused.

"So, what's the plan?" I inquired quickly, perching on the edge of a chair. "How much are you short for the deposit?"

Sam took a huge bite of her makeshift sandwich and swallowed. "We have three hundred dollars, and we need five. But we just need it through Monday, because Monday the check's coming. If the stupid city services hadn't fucked it up, we wouldn't need anything! And we didn't want to ask you for it—that's why we didn't call. You already did so much for us."

That much I believed—they really didn't want me to have to bail them out again. They would rather have resorted to eating food in the store and camping out in the park. "So how were you planning to get it?"

Sam and Valentina looked sideways at each other. If they were planning to employ subterfuge to get the money, they were going to have to learn to communicate more subtly. "Uh, we thought maybe Alita could wire it to us, Valentina's trans mom, but she hasn't called us back. Or I could walk some more dogs, see if I could raise some cash that way. We haven't figured it out yet."

"I see that." I looked at the clock: almost 3 P.M. Time to act, before the day faded away and they were rolling crackheads for nickels, or I was paying for another hotel room. I stood up, and they looked up at me, expectant. "All right. Let's go meet this broker."

"What?"

"I said, let's go see these rooms for rent, and if you haven't heard from Alita by then, I'll put down the deposit. Finish your sandwiches, and we'll go. And leave your bags here. You can pick them up tonight."

There. Look at me, solving things again. I wanted to brush my hands together—*finis.* Maybe I wasn't a trans mom, but I was some kind of mom. Sam and Valentina exchanged another look, happier this time. "Awesome. Thanks so much, Janice. You shouldn't have to do this—"

"Come on," I interrupted. "Time's a-wastin'."

It was a merry subway ride uptown to the broker's office, the girls taking turns one-upping each other with gross stories about the residents of their former home. "How about *Wally*," said Sam, eyes gleaming. "When he first came, he had, like, *orange wax* dripping out of his ears. And the wax had these *dead gnats* in it. *So* disgusting." We got off the train in Harlem, walked a few blocks to the Broadway address Sam had written on an index card. It was a barbershop, with an easel in front reading CUARTOS PARA ALQUILAR, ROOMS FOR RENT, IMMIGRATION LAWYER, NOTARY PUBLIC.

We walked past the haircutting chairs to the small, walled-off office in the back, where several people sat slumped in plastic chairs as two women at desks made phone calls and photocopied IDs. "Can I help you?" asked one of the women, hand cupped over her receiver.

"We called before," said Sam. "You said you had some rooms in the Bronx?"

The woman nodded, said something in Spanish into the phone, hung up, and pulled out a few index cards, which she sorted and dealt on her desk like a blackjack dealer. "Here they are."

I peered over their shoulders to read the cards. *1 bedroom, window, clean, near D train, one person $100, two $150/week. 1 bedroom, no window, TV, quiet, near 4 train, one person $100, two $150/week.* A sign on the wall read NO REFUNDS ON BROKERS FEE. Sam and Valentina debated the merits of the places, as I watched the woman at the next desk complete her transaction with a customer—she photocopied his ID, he signed an agreement, and off he went with his index card.

"What if they choose a place and they get there and they don't like it?" I asked our broker.

"They come back and get another for the same price. But no refund on the fee if you don't take any place at all."

"We want this one," decided Valentina. *Clean, window, TV, shared bath, near 4 train, two $150/week.* Two weeks in advance, plus the broker's fee. Valentina opened her coin purse and pulled out a roll of bills held together with a rubber band, as I counted out a stack of twenties from my wallet.

"I need your ID and signature." Valentina pulled out a nondriver's license bearing the name Jesus Colón and a picture of someone who could have been her brother; she tittered to me and Sam when the broker reacted with the slightest look of surprise. The broker made a photocopy of the ID, and Valentina signed the typed agreement as Jesus. Meanwhile, Sam was writing her own agreement on a blank index card. *I owe Janice Erlbaum two hundred dollars, July 16, 2005, signed: Samantha Dunleavy.* "Okay," said the broker. "And if you don't like it, come back for another one. We're open till seven."

"Congratulations," I said to them, shaking their hands. "You're one step closer to living indoors."

Unbelievable, I thought, as we walked toward the subway together; they were really going to pull this off. I thought the cheap, readily available room for rent was a myth; I had no idea what kind of real estate deals went down in the backs of barbershops. Valentina's benefits could cover them both for a few weeks, and at seventy-five dollars a week for rent, Sam could easily live off her own benefits—since she was HIV-positive, she was entitled to a few. Of course, she was already talking about the jobs she was going to get.

"This one place I'm going on Monday, they give you paid training to be a security guard. I'd be great at that. Then I'm going to this other place to be a foot messenger, then I got an interview to be one of those street canvassers that raise donations for the environment."

"I hate those kids," I said. "They make me want to club seals."

"You make a good commission, though. You can also do it for gay rights. Everybody thinks I'm gay anyway; maybe they'll give me more money."

We got to the subway, and I checked the time again: almost five-thirty already. No time for me to look at the room with them, but it seemed plausible that they'd actually find a place to sleep before nightfall. "Hey, I'm going to have to go downtown; I have wedding stuff to do, and then we're going to a friend's party tonight. But you guys *have* to call me this time, ha ha, because I have all your stuff. So let me know when you're in your new place, and you'll come down and get the stuff late tonight or in the morning, okay?"

"Okay." Sam was grinning again, only slightly abashed. "Thanks,

Janice. I know I say that a lot, but I mean it. And I promise I'll call later. I would have called before. I just didn't want to bother you."

"Always bother me," I instructed. "Good luck, and call me later."

I was optimistic on the way downtown—this was working; this could actually work. On Friday morning Sam was still incarcerated with no contact in the halfway house until god knew when; now here it was Saturday night, and she was getting ready to turn the key to a room of her own. Well, a shared room of her own. Better than the last room she shared with Valentina.

Bill met me outside the printers. "Let's hear it," he said, upon seeing my face.

"Okay, so I leave you this afternoon, right, and I go to Food Emporium . . ." I caught him up on the story—running into them, the missing welfare check, the barbershop, the index cards. "Anyway, they just left me a message while I was still on the train; they got to the place, they liked it, they're taking it. They want to pick up their stuff tonight around midnight, after we get back from Noah's party."

"Great." He swung the door open and held it for me. "Good thing you decided to do the grocery shopping, *wife*."

We entered the printers, and the clerk showed us the programs Bill had designed, the picture we took on the night of our engagement on the front. "Don't you look happy," the woman said.

Didn't we, though? We'd just handled a successful elopement. Bill looked at me and grinned, rakish.

"We are," I said, my hand over his. "We really are."

Chapter Ten

Make a Wish

I was sitting with Sam on a thick log bridging the Bronx River, our feet dangling above the black water. Sam had led me here from her new place—a clean, decent-sized bedroom with wood floors and a window, a double bed and a TV, in a nondescript apartment carved into three Sheetrocked spaces, each locked from the outside with padlocks. There was a small, shared kitchen, and a shared bathroom with no toilet paper; the residents of the three spaces supplied their own. Sam showed me around the place like it was Trump Tower. She'd been particularly proud of the "balcony"— actually a fire escape, accessible from their window, which overlooked the busy street below. "This is better than the TV," she bragged, inviting me to climb out and see for myself.

"It's great," I agreed. "I'm really happy for you guys."

The log was the next stop on our tour of their new room and its environs. "This place is awesome," Sam promised, as we descended a stone staircase by the Grand Concourse, shuffled down a steep, muddy embankment, and navigated through the muck to the banks of the river, where we clambered up the damp branch. And now here we were, sitting comfortably on the smooth, curved limb, surrounded by the dark green summer trees, the river hurrying excitedly under-neath.

"This *is* awesome," I marveled. "How did you find it?"

Sam's mouth twisted into a suppressed smile—she'd impressed me yet again. She shrugged, like it was nothing. "Me and Valentina found it the other day. We were fencing with sticks right over there; it was so fun."

"Ah." I smiled, enjoying the idea.

We sat and watched the river, let our toes point, felt the slight mist from the stream tickle our legs. I had something to ask her, some-thing Bill and I had been discussing, but I had to work my way up to it. "So. You saw the pulmonologist on Thursday?"

She gave me the shrug again, and I saw how bony her shoulder was getting, the weathered PSALMS 22 tattoo sticking out from her sleeveless black shirt. "He says I'm doing all right. I just have to be careful about infections aggravating the asthma. As long as I take the prednisone and stuff, I should be all right for a while."

For a while—that was the catch. I nodded, stared straight down at the water, as she was staring. Tried to see her peripherally, to look without looking.

"And what'd your . . . other doctor say?"

Her mouth twisted again, suppressing something that wasn't a smile. "She says . . . I'm doing all right."

Sam had been resisting this all week, since she left the halfway house; she wouldn't talk about her AIDS. I'd hounded her about it, as gently as I could—"When are you seeing the doctors again? Do they want to retest your T cells? Do they think the antivirals are working?"—but she was evasive, gave the minimum amount of infor-mation, changed the subject—"I don't really want to think about it too much. I just want to keep taking my meds, and focus on, like, life and stuff. I start training for that street canvassing next week. And I applied at this place that's like a dog-walking service. They said I could probably start real soon."

I didn't want to push her now, but I had to know. "Any more news about the numbers?"

I sneaked a look at her, caught a little wince as it passed over her face, watched her slump forward a few degrees. "They haven't really improved."

"But they haven't gotten worse," I noted, optimistic. "Stable is okay. Maybe once the antivirals start working . . ."

She slumped a few degrees more. "They actually got a little bit worse," she confessed.

I slumped too. "Huh. Well . . ."

The river raced underneath us; it was giving me vertigo. I wiggled backward on the log, steadied myself.

"So listen," I said, clearing my throat, "since we're talking about all this doctor stuff . . ."

I could feel her stealing a sidelong look at me, her elbows resting on her thighs, her head drooping. "Uh-huh."

"I think it would be a good idea if you had someone to help you deal with all of this, you know?"

She frowned at her lap. "You mean, like a shrink? 'Cause I don't wanna see a shrink, I'm seeing enough doctors, and the shrinks didn't do shit for me when I was in the psych ward. And I mean, I got you, and Maria, and I called Jodi the other day, we're gonna get together soon, I think—"

"Not like a shrink," I interrupted. "Like a guardian. A legal guardian."

I sneaked another look at her. Her arms were wrapped around her knees, and she gripped her own wrists tight. "Like . . . how do you mean?"

"I mean, I'm saying that you need somebody to look out for you right now. And I know, you've been taking care of yourself since you were twelve, and you've gotten this far, and you know nobody's more impressed by that than me. I'm not saying you can't take care of yourself, I'm just saying that you don't have to anymore—you have me, and you also have Maria and Jodi, and I know all of us want to make sure that you're getting all the right treatment, all the right assistance, all the right everything. You know?"

She nodded into her knees, the lower half of her face obscured. "I know."

"So, what I'm saying is . . . I mean, we've known each other for close to a year now . . ." I stumbled on my words—why was this so hard? I'd just proposed to Bill last month; you'd have thought I'd be used to proposals by now. "I'm saying, why don't I become your legal guardian?"

She was quiet. Which I couldn't stand—she was supposed to say yes right away!—so I kept talking. "That way, if something were to ever happen to you, god forbid, I'd be there to help you deal with it. If you went back into the hospital again, or had any kind of emergency—like the room deposit—whatever you need. And, you know, even when you're feeling well, it's nice to have a guardian, right?"

She laughed, and her face came out of her lap, turned toward me, her eyes so clear and open. "Yeah, it is. I mean, knowing that I have you in my life, and Maria and Jodi, it makes such a big difference to me."

"It makes a big difference to us, too." I looked at her lovingly, wishing she were short enough and young enough to permit me to stroke her hair when she wasn't lying in a hospital bed. "And listen, if you'd rather elect Maria to be your guardian, as long as there's *someone* who can act on your behalf when you need them to, I totally understand."

I totally understand, I told myself. *Maria's single, I have Bill at home; Sam might want someone who's all her own.* And Maria was just as devoted to Sam as I was, if not more. Sam was certainly devoted to her—she'd once let it slip that Maria was the one she thought of like a mom, and I was like a cool older sister. *But I'm older!* I wanted to protest. *And besides, I met you first. You have to pick me. Pick me!*

Sam stared straight ahead downriver, her chin on her knees. She didn't say anything, and neither did I. It was a beautiful place to sit, hearing the soft *shush* of the water underneath us, watching the silver ropes of the stream over the rocks.

"You would really want to be my guardian?" she asked. Her voice was soft and incredulous, as sweetly disbelieving as a kid's on Christmas morning. *Is this for me?*

"Well," I told her, bumping her with my shoulder. "What the hell, I'm stuck with you anyway. I might as well horn in on your family fortune."

She bumped me back, openly smiling. "Right? Ha ha."

Then she leaned back, and we sat, side by side, quiet for a moment. She was doing the math in her head; I watched her add it up. I was only a year younger than her real mom, the junkie who sold her for drugs. *Mom.* My heart got louder in my chest. I wasn't ready to be anybody's mom; I'd never planned to be. Bill and I had agreed long ago, we never wanted to have kids. But then, I'd never planned on meeting Sam.

She balanced her chin on her knee, affecting an underbite. *She looks good*, I thought. She was thin, but the circles under her eyes weren't too bad, and her skin was tawny from the sun. She looked peaceful, and determined, like she was looking forward to the rest of her life.

"Can I think about it?" she asked.

"It's a standing offer," I said.

"Cool."

Cool. Okay. She needed to think about it. I was a little disappointed, but I shouldn't have been surprised; I should have known the idea of *family*, of *legal*, of *guardian*, would be hard for her to swallow. She couldn't hear those words without feeling the sting of the belt. And she knew why I was asking her now, when I'd never asked before; she knew I was thinking ahead to the time when she couldn't manage alone. I didn't want to face the fact that the day was coming; why should she?

I'd give her some time to think about it. She didn't have to decide that very minute—in a way, she'd already decided. I was here, wasn't I? Just like I told her I would be, all those months ago at St. Victor's: *I'm going to be in your life from now on.*

I spread my hands on either side of me, leaned back, and felt the breeze on my face. Sam sat silently next to me, on the thick log over the deep water, looking down at the Bronx River, running away.

Late July, 2005. This is when Sam and I saw the redhead on my corner, when we were heading from my house to the bookstore at the north end of Union Square. This is when I took her to an open mike at a poetry club, but she decided she didn't want to get up and read, so we just sat and listened. This is when I carted a bunch of Bill's old housewares from his bachelor apartment in Queens up to Sam and Valentina's place, and Sam used her new pots and pans to make us coconut curry shrimp. That's when I met one of the other families sharing the apartment—a Mexican couple with two kids under the age of four. The couple didn't look much older than Sam and Valentina.

Sam and I saw each other every three days or so, and I heard from her daily. She'd started a few shifts a week as a street canvasser, stopping people on the sidewalk to raise donations for impoverished kids. "'Scuse me, sir? Do you have a minute to help starving children?" Ironic; in a way—she was still panhandling for food.

She didn't mention my offer to become her legal guardian, and neither did I. But something had been agreed upon between us, it seemed. She was dutiful about checking in with me, and she was way more forthcoming with the information from her doctors; she even offered me the name of her pulmonologist, the one who'd sounded the alarm in the first place. "But I'm switching doctors next week, to someone at the hospital nearby," she said. "It's a pain, going all the way to Brooklyn all the time."

She still called with emergencies—she sprained her good wrist while skateboarding; thank god it didn't need surgery. She was feeling hopeless and depressed—why did she decide to get sober at the exact moment when drugs would have come in so handy? She and Valentina drank a bottle of Baileys Irish Cream down by the banks of the river; it made her puke her guts out. I gave her a pass on it—*one* pass, because she was honest about it, and she said she hated the experience. "But if you do it again," I warned, "you're blowing the Disney World deal."

All in all, though, I had to admit that Sam and Valentina had managed to surpass everyone's expectations — they'd found a place to live, and they were maintaining it. Valentina worked as a messenger during the day, then in the evenings she put on her blouse and pumps and brushed out her hair and went to business school. Sam, too, was working; aside from the Baileys, she was seven months sober. Almost three weeks into their experiment in independent living, it was looking like a success.

And then, of course, another phone call came. Monday, August 1, noon. I was at my desk when my cell phone buzzed with a number I didn't recognize. "Hello?"

"Hi, Janice, it's Maria." Her tone was friendly, but I could tell this wasn't a social call. "Just wanted to let you know, Samantha's been admitted to Mid-Bronx Hospital. They think she has meningitis, but they're not sure if it's bacterial or viral yet. I saw her for dinner yesterday, and she wasn't feeling so hot; I tried to get her to go to the emergency room last night, but she wanted to give it until the morning to see if she felt better. But apparently she fainted on the way to work, and she managed to get to the nearest hospital, and they admitted her right away."

"Oh, wow." I was momentarily stunned, woozy. If it was bacterial meningitis, I knew, she could be dead within days. Bacterial meningitis can kill a healthy person who contracts it; without an immune system, she had no chance. Viral meningitis is less deadly, but for someone with AIDS, it's still very bad news. "Do you know when they'll know more?"

Maria was trying to sound calm and rational, despite the facts; I recognized this from my own attempts at the same. "Tomorrow, I think. In the meantime, you can see her, but you'll have to wear a mask and gloves and everything. It may not be the best idea to visit. And I don't know if she can handle calls right now — I just spoke to her, and she said her head is killing her."

"Of course." And yet she'd managed to call Maria, I noticed. What a stupid time for me to be jealous, when her life was at risk. I was in shock, that was my only excuse; I wasn't thinking straight. "Thanks, Maria."

Bill came home that night to find me smoking and surfing, smoking and surfing, dripping ashes all over my keyboard, relentlessly clicking. "Sam's in the hospital again," I told him, distracted by a flashing banner on the New York State Department of Health AIDS services website. "Oh, and I heard from the deejay; he got the check from my dad and everything's set."

Bill shook his head at me. "See, in my business, they call that 'burying the lede.' What happened this time?"

"Meningitis." I took another hit off the joint and starting coughing up a lung. "Not sure what kind yet," I wheezed.

"Oh, babe." He sought refuge in the easy chair. "This is happening way too fast."

"I know." Although, according to the Internet, this was how things went when you had advanced AIDS. You got infections, and sometimes you recovered from them, but they always left you weaker than when you started. And then you got another infection, and maybe you recovered from that one, too. But only 60 percent of your full health. And you kept getting sick, and never fully getting better, until finally you just died. That was how things went.

I tortured myself all night—I should have been spending more time with her, knowing how short time could be; I shouldn't have let her get this sick. I was supposed to be keeping an eye on her; instead, I'd been letting her run around working a part-time job, smiling at her stories about riding her skateboard and wading in the Bronx River. I should have warned her to take it easy. I should have been more conscious of her health. I should have talked to her pulmonologist. I shouldn't have let her and Valentina live alone.

I thought about those Disney reservations. *She might not make it to December,* I realized. *She might not even make it the six weeks to the wedding.*

The next day, I rode the subway for an hour to the hospital in the

Bronx, where they'd determined her meningitis was viral—good news. Or, goodish—none of it was really "good." I came into her room just as she was waiting for a spinal tap.

"Hey, babe."

Sam was in the fetal position on a flat bed, shivering, white as an eggshell, face contorted with pain. She couldn't answer, could only open one eye in acknowledgment, but I knew she was grateful to see me. I dropped into the visitor's chair, and she extended her hand, which I grasped and held. It was clammy and cold, like she'd been squeezing ice in her palm.

"Thanks," she croaked feebly.

"Shhh," I told her. "Save your strength."

The door to the room opened, and a nurse and a doctor entered, bearing a tray of hideous implements: a long, wicked, pointy metal pick, and a needle and syringe the length of my forearm. I was glad Sam's eyes were closed. The doctor, a stout blond guy, smiled at me as he addressed Sam. "Okay, Sam, I'm glad your friend's here, but we're going to try the tap again. I know this isn't fun, but we'll make it as quick as we can."

"Should I go?" I asked, hopeful.

He glanced at me, as the nurse applied a local anesthetic to Sam's lower back. "Well, you can stay, if she wants you to."

Sam gave my hand a faint squeeze—*Stay*. "I'll stay," I decided, bracing myself.

"Ow!" she chimed, as he dug in the needle, a sharp, bright note of pure pain, and her hand clamped onto mine. "*Ow!*"

The doctor winced along with her. "I'm sorry, Sam, I know it's uncomfortable. We'll get it as fast as we can."

"Ow!" Her whole body spasmed and flailed, her bony hand jerking mine in its tight grip. I could feel the pain flowing through her body; I felt sick just witnessing it.

"Try to stay still, if you can; I know it's hard."

"Ow!" *Jesus!* Sweat and tears poured from her face; her mouth was open and distended in agony. What were they doing to her? It looked like torture, actual torture, like what evil governments do to political dissidents in back rooms. I wanted to close my eyes, but I couldn't close myself off from the sound, the grip on my hand, the waves of pain coming off of her. "Ow!"

Both the doctor and the nurse looked miserable, brows furrowed, wincing as she did. "We're really sorry, Sam, we're almost done here." "Ow!"

I felt the blood rushing from my head, the clammy nausea coming over me. I kept my hand on hers, tried breathing deeply. "It's going to be over soon," I crooned. "It's going to be over soon." Sam gave another jerk and cry, and I cried out with her. "Ow!"

"All right, all right. I think we got it." The doctor pulled out the needle, put it on the tray. I didn't dare look at it. Sam gave one last cry as he withdrew, then her hand went heavy in mine. "That was tough, I know."

He pulled off his gloves and mopped his brow. Sam looked as though she was about to faint dead away. "Okay, honey," said the nurse. "You rest now, all right?" They prepared to leave the room with their infernal tray, but I interrupted.

"Is she . . . is she going to be okay?"

The doctor gave me a blank smile. "We think so."

The nurse opened the door. *Wait!* They couldn't leave without giving me some information, some idea of how bad this was or wasn't going to be; they had to tell me whether she was going to make it through this or not. "Is there any idea how long she'll be here?"

Either the doctor didn't know, or he wasn't going to answer. "Until she gets better. Okay, Sam, we'll see you later."

Sam was limp, her breathing shallow, her wet hand dangling in mine. I sat alone in the room with her, listening to her monitors beep, watching her chest rise and fall. Just three days ago we'd met downtown in the park, walked around and browsed the magic shop on Fourth Avenue, talked about her taking the October SATs. Now here she was, drained of everything vital, stuck like a soggy noodle to a dampened hospital bed she might never get out of.

Her eyes fluttered open, and she twitched and pulled her hand from mine. "Hey," I said, frowning.

"Hey," she said thickly. "Hurts . . . so much."

"I know, oh god, I'm so sorry. I'm so sorry you're going through this right now." *Right now*, as opposed to when? The ten times she'd already gone through it this year, the ten times yet to come? "Just rest. Is there anything I can get you?"

She couldn't even shake her head no. "Thanks. I'ma . . ." She settled in a little, face screwing up as she bumped the site of the spinal tap. "Eeeyagh."

"Oh god." I could feel the pain in every pore, every muscle of my own. I writhed in my seat. "I'm so sorry, babe. I'll just sit right here and be quiet while you sleep for a while, okay?"

Nor could she shake her head yes. "Thanks," she said again, her heavy eyes closing.

I sat and got familiar with our new room, a room I knew I'd be seeing for a while. It was a children's hospital she'd been admitted to—she was on the floor for teenagers—and the perimeter of the room was bordered with a historical time line of New York City: dinosaurs and rocks in one corner, crowds cheering at Yankee Stadium wrapped around the other. The TV on the wall was flat-screened, and there was a wireless keyboard on the nightstand—they must have had some kind of child-safe Internet access here. A stack of kids' books sat on the far windowsill. I strolled over and browsed the titles. One of the *Chronicles of Narnia* books, favorites of mine in grade school; a book called *McGrowl*, about a crime-solving robotic dog.

Sam stirred in her bed, made an unhappy noise, went back to sleep. I looked out the window at the neighborhood below. Her apartment was only four blocks that way. I thought of her as I'd seen her just the week before, when I came up to take her out for Chinese food, and she answered the door with the toilet brush in her hand. "Just cleaning up," she announced, beaming, so proprietary, so proud. "Would you mind taking off your shoes? The floor's wet."

I picked up *McGrowl* and sat down again at Sam's bedside. Might as well make myself comfortable. It was going to be a long week.

• • •

"Hey, Janice, it's Maria. Just wanted to see what time you were going to be at the hospital today. I have to work until five, but I should be there by quarter to six; if you're still there, maybe we can talk about a few things. Thanks. Take care."

"Hey, Maria, it's Janice. I'm on my way home now; sorry I missed you today. But she looks better; she's keeping down clear liquids, and they're hoping the seizures were just a fluke. Um, I'll be there tomorrow around six. Maybe we can connect then. Hope all's well, and I'll see you soon."

"Hey, Janice, it's Maria. I'm not going to be able to make it today; I'm working a double. I didn't want to call Sam because I know the headaches are still pretty bad, but if you could give me a call when you can, let me know how she's doing, I'd really appreciate it. Okay. Take care. Thanks."

"Hey, Maria, it's Janice. They moved her to the ICU because of the seizures; I was trying to get a doctor to tell me what was up, but no luck. But she's definitely improving, aside from the seizures—the antibiotics seem to be working on the meningitis, she's eating again, and she seemed like she was feeling better, painwise. But, um, I hope we'll see each other soon; we should definitely talk. Hope you're well. Catch you soon."

This was how the first ten days of August went: Every day after work, I got on the subway uptown, with a book and my notebook and my cardigan in my bag, because the train and the hospital were both freezing cold, and I rode for an hour to the Bronx, then walked the six blocks through the wilting sun to the hospital. If Sam had been able to take liquids or food the day before, I stopped and bought her a rainbow ice pop from the Mister Softee truck; if not, I just went straight to her room. Sometimes she was sleeping, or she was out of her room while they ran a test on her, a scan or a sonogram or an X-ray; if so, I just wrote in my notebook or read. Then she'd wake up, or return, and I'd hear about her day.

"I feel better than yesterday, but it's still painful sometimes—like, I still can't read or watch TV, or my head starts killing me. But the doctors say the infection's getting better, and I haven't had any seizures since yesterday, so that's good. And Maria came after you left. She said to tell you hi."

Or, "They did the CAT scan, and it looked normal, but they still want me to wear these stupid discs on my head. I look like an alien. And it's uncomfortable when I lay down, but it's worse when I try to keep my head up. I just want to it stop hurting, already."

Or, "Last night was real bad. I kept throwing up my food, and my head was really aching, but I feel a little better today. And Valentina stopped by, she said the apartment's boring without me. I signed over my last paycheck to her, so I'm covered for the next two weeks. But I think the social worker here is going to help me apply for benefits."

And I'd try to sort through all of it. "So, wait. The neurologist said he thinks the seizures *weren't* linked to the meningitis? Or they *were*? Okay. And the internist says what? So he thinks they probably won't recur, once you're done with the antibiotics? And they're keeping you on those for how long? And wait, how long does the social worker think it's going to take for you to get benefits? Did she talk to you about the health-care proxy?"

I'd filled out a health-care proxy form with my name and information (*Relationship to patient: Friend*); it would entitle me to talk with her doctors about her care, and to make decisions for Sam, should she become impaired. Until she signed it, though, I was stuck trying to cadge information from nurses and orderlies, who took increasing pity on me the more they saw me sitting in that chair in that darkened room, squinting as I read. "Your girl is doing better today," they'd say as I passed them in the hallway. "They took the electrodes off last night, and she got some decent sleep. She could go home in a few days, if she keeps this up."

At the mention of the proxy, Sam pressed her lips together tight. "Yeah, the social worker said something about that, but we didn't really get around to talking about it, 'cause she had to go."

I conferred with Maria one evening when we'd overlapped, while Sam was busy getting a sponge bath from a nurse. We ducked into the hallway, leaning against the wall like smokers without cigarettes. "She doesn't want to sign the health-care proxy because she doesn't want to face it," said Maria. "You know how sensitive she is about talking about her AIDS."

"I know. She always calls it 'my diagnosis,' or 'that other thing.' It's like she doesn't even want to say the words."

Maria's lively brown eyes were drooping at the corners, I noticed; she looked like she'd been awake for days. "Well, she may want to stay in denial about it, but I don't know how long she's going to be able to. They say she's getting better, but this thing knocked her flat on her ass. Last time I got her to talk about it, she said her T cells were around a hundred—that's *awful*. I want one of us to be able to talk to her doctors, soon."

"Me too. I mean, I don't want to push her, but—"

"You're going to have to. We both will."

Maria was right. I was going to have to be more forceful. Just the day before, one of the doctors had dropped by when I was there, and Sam asked if I could "give them a minute." And I thought, *Take all the time you need; I'll just be right here listening and asking questions.* But then I realized she wanted me to leave the room. "Oh," I said, hopping up from my chair. "Sure, I'll be in the lounge." I sat in the lounge for ten minutes, my face hot with mortification and resentment. How dare she ask me to leave? What did she have to discuss with the doctor that she couldn't discuss with me? What was I, chopped liver? I had to compose myself before I walked back into her room with a smile. *So, what'd he say?*

"So I'll nag her again tomorrow," I said to Maria. "And you stay on her, too."

"Right." She touched my arm, the signal to go back into the room. An almost wifely gesture, from my co-parent.

I didn't know what I would I have done without Maria, without somebody holding my hand through this every step of the way. At least Maria was right there next to me, going through the same experience. Jodi, meanwhile, was busy with her new job and her own kid, and though she tried to call and visit when she could, she lived way out in Brooklyn with no car; it was more than an hour and a half by subway to get to the hospital. "And frankly," she'd told me over the phone, matter-of-fact, "I can't really handle what's coming. I can't stand to watch. You know, besides my son, I've got a daughter only a year older than Sam. I've seen what happens to these kids before, and I know I'm not going to be able to bear losing her like that."

I looked across the hallway of the Intensive Care Unit, through the open door of the room there, saw the crib, the electrodes, the monitors. The toddler sleeping fitfully, its thumb in its mouth. Poor baby.

I put on my brave face to match Maria's and reentered Sam's room, smiling. "So, kid, you smelling any better?"

By the next week, Sam was looking so much better that the doctors moved her from Intensive Care back to the teenagers' floor, and started saying that magical word—*home*. Home! Our visits, and my phone calls with Maria, took on a celebratory air—she'd managed to kick meningitis while severely compromised—look how strong she was! That was Sam for you: give her odds, and she'd defy them for you. If anybody was going to exceed her doctors' expectations, it would be Sam.

She was full of plans for her release. "It's gonna be a week or two before I can go back to work, but I already called and they said to come in whenever I'm feeling better, so that's good. And Maria said she was gonna get us tickets to see a Yankees game. I never seen a ball game in person—closest I ever been to Yankee Stadium was to cop some dope on a Hundred Eightieth Street first week I was in town. It's gonna be so cool."

"I bet it is." I smiled—I could afford to again. I didn't have to watch her monitors and worry, or writhe with her through a spinal tap, or nag her about the health-care proxy—not right now, anyway, since she was on an upswing. "Did you give that money to Valentina?"

I'd taken the liberty of giving Sam $150 to give to Valentina to cover the next two weeks of her rent. I figured the "don't give them money" thing didn't apply as much anymore, not when we were trying to keep Sam living indoors. "Yeah, I did. Thanks so much, Janice. I swear, I really am going to pay you back for all this."

"I know. Don't worry about it. I'm glad I can help."

She nodded and settled her head back against the pillow, eyes heavy. She still got worn out so easily; twenty minutes of animated conversation could sap her strength.

"Do you want me to read to you?" I suggested. We were reading *McGrowl* together, only a few pages every day, as she tended to fall asleep. Then I'd stop reading aloud, and she'd wake up enough to chastise me in a murmur, "You're not reading."

"No, I don't want to fall asleep. I want to wait until you have to go." She repositioned her pillow, leaned back again. "It's so boring here. I'm so sick of being in the hospital. All I do is look forward to seeing you and Maria."

"We look forward to seeing you, too," I assured her. "Although we're kind of sick of the setting."

She gave me a little smirk, like, *Tell me about it.* "And when I'm out of here, we have to go to Coney Island with Bill, like you said."

"Absolutely. He's looking forward to it. It'll be advance training for Disney World."

Sam looked pleased, her calendar in place. "How's the wedding coming along?"

"Great. I think it's going to be really great. A lot of our really good friends will be there. I can't wait for you to meet everybody." They'd certainly heard enough about her. The legendary Samantha was going to be one of the main attractions among my friends and family—her, and my legendary mom, if she would ever RSVP.

"Yeah. Valentina's real excited about coming with me. She's getting a new dress and shoes and everything. I said I might even let her put makeup on me, just to see how it looks." She couldn't contain a laugh at the idea. "Can you even imagine me in makeup?"

"That would be something," I said, laughing along. Thinking, *It'll be something if she makes it to the wedding at all, much less in makeup.*

But again, she looked all right now, if not fully robust—too skinny, but red-cheeked and high-spirited, talking about all the writing she was going to do now that she could sit up and hold a pen again. "I still really like the idea we came up with together," she assured me, "but I think I might want to write my own book first, about my life, and everything I been through."

I remembered the excerpts she'd sent me from the halfway house, the pieces she'd shown me since then. *Baby Dunleavy was born seven weeks premature. Her mother told the nurses to give her an American name . . .*

Write fast, I thought. "I can't wait until you do."

Sam closed her eyes and leaned back against the pillow again, a slight smile on her face. "Then I'll be totally famous."

I laughed. "Just remember who your friends were."

Her hand snaked out toward mine, her grasp bony but firm. "Always. I'm always going to remember what you've done for me, Janice."

I gripped her hand tight in reply. "And you for me."

Her hand got heavier in mine. She was fading for the day. "Do you want to read some more *McGrowl* now?"

"Sure." I picked up the book, tented on the nightstand next to me, and found the place where we'd left off. Sam snuggled deeper into her bedclothes, satisfied. " 'Even Mrs. Wiggins had to admit that Thomas had a special way with animals . . . ' "

Two days later, Sam went home to her apartment. She called and left me a message: "Hey, they let me go this morning. You can come up if you want, but I'm just gonna take it easy today. Give me a call if you wanna hang out this week. Thanks for everything, and I'll talk to you soon."

But it was Maria's call I returned first. "She's home!" I exulted.

"Hallelujah!" she agreed. "I just hope she stays there for a little while."

"Seriously." I looked over at the FRIENDS plaque on my bookshelf and sighed with relief. "That was a hell of a scare, there."

"It probably won't be our last."

I got that familiar seasick feeling I got every time I looked too far ahead. "I know. I wish we had a better idea of what to expect. I mean, we know what to expect, but when to expect it."

Maria's voice stayed firm and counselor-like. "Me too. Me too. But we'll stay on top of her this time, and you and I will stay in touch, too. She doesn't get to go back to work until she's feeling a lot stronger. And any time she's not feeling well, she goes straight to the ER."

"Agreed."

"She's *got* to take it easy," Maria emphasized.

"I know."

And yet we both knew that we couldn't contain her, we couldn't slow her down. We couldn't ask her not to run around and ride her skateboard while she was still able, even if it shortened her life. We were going to take her to Coney Island, to a Yankees game, to Disney World, if we could; we'd take her everywhere she wanted to go. Maria and I would become a two-woman Make-A-Wish Foundation — wishing as hard as we could for Sam to survive.

Chapter Eleven

Good Times

Bill and I sat in the private dining room of a hotel near Union Square, a surfeit of dishes in front of us, the banquet manager seated across the table. A waiter stood by proffering a towel-wrapped bottle of wine.

"Would you like to move on to the white wine?" he asked. "Or do you prefer to stay with the champagne for now?"

"The white would be great," said Bill, already two glasses deep into the champagne.

"Just a little for me, thanks," I said, trying not to slur my words. It was two-thirty in the afternoon, and I was hammered like a bent nail.

"So you can choose three of the cold appetizers, and three of the hot ones," explained the banquet manager, waving over two more waiters with trays. "And then we've got a selection of pastas and salads for you to try."

"Ucccch," I complained to Bill. "This is all so good. I can't stand it."

He dug into a plate of gnocchi. "Suck it up, Champ, we've got three more courses to go."

"It's a lot of food," the manager agreed. "It's a shame your parents weren't available to join us this afternoon. We made enough for four people."

"I should have asked Sam and Valentina," I said to Bill. They would have loved sitting around in this exquisite room, being served by jacketed waiters; what a treat it would have been. "I can't believe I didn't think of it."

"Who are Sam and Valentina?" asked the manager politely.

Bill and I caught each other's eyes. "They're our . . . hungry friends."

They're our homeless kids! I wanted to say, full of boozy bravado. *They're ex-hookers and junkies, and they broke out of their halfway house, and I got them an apartment in the Bronx! Sam's a genius, and I'm going to adopt her! She has AIDS!*

"Would you like to try the red as well?" The waiter started filling yet another glass in front of me.

"Oh." I smiled at him warmly. "Maybe jus' a little."

We finally wobbled out of the hotel at about four-thirty, utterly ruined. "Good thing I swapped days with Ted," Bill groaned, holding his stomach as we walked across the park. "I'd hate to have to go to work right now and throw up on everyone."

"Well, I'm supposed to meet Sam in a half hour," I reminded him. I tried using my thumbs and forefingers to open my sleepy eyes wider. "I gotta sober up." She'd seen me stoned before—everybody in my life had seen me stoned—but stoned was my default setting; I covered for it well. Drunk, on the other hand, I wasn't so good at hiding.

"I'm drunk," I announced to Sam, meeting her by Valentina's school in Chelsea. "I totally apologize. It was an accident. It should wear off soon. In the meantime, though, I'm totally drunk."

She looked me over and laughed. "So I guess you had fun at your tasting."

"Uccch." I put my hand on my belly, as Bill had. "A li'l too much."

We started walking toward the subway, Sam filling me in on the events of the past few days. "I been feeling pretty good, mostly, a little tired sometimes. But that's probably because I haven't been sleeping so good." She shot me a look, like, *you know what I mean*. Nightmares again.

"That sucks. You think you could get something from the doctors to help?"

She twisted her mouth to one side. "I dunno. I don't want to start messing with too much prescription stuff like that; it'd be real easy to relapse into everything else. Like, every time I go into the hospital, and they give me painkillers, it's hard when I come out not to just go pick up."

Pick up. That's what they said in 12-step groups. Which reminded me—"You still going to meetings?" It was absurd, me wobbling like a wino and wagging my finger at her about sobriety, but she took it seriously.

"When I can. If I'm not at the doctors, or doing something. I probably won't go today, because I'm seeing you, but maybe tomorrow I'll go. There's this one at this Quaker meetinghouse, I really like that one."

"That's cool." I liked the image of Sam sitting in silence like the Quakers do, in an airy meetinghouse full of natural light, watching dust motes rise through the sunbeams. "I'm glad to hear it."

The rocking of the train on its way uptown made me drowsy—too much wine, too much food. "Close your eyes," Sam suggested, playing the parent for a change. "I'll wake you up when we get there."

"Nonsense," I said, blinking and stretching my eyes some more. "I'm wide awake. What were you saying again?"

We walked to her apartment, the hospital looming over the tops of the other buildings. She was telling me about the nightmares she'd been having, and I was starting to sober up. It was no wonder she was having trouble sleeping, with everything that had been resurfacing lately—the leering faces of unwashed men, her mother's fingernails clawing at her, *Go make me some money*. And then there were the existential questions—What had she done to deserve this? Was this, again, punishment for her sins on the street? Is your life predetermined?

Was this all her inescapable fate? Why did she even bother waking up in the morning, staying sober, taking her meds?

"Of course, I'm gonna keep doing all that, because when it comes down to it, I don't really want to die. That's one thing this whole thing has taught me. It's like, I never knew how much I wanted to live until I found out I was dying."

You're not dying, I wanted to protest. *Not any more than the rest of us are. Not yet, anyway. Not yet.*

We reached their apartment and walked the two flights up the stairs, which winded Sam a little. "I'm all right," she said, opening the front door and then the padlock to their room. Valentina's messenger clothes lay strewn on the floor near a box of cereal and a pile of library books. "Sorry about the mess—I haven't been real good about cleaning up lately."

"It's cool." I pushed a pile of clothes aside and sat down on their bed. There was some kind of board game tangled in the sheets. "What's this?"

"Oh, it's so cool, it's called 'Would You Rather . . . ?' Some guy gave it to us outside the bookstore the other day. He was like, 'I went to return this, but they wouldn't take it back, and I don't want it, do you?' And we were like, 'Yeah!'" She reached out and grabbed a stack of game cards with questions on them. "You wanna play?"

"Sure."

She sat down cross-legged on the bed; I turned to face her. "There's a whole part with rolling the dice and everything, but mostly it's just questions."

"Okay. Shoot."

"Okay. Let's see." I smiled, watching her scrunch up her face in concentration. This is what she was supposed to have been doing all those years when she was out on the streets—doing jigsaw puzzles, playing board games. "Here's a good one. 'Would you rather have to kill Winnie the Pooh, or Bambi?'"

"Mmm . . . Winnie," I decided. "But only if I absolutely had to kill one of them. I'd put barbiturates in the honey; it'd be a peaceful, delicious death. How about you?"

"Um, probably Bambi, 'cause then I could eat him." She grinned. "Okay. Now you pick a card and ask me one."

"Okay." I frowned at the card I'd selected, wondering if I was still drunker than I thought. "Okay, I swear to god, this is what it says— 'Would you rather pee out of your nose, or poop out of your ear?'"

We both started laughing; Sam fell over onto her side. "'Poop out of your ear?' Are they serious?"

"I know. What kind of twelve-foot bong were they smoking out of when they came up with that one?"

"It's like, 'I can't hear you, I have to take a crap!'"

"Or, 'God bless you, would you like some toilet paper?'"

"What if you're wearing a hat 'cause it's cold out? Then it's like a diaper, and you've got poop smooshed all over your head!"

"And all your Q-tips are covered in shit!"

We laughed until tears came out of our eyes, which was at least better than poop coming out of our ears. "Okay, okay, gimme another one."

"Okay." She settled down and sifted through a few cards to find a good one. "Okay, would you rather hide a deep dark secret from your loved ones, or tell the truth and go to jail for twenty years?"

"Jesus, twenty years." I contemplated it for a minute. "What'd I do, kill somebody?"

"Probably." She shook her head sadly. "I warned you about your temper."

"Huh." This was harder than I thought, this game. I wanted to be a good role model for Sam, to say, *I'd tell the truth, of course; I'd never lie to the people I loved.* But of course I'd done just that, more than a few times; I'd even lied to her. And to go to jail for twenty years? "Honestly? I'd probably hide it."

"Me too," she confessed. "Like, I'd like to think I'd be all noble and everything, but if you think about it, you're hurting your loved ones more by going to jail for twenty years than by not telling them the secret."

I smiled at her pragmatic approach. "Still, can you imagine? Not being able to tell the people you're closest to the truth? How totally alienating would that be, having to lie to everyone all the time." I shuddered. "I bet I'd break down at some point and just let it slip."

"But you can't, though, or you'd go to jail." Sam's face was earnest. "You have to keep the secret."

"Okay." I laughed. "I'll lie my head off, then. Sorry—I'm not a very good mentor, am I?"

"No, you're good. Now ask me another one."

We played Would You Rather . . . ? for a while, then Sam wanted to show me some more writing she'd been working on. "Look what Maria got me. It used to be her sister's."

It was an old word processor, the kind I hadn't seen since the early nineties—more of a typewriter than a computer, but it still worked. "Cool, that's awesome."

"Yeah, I wrote a bunch of pages so far this week. Working on my life story." She handed me a sheaf of pages, and I started devouring them right away:

My earliest memories: a harsh animal smell, a wet diaper, a hollow in my stomach that made me scream. Shivering next to my brother, pressing myself into the warmth of his back. My father's face floats over mine, and my whole body tightens.

This was it, the start of the autobiography I'd been nagging her to write since I'd met her. This was her golden ticket, her writing—if she could finish a book, she'd have no problem finding a buyer. I skipped ahead a few pages:

I was in the backseat of this guy's car, jiggling my leg, wondering what kind of pervert he would turn out to be, not that it mattered. I was hungry. My cut-off jeans were swimming on me, and the gun tucked in my waistband was in danger of falling down my leg.

I put the sheaf down. "Wow, it's great. Can I get a copy for myself?"

"Thanks." Sam looked gratified. "You can keep that copy, if you want."

"Great, thanks." I slipped the pages into my bag, kept my voice casual. "Can I show it to people?"

She wrinkled her nose. "Mmm . . . not yet. I want to wait until it's finished."

"All right." It was like being given a bag of gold doubloons and being asked not to spend them. "Whenever you're ready."

We hung out for a while longer. Sam asked me about volunteering, and I confessed that I hadn't been to the shelter the past three weeks. I missed the first Wednesday she was in the hospital, and then the next week I left her bedside in time to make it there after dinner, but I felt exhausted on the subway downtown; I skipped the stop and went home. By last Wednesday, I'd decided to admit it—I was burnt out. I needed a break. "Besides," I told her, smiling. "I'm more involved in one-on-one mentoring these days."

"Too bad for them." She smiled back. "But good for me. Now I don't have to be jealous of any of your other favorites."

When it was time to go, she wanted to walk me to the subway, and though I thought she was getting a little peaked, she insisted. "Just let me change my T-shirt." She opened the closet door, and there was a construction-paper collage taped to the inside. "EILEEN," it said, in ornate script letters down the side; in the center was a ragged-edged oval picture of a teenage girl that looked like it had been cut out of a larger photo. I peered at the picture—a girlier version of Sam, with long dark hair and a sweet, rueful smile. Her younger sister.

"Wow, that's Eileen, huh?"

"Yep. I been thinking about her a lot lately." She gazed at the collage, drifting into reverie. "Wondering . . . how she's doing."

"It must be hard, not knowing. I guess there's no way to find out." I remembered what Sam had said about her sister, back in January when she was at the psych ward—how Eileen had been diagnosed HIV-positive after running the streets with Sam, how she'd tried to kill herself and wound up in a coma for a few weeks. She was in a group home now, but nobody in the Dunleavy family was allowed to know exactly where she was, because of the abuse in the home. "Maybe I could try to track her down, find out where she is."

Sam looked at me strangely. "She's in a coma ward in a hospital in Colorado," she said. "At least she was, last time I heard."

"Really?" I frowned. "I thought you said she came out of the coma, and child welfare put her in a group home."

She frowned back at me. "No way, I never said that."

Really? Because I remembered the conversation so well; I even wrote it down in my notebook. "Huh," I said, casual. "I must have gotten it mixed up." I shrugged, like, *You know us potheads; we can never remember anything.*

"Yeah," she said, still frowning. "'Cause last I heard, before I went to the shelter, I called a friend of hers who stayed in touch with her, and she said Eileen was still in a coma. She said they thought she was gonna be a vegetable all her life. Anyway, you ready to go?"

"Yep." I smiled. "Ready when you are."

We walked to the train together, the streetlights waking like stars in the darkening sky, and talked about the wedding. "Did your mom say whether she's coming?" Sam wanted to know.

"Haven't heard yet. But I'm going to send her a card for her birthday next week; I'll remind her then. I don't think she wants to come, to tell you the truth. I think it's too hard for her to deal with." I sighed. "But you'll get to meet my old friend Adam; he's your age; I told you about him before, right? He's one of the only people I know who's even remotely as smart as you are. I've known him since he was thirteen. We met back at this dot-com I used to work for. He's brilliant—he used to be a hacker when he was a kid. He hacked the MTV veejay contest back in 'ninety-six. It was in all the papers."

She narrowed her eyes and dug her hands deeper into her pockets, a look of discomfort on her face. I must have upset her, going on about Adam too much. "That's cool," she said.

We reached the subway, and Sam stopped before hugging me good-bye, turned her head to the side, and gave a few deep, raspy coughs. I frowned again.

"Sounds lousy," I noted. The coughing had made her go pale for a second. I'd done it again—I'd worn her out, when I was supposed to be looking after her. I shouldn't have let her walk me to the train. "You sure you're all right?"

She shook her head. "Naw, I'm good. I'm just tired from work and everything. I'll go home and lie down for a while."

"Okay. Definitely rest up, though, and if you're not feeling a hundred percent well, don't go anywhere tomorrow. You've got to take it easy, okay?"

"Okay. Thanks, Janice. I'll call you this week."

"From your house," I instructed. "Not the hospital."

"Right." She laughed. Then she coughed again, that ripping, wet cough. "I'll talk to you soon."

I hugged her gently, then climbed the stairs to the subway, watching from the elevated platform as she walked away down the littered sidewalk, her hands in her pockets and her head down, shrinking with every step.

August 21, 2005

Dear Mom,
Happy birthday! I hope it was a wonderful year for you and Jerry, and I hope the year to come will be happy and healthy as well. I got your message about the engagement—thank you so much for the congratulations—and I hope you got our invitation to the wedding. I know it's a busy time of year for you and Jerry, since you're opening the new store, so I will certainly understand if you're not able to make it—I do hope you can come, but if not, the four of us can always plan to have lunch when things are a little quieter. In the meantime, I'm thinking of you with love, and hoping you're very well.
    Janice

I dropped my mother's birthday card into the mailbox on the way to the subway, then rode the train uptown to pick up my altered dress.

It was really happening, this wedding thing; I was actually getting married to Bill. Two years ago, if anyone had said the word *marriage*, in relation to me, I would have clutched my neck and made strangling noises. Now here I was, standing in front of a three-way mirror in a Fifth Avenue boutique, wearing a white dress and gold high heels and clutching a prop bouquet.

"You look *gorgeous*," gushed the salesgirl, as she was contractually obliged to do. "Oh my god, it's going to be *such* a special day."

I smiled nervously at myself in the mirror. I wasn't getting cold feet, but I was definitely getting sweaty palms. I knew I was making the right decision; there hadn't been a moment since the engagement that I didn't look over at Bill and think, *I am so lucky, and I am so smart. Marrying Bill is the best idea I ever had.* At the same time, I was getting a little frantic about the big day—it was coming so soon, and there was still so much to arrange. More than anything, I wanted our friends and family to have a good time, to share our great happiness; I wanted this to be a celebration for everyone. And if my mom wasn't going to have a good time, I wanted to let her off the hook.

"Great," I said, admiring myself for one last second. I barely recognized this woman in the mirror, wearing this elegant dress, her chin high, her gaze strong. I looked so grown-up. I didn't even look like I was faking it. I *wasn't* faking it. I was thirty-five years old, damn it; I had a partner and a career and friends and three cats, and an unofficially adopted daughter. "Great."

I slipped out of the dress and back into my sneakers, accepted the garment bag carefully in both arms, and allowed the doorman to hail me a cab home so I wouldn't get trampled on the subway with my pretty dress. I was halfway to my place when my phone rang: *Sam.*

My heart, as always, sped up. *What now?* "Hey there," I answered.

"Hey!" She sounded fine, happy even. I relaxed. "How are you?"

"I'm good, how are you?"

"I'm good. But I don't think I can make it to Coney with you and Bill this weekend, because Maria's staying over. We're gonna go to a Yankees game on Saturday, and then we're going to church on Sunday."

"Oh, cool!" *Wow,* I thought. A sleepover, and *church.* Maria was really winning the battle for Sam's soul. Suddenly the dress bag felt heavy on my lap. "That sounds great. Maybe we can go to Coney next weekend instead, okay? And ask Valentina if she wants to come, too."

"That'd be great, thanks, Janice."

Bye.

I hung up, strangely unfulfilled. Here I'd been prepared for some fresh catastrophe, ready with my running shoes to go flying up to the Bronx, or Larchmont, or deepest Brooklyn, or wherever she needed me to go, and it turned out she didn't need me after all.

So instead of going to Coney Island that Saturday, Bill and I went to my dad and stepmother's house in New Jersey to finalize the wedding plans. My stepmother, Sylvia, the lithe and lovely woman my dad was lucky enough to marry when I was twelve, poured us some champagne, and we sat in the den with our flutes, poring over the folder Bill and I had been keeping, their shih tzu sneezing on our feet.

"I like the smaller tables," suggested Sylvia, looking critically at the ballroom diagrams with her keen aesthetic eye. "They make for more mingling."

I agreed. "And here's the invite list, so you can see how many guests we're expecting."

Sylvia scanned the page I handed her. "Honey, is your mom coming?"

"Still no word," Bill reported. "We're thinking no."

My father and Sylvia exchanged a look but tactfully declined to comment. "How about your brother?" asked my dad. "We haven't seen him since he was a kid."

"Oh, yeah, Jake's totally coming. I can't wait for you to see him, he's like six foot three now. I guess he looks more like his dad than like our mom. And he's got the most beautiful girlfriend."

"Wonderful. I can't wait to meet her." My father smiled, extremely pleased. "And I'll tell you who I really can't wait to meet—Samantha."

"Oh, yes," said Sylvia. "We've heard so much about her."

Time for Bill and I to exchange a look. I'd only recently broken the news about Sam's diagnosis to them—*Hey, you know that homeless junkie I've been spending way too much time with? She's also got AIDS!*—and they were being very cool about it, exhibiting true *sangfroid*. Still, I knew they were worried about me, for any number of good reasons. To wit: I'd already picked up an ear-and-throat virus from hanging out at the hospital so much.

"I can't wait for you to meet her, too. Maybe you can talk speculative physics with her, Dad; god knows I can't."

My dad looked impressed. Sylvia shook her head. "She just sounds so extraordinary."

"She is. She was telling me the other day—"

Bill cleared his throat. We didn't have time for another ten-minute sermon on the miracle of Samantha; we were still discussing the logistics of our union. "So, I'm with you on the small tables," he said, "but we want to make sure there are enough seats for everybody. What are the dimensions of the room, again?"

It *was* hard for anyone to get in a word that wasn't about Sam. Even now that the crisis had abated, now that she was two weeks out of the hospital with no ill consequences, I was still jumpy at the sound of my phone, still spacing out when we were talking about the honeymoon, wondering how Sam's health would be by then, and what we'd do if there was an emergency. But most of her calls that week were innocuous enough: she wasn't working, and she was bored; she wanted to know what I wanted for my thirty-sixth birthday at the end of the month.

I wanted a piece of paper that said I was her guardian, that's what I wanted. I wanted to be formally recognized as more than just a friend. I wanted to be able to talk to the doctors when she got sick, to say to them, "I'm her legal guardian."

We talked about it some more when we met in Union Square one evening that week. "I only have an hour," I'd warned her in advance. "I have to get a whole bunch of wedding stuff done; I'm really behind."

"That's cool. I'll just be hanging out by the dog run. I'll see you when you get here."

And there she was, eyes gleaming as she watched the dogs playing, a scruffy black-and-white mutt barking joyfully at the discovery of a stick. We took a seat under a tree, and Sam started dissecting a fallen leaf along its veins.

"I don't know," she said. "I mean, the only thing that freaks me out about the guardian thing is, what if the court wants to talk to my parents, or notify them or anything? I really don't want them to know where I am. I don't want any contact with them at all."

Eesh. "I understand." I didn't want any contact with them, either. But I wouldn't back down from them in a court of law—hell, I'd relish the opportunity to indict them for what they'd done to their children. "I don't think that's an issue, since you're over eighteen, but I'm not sure how it works. I've been waiting to hear from you before I called a lawyer to look into it."

She nodded, picking at a scab on her knee, visible through the rip in her cargo pants. "I'll think about it some more," she promised.

"Okay. In the meantime, though, you could sign the health-care proxy."

"Oh, yeah, I meant to do that. It slipped my mind." She looked up from the fascinating scab. "I guess I've had a lot on my mind lately."

Yeah, I guessed she had. No skateboard with her today, and her arms were getting bony again. I wondered if she had kicked last week's rheumy cough. "How was your checkup the other day?"

Shrug. "It was okay. The numbers are low, but they're stable. And I been feeling all right. I mean, I haven't been working or anything. . . ."

I started feeling for my wallet in my back pocket. "If you need anything—"

She held up her hand. "No, I'm good. Seriously, I don't want to keep taking money from you, Janice. You've done so much for me already."

I shook my head, peeved; we'd been over this a hundred times. "See, but that's what a guardian is for. That's what we do. We're like parents are supposed to be; we look out for you, and we offer to help pay for stuff. You think my parents didn't help me pay for stuff sometimes? I wouldn't have gotten my apartment without my dad's help; now I'm trying to help you." I put my hands out in frustration. "Will you let me help you?"

She let her head hang, biting her lip, eyes obscured by her shaggy hair. I drew back, too late; I hadn't realized how much I'd raised my voice while making my point.

"I'm sorry," I said. "I'm not trying to harangue you."

"I know," she said softly. "I just . . . I want to be able to take care of myself."

Two tears fell from under her hair to the dirt below, and she pulled her knees into her chest. "Oh, babe." I crawled to her side, put my arm around her back, felt the lumps of her vertebrae through her shirt. "I know."

"Why," she said, into her knees. "Why did this happen *now*? Just as everything was going so good. I got an apartment, a job, friends; I been sober; I got everything I worked so hard for. Don't I deserve a chance at a good life?"

I rubbed her bony back in circles. "You do, Sam, you do. And you're going to have one."

She shook it off—*no*. I could spout all the wishful thinking I wanted; she had only a few months to live, and she knew it. There was no right thing to say in this situation, no helpful advice, no mentoring I could offer her to assuage the fact that she was going to die within the year, and she was powerless to stop it. I could try to be her guardian, but I couldn't guard her from dying.

We wound up spending a few hours together, browsing the bookstores, watching the crowds. Any errands I needed to do could wait; right now, I had the chance to be with Sam. I tried to buy her some ice cream, but she wasn't hungry. "My stomach's been not so good today."

"You better rest up for Saturday," I fretted. "If you're not feeling well, I don't think we should go to Coney."

"Oh, we're *going* to Coney," she insisted. "I never been on a roller-coaster before, and that's one of the things I gotta do."

Right. On the list she must have made. Like the list she made

before she went to rehab, of things she wanted to do before she left—
fly a kite, learn how to yo-yo. Now it was things she wanted to do before she died. *Jesus.* I knew she shouldn't exert herself, but if riding a
roller-coaster meant taking a week off the end of her life, it would be
worth it. "Okay," I said, pretending to lecture her. "But I want to see
a note from your doctor saying you're okay to go."

"I promise I won't go if I'm not feeling good." She held up her flat
palm like she was on the witness stand. "I swear. Oh, but listen,
Valentina can't make it—Alita is in town from Miami with a bunch
of the other girls; one of her clients flew them all up for this all-
weekend trick on Long Island."

"Oh." I frowned again. So instead of going to Coney Island with
us, Valentina would be going with her trans family to a two-day trick
in the suburbs. She wasn't supposed to be tricking anymore—she was
supposed to be going to school, doing her homework, fencing with
sticks by the Bronx River. "Well, I'm sorry she can't make it."

"Me too," said Sam. "But it's still going to be *awesome.*"

Over the next few days, I monitored both Sam's health and the
weather anxiously, but Sam stayed hearty enough, and Saturday
dawned with a golden sun, beaming bright but not too hot through a
few pudgy clouds. Bill and I woke up, ran, showered, and tossed
down some breakfast just as Sam rang the bell from downstairs. "Be
right down," I called, strapping my fanny pack around my waist.

In the elevator, I rifled through the pack—water, alcohol wipes,
hand sanitizer, Band-Aids, Tylenol, tissues. A mini-pharmacy, in case
Sam needed some kind of treatment during the day. And germ
prevention—she had to be wary of viruses, infection, all that. All I
needed was a bottle of Lysol hooked onto my belt like a firearm.

Sam was standing in the lobby, grinning from ear to ear. Thin,
maybe, but full of energy, practically bouncing on her heels. "Hey
there," she hailed us. "Hey, Bill."

"Hey, Sam." There was a second of awkward foot shifting between them—how should they greet each other? Sam didn't accept
social kisses—she was more of a hand slapper. She and Bill settled on

a firm shake, and we started moving toward the door, down the block, to the subway.

Again, conversation was easy between them. Bill and Sam shared an interest in forensics and the science of death, so we spent most of the train ride grossing out the riders around us, talking about the infamous "body farm," where scientists study decomposing humans under varied conditions. "You know what would be a cool job," said Sam, "is the person who studies the bugs that feed on dead people. 'Cause they can tell how long you've been dead by how fat the maggots are."

They laughed and drew diagrams in the air, now moving on to the subject of victim disposal and the perfect murder. "Cruise ship," I volunteered. "Right over the side. They never recover the bodies out there."

"Remind me never to take a cruise with you," said Bill.

"We're taking a plane to Disney," Sam asked with mock concern, "right?"

So it went all day long—the chatter, the perfect murder scenarios, the jokes. We went straight from the subway to Nathan's Famous, and I claimed a table for the three of us, watching as they stood in line, gesturing and smiling. *Look at Bill*, I thought; *look at how fatherly he can be*. And not in a patronizing, heavy-handed way; he was just a natural—elbowing her to point out one of the freak-show performers, blocking a path for her through the crowd as they exited the line. They brought over three cardboard trays of hot dogs, fried shrimp, and French fries. "Gotta get a good, solid base of greasy food under you for the day," said Bill.

I kept an eye on Sam while she ate—*Good, a whole hot dog, and a bunch of fries*. So her appetite was okay, at least for today. She wiped ketchup from the side of her cheek and belched loudly, content. "So what's first?"

We took a digestive walk down the pier to start; a group of sun-bronzed men in open shirts played instruments at the far end, singing and rapping sticks together, using an overturned bucket as a drum. Seagulls cawed overhead, children shrieked in the surf below, and the breeze was briny and damp against my cheek. People fished from the sides of the pier using poles, or small wire cages full of raw chicken. "Look," said Bill, pointing. "That guy's using a bucket of KFC to catch a sardine."

Then it was time to get serious. "Let's start with the International Speedway," I suggested. We hastened to the track and threw ourselves into consecutive race cars, decorated with the flags of various countries. Sam was Germany, Bill was Italy, and I was the United States. "I'm going to kick your fascist *asses*," I promised.

But the two of them were just as determined and lead-footed as me, and in the end we were all thwarted by the kid driving for Brazil. Undaunted, we moved on to the Polar Express, one of those rides that whips you around a circular track until the centrifugal force pushes you practically into your seat mate's lap, tossing you in the air and catching you with each revolution. This version featured a mural of hip-hop polar bears spinning records and driving Beemers, with the disembodied heads of Biggie and Tupac floating in between; it also featured a live deejay playing ear-blasting Beyoncé and exhorting everybody to "say ho! (*Ho!*) Say ho ho ho! (*Ho ho ho!*) Say ho ho ho! (*Ho ho ho ho!*) Now screeeeeeeam!"

"Aaaaaahhhhh!"

After the Polar Express, it was the Wonder Wheel, the Break Dancer, the Top Spin, and the Zipper, which scared me so badly my shirt was drenched in pungent sweat by the end, though I laughed my ass off, between screams. The Zipper bore a sign advising against the following people riding: pregnant women, people with heart conditions, people with a history of seizures. . . .

I pointed it out to Sam, and she scoffed. "I haven't had seizures in weeks!"

Then it was time for ice cream and candy. We stopped at an arcade for a few games of Skee-Ball, and Sam started in on a giant blue jawbreaker the size of a small child's fist. It stained the entire lower half of her face blue.

"Okay," said Bill, serious. "Enough screwing around. It's time for the Cyclone."

Yeah. Time for me to stand and watch them go on the Cyclone from across the street. Just the previous summer, Bill had talked me into trying the rickety old wooden coaster, and I'd spent the entire three-minute ride cursing his name and threatening his life, in between weeping in terror. "I'll be waving to you from over here," I said.

I watched Sam and Bill go through the turnstile, waited a few minutes while they stood on line, then saw their car start to rise—*chik-chik-chik*—up the first hill. They turned and waved. I waved back.

Then the car stopped. I knew for a fact that it was not supposed to stop there, halfway up the first hill. Everybody in the car turned around, started craning their heads. Bill leaned over and gave me an exaggerated shrug. I gave an exaggerated shrug back.

A mechanic in overalls started to climb the tracks. *Oh my god.* They were stuck. The ride was malfunctioning. This was going to be a disaster, I was going to see it in the *Post* the next day, KILLER CYCLONE! CONEY COASTER KILLS TWENTY-SIX ON OTHERWISE IDYLLIC DAY. I shaded my eyes, sweating, watching the mechanic kick the tires of the car. I wondered if I should take a picture with my cell phone. It could be the last picture of the two of them, ever.

Just then the car started to move, and everybody cheered. Sam and Bill waved again as they resumed the climb up the hill. *Chik-chik . . .* "Aaaaaahhhhhhhhhhhhhhhh!" I kept my eyes on them, their arms up in the air as the car screeched and jostled along its track, whipping over the camelback humps, ending in a pneumatic hiss. A glut of riders emerged from the exit, but Sam and Bill were not to be seen. Until the car started up again, and there they were, this time in the very first seat.

I had to wipe away tears, watching them together, hearing their yelps of surprise, seeing their grins flapping in the wind as they tore around the track. I managed to get it together by the time they came through the turnstile again, Sam's eyes the size of saucers.

"That was AWESOME!" she confirmed. "I LOVE roller-coasters!"

The shadows were getting longer as we walked along the board-walk, taking in the karaoke stand and the guys with giant snakes around their necks and the Shoot the Freak booth. Bill let out a yawn, and I saw Sam stifling the same.

"It's getting late," I said regretfully. "We should probably head home soon. You've got a long ride back to the Bronx."

I expected Sam to quibble, but she agreed right away. "Okay."

We made our way to the subway, ears still ringing with the swinging sensation of the Zipper, the Break Dancer, the Polar Express. My fanny pack bulged with the prizes we'd won at Skee-Ball—miniature Slinkys, Magic 8-Ball key chains, and Day-Glo tubs of squishy "moon goo." I smelled like French fries and sea brine.

Bill took my hand and smiled at me, sidelong. *I love you,* he mouthed.

I love you, too.

"This was one of my best days ever," said Sam, her teeth faintly blue in her smile. "I'm never going to forget today."

Chapter Twelve

Unlucky

August 29, 2005

Dear Janice,

Happy Birthday! I was very happy to get the birthday card
and photos that you sent, and I'm glad you understand
how busy Jerry and I are these days—we're planning to open
our new store on the day of your wedding! I wish the timing
were different, but I am afraid we will have to miss your big
day. But I'm delighted that you've found someone to love
and be happy with, which is what you deserve. We will be
thinking of you, and send love to you and Bill!

    Love,

    Mom

————————⬤———————— I reread the card from my mother, closed it,
and put it in the out-box on my desk. I'd figured as much. I was relieved, really; I didn't want to spend the whole wedding worrying
about whether my mom felt awkward around my dad and Sylvia,

whether she was having an okay time. I felt protective of her. But part
of me had hoped maybe she'd come, just for a little while, just long
enough that I could get a picture of the two of us, my mom and me,
on my wedding day.

Well, my dad and Sylvia would be there, and my brother, Jake. So
would all my honorary aunts and uncles; my stepsister, Satia, from
Georgia; Bill's family; and all of our friends—Edward from the museum, Jay the volunteer, Adam the ex-hacker—friends and col-
leagues from high school, college, and old jobs; folks from North
Carolina, Los Angeles, Oregon. And, of course, Valentina and Sam.

Only three weeks to go.

But first, I had to celebrate turning thirty-six. Bill took me out for
dinner that night, squiring me down the block on his tweed-jacketed
arm to the cab he hailed. I wore the same dress I wore the night we
got engaged, just ten weeks earlier, and the same candlelit glow, as he
held my hand and I hooked his leg with mine under the table.

"Happy birthday," toasted Bill. "To the future Mrs. William K.
Scurry, Jr."

I pretended to choke on my drink. He laughed and amended himself. "To the future Ms. Janice Erlbaum. Happy birthday, Shmoo."

We clinked, kissed, and sipped, our gold rings gleaming in the
candlelight.

I clung to his arm as we walked toward home, done in again by
two glasses of wine and an extravagant meal. The doorman stopped
us on our way through the lobby. "Got something for you." He
handed me a small gift bag, an envelope with Sam's handwriting on
it sticking out of the top.

I opened the card in the elevator.

Dear Janice,
Happy Birthday! You're such a great person, and I'm really
grateful for all that you've done for me. I hope you're having
fun—remember to take time to take care of *yourself* today.
Have a great birthday, and I'll talk to you soon.
    Sam

Inside the bag was a vanilla-scented candle. "Look at her," said Bill, kvelling. "So thoughtful."

My eyes filled, mascara threatening to run from the corners. She wanted me to take care of myself. What a sensitive and loving girl she was; how lucky I was to have found her. I'd have to call her in the morning, thank her for the gift, maybe see if she wanted to meet me in the park after work and browse the bookstore. "She is."

And yet I didn't call her the next day—I got up, ran, and sat down at my desk, where a pile of overdue projects sat steaming and attracting flies. I meant to call her at lunch, but I called my dad first, and we wound up talking for a while; then my friend Emilie came by after work and we split a bottle of wine in celebration of my aging. By the time she left and Bill came home, I was all giddy and sloppy and laughing excessively, and we picked at leftovers from the fridge in front of the TV until I fell asleep, my head in his lap.

But I meant to call Sam—I kept thinking of her, as I always did, when something reminded me of her lopsided smile, her loping stride, the way she'd turned her face upward to the sun last weekend at Coney Island, closing her eyes and basking. *I'll call her after I finish this one thing*, I kept thinking. *After I scoop the cat litter. After dinner. After this show.* And then the day ran away from me again, and I still hadn't called.

I was at my desk on the morning of September 2, alternately working and checking the news, which was sickening. The entire city of New Orleans was drowning in the wake of Hurricane Katrina; stadiums full of people suffered without water, food, or care; people were dying in attics, on roofs, on the streets, in hospitals, and nobody was helping them. It was a codependent's nightmare.

My cell phone buzzed: *Maria.* I braced myself and answered. "Hey there."

"Hi there!" She sounded like she was walking somewhere in a hurry. "Guess why I'm calling."

Great, another tragedy. I should have called Sam; I should have been suspicious that she hadn't called me. "She's in the hospital again," I said.

"Yep. Same one as last time. She just called me. She was running a fever, so she went to the ER, and they admitted her right away. Apparently, she almost hit 104."

"Ay yi yi." I put my head in my hand. "So what's the drill? You're on your way there now?"

"Yep. I'll call you when I know more."

I looked at the calendar over my desk, already blocking out the next week of evenings to go spend at Sam's bedside. "Thanks, Maria. I guess I'll talk to you soon."

And often, I predicted, closing the phone.

Sure enough, I'd heard from Maria twice more by the time I got on the subway the next afternoon, armed with my cardigan and my books and best wishes from Bill. And I called Jodi on my way uptown; we hadn't spoken in weeks. Sam had told me she'd visited Jodi's recently, played Xbox with her son, Evan; they were thinking they might want to join us at Disney World, if Jodi could get the time off from work.

"Just wanted to let you know," I told Jodi's voice mail, "Sam's back in the hospital. Same one as last time. She had a high fever, but she's stable now. I'll give you a call when I know more."

The familiar walk to the hospital; the same brightly lit liquor stores, fast-food joints, and unisex salons; the same old drunk slumped over the mailbox on the same old corner. The guard at the hospital entrance nodded at me—no need to sign in; he recognized me from last month. Same elevators opening onto the same mural—planets, comets, stars.

Sam, attached to the same battery of machines, her mop of hair damp with sweat. "Hey," I said, coming around her bed to the visitor's chair, studying her face. Pale, very pale, with bruise-colored circles under her eyes. "How're you doing?"

"Not so good." She spoke with effort; I could hear phlegm in her lungs. "Dr. F. just stopped by a few minutes ago. I told her you were coming, but she had to go."

Dr. F. was the AIDS specialist, the one Sam had been seeing on her last visit here, the one in charge of the antivirals. She had a complicated last name, Eastern European or something, so Sam called her Dr. F. I'd missed meeting her the last time around, but I was looking forward to tracking her down as soon as I could. "What'd she say?"

"Dunno. She said it looks like MAC, but they're not sure yet. They gotta do some more tests."

"What's MAC?"

Sam indicated the flat-screened monitor on the wall. She'd looked it up on the hospital's kid-safe intranet. I took the wireless keyboard off the nightstand, moved the cursor to activate the darkened screen, and the page bloomed into view. MAC, it said on the screen, in cheerful purple letters accented with cartoon flowers. "(Mycobacterium avium complex): A group of germs found in food, water, soil, or air that affects people who are living with AIDS."

"Is that all it says?" No prognosis? No suggested course of treatment? I determined to look it up myself when I got home, get the unflowered version for adults.

Sam's eyes looked cloudy, lost. "Dr. F. says it's like an infection you get when your T cells get real low. They're giving me these." She indicated the bag of antibiotics with a tired nod. "Painkillers, too."

"Good."

"Well, not good . . ." *Right.* Because she didn't want to relapse upon leaving the hospital, the way she had in the past.

"Don't worry about that now," I told her. If she made it out of the hospital this time, I'd buy her as much heroin as she wanted.

She was exhausted, her heavy lids closing, but she didn't want to sleep while I was there. "Talk to me," she said. "Tell me about Disney again."

I smiled. Finally, something I was qualified to do to help. I could tell stories all day and all night; I could be Scheherazade, keep her alive just by drawing out the plot. "Well, it's going to be great. Except you and Bill are going to have to put up with me on the plane ride down there—I hate flying. I get so scared. Remember how much I screamed on the Zipper?"

She nodded, barely, and a faint smile crossed her face. "You were screaming so loud."

"That's how loud I feel like screaming whenever I'm on a plane. The whole way down to Florida. I'd be like, '*Aaaaaaahhhhhhhh!*'"

"Except . . . except they'd throw you off. Out the window."

"Yeah, they'd make me go sit on the wing."

Her head drooped, and I fell silent for a minute. "Tell me more," she murmured.

"Well, so we'll get to the airport in Orlando, and we'll take the special Disney bus to the hotel, and we'll put our bags in the rooms, and then we'll get right on the monorail, which is like a really clean, quiet, above-ground subway, and we'll take it to the Magic Kingdom. And we'll go straight to Space Mountain—I'll be screaming my head off on that one, too, but in a good way—and we'll ride it as many times as we want. And when we're done with that . . ."

Sam's mouth had fallen open a little bit, and her eyes were fully closed, a slight buzzing sound coming from her nose as she fell completely asleep.

And when we're done with that, Sam, we'll hop onto the back of a unicorn and ride it all the way back to fairyland. I wanted to believe it so badly, the story about Janice and Sam and Bill in Disney World, running around and laughing like we did at Coney Island, just a week earlier. It was the only story I wanted to tell. But for now, all I could do was sit and watch the orange line of her heart monitor, rising and falling like an amusement park ride.

I rode the train uptown the next day, and the day after that, and the day after that. I sat by her bedside and watched her sweat, writhe, vomit bloody bile into a kidney-shaped trough. Watched her sleep, watched the heart-rate monitor, the breathing monitor, both of them so slow. When she was awake, she was in pain, she was afraid. She held my hand and rasped to me, "I don't want to do this anymore, Janice. I'm scared."

I didn't want her to have to do it anymore. "I know," I told her. "I'm so sorry, babe. I'm right here."

Once again, everything else fell off my calendar—I sent e-mail after e-mail canceling, apologizing, rescheduling. *Of course*, said my friends, *you have to be there for Sam.* Fortunately, most of the wedding plans were already set; there were only a few last details to take care of over the next two weeks. The week after that, we'd be leaving on our honeymoon.

If we'd be leaving on our honeymoon. I didn't want to bring it up with Bill, but I was worried that when the time came, Sam might be at the very end of her life, in which case I couldn't possibly go away. I had to be there for her. I was supposed to be her guardian. I'd promised her all those months ago: *I'm going to be in your life from now on.* Now was not the time to renege. I couldn't flake out on my dying adoptive daughter, not even for an afternoon. I couldn't tell her I was busy, or I had to meet my stepmother at the florist to pick out flowers. And when I was desperate to go home and get high and get away from the stinking chill of the recycled hospital air, and she reached out her fevered hand and said, *Please stay, just a little longer,* I had to stay.

Bill watched me fidget through dinner at night, watched me smoke joint after joint on the sofa, waiting for an unwanted call from a nurse, or from Maria—*Come quick, there's an emergency.* He knew what I was thinking, especially after I hinted around to him about it one night.

"I don't know if I feel great about leaving Sam right now," I ventured.

"Well," he said, his top lip stiff as stone, "you don't have to leave her right now. You have to leave her in three weeks."

I didn't mention it again. It would be a terrible precedent, I knew, to start my marriage to Bill by canceling our honeymoon to stay home with Sam. I *had* to go on our honeymoon; I *wanted* to go on our honeymoon. I wanted it more than anything—I could have skipped the wedding and gone straight to Bermuda with him, right then and there. We could have thrown ourselves into the warm ocean, bobbed in the waves; wrapped ourselves together in a big beach towel, sharing one chair in a sandy cocoon. I could have pressed my cheek against his chest, heard his heartbeat, felt his toes wiggling under mine.

I could, and I wanted to, and I would. Sam just had to get better, that was all.

I entered Sam's room the next evening to find her sitting up in bed, the wireless keyboard on her lap, squinting at a picture of the Coney Island Cyclone on the flat-screened monitor. She'd hacked through the child-safe intranet to get to the real thing; she'd even signed up for a freebie e-mail account, so I could send her e-mails when I wasn't there by her side.

"Uh-oh," I said as I came around the bed to hug her. "What're you rotting your brain with today?"

She grinned—she was having a good day, a better day than she'd had all week. She'd worked her way up to ecru on the Pantone chart of sickly skin colors, and her face was lively, even if her eyes were dim. "I was just reading about Coney Island. That place was awesome."

I dropped into the visitor's chair, grinning back. "Except for when the Cyclone stopped, and I was across the street, like, 'Oh my god, they're gonna die!' "

Sam looked happy. "I was reading the Disney book again last night after you left. But my eye's getting real bad, 'cause of all the bacteria floating around. They're taking me down to the eye clinic soon, they gotta give me an injection."

An eyeball injection—I tried not to make a nauseated face. "Oh, wow. They can't do that here?" Every time they moved her for a test, she came back significantly weakened. I'd taken to riding along with her to X-rays and sonograms, when I could, just so I could noodge everybody to hurry up, get her back into bed ASAP, not make her sit up in the wheelchair too long or she'd start dry heaving, or going cold. Now they were planning to put a *needle in her eyeball*—and they couldn't take the elevator up here to do it?

"Naw," said Sam, and I stole a look at the eye in question, which was definitely lagging behind the other one when she shifted her gaze. "I wish they could do it here. I mean, I wish they didn't have to do it at all."

"I bet." If you told me that someone was going to put a needle anywhere near my eyeball, I'd be sobbing and begging to be knocked unconscious. Sam contented herself with a resigned chuckle.

"Oh, well. Won't be the worst thing I been through."

Maybe not, but it was one of the worst things I'd been through in a while—standing next to her wheelchair in the darkened room in the eye clinic while the optometrist forced her into a gruesome face mask with *Clockwork Orange*–style eye props. She squeezed my hand, and I squeezed back, just as scared as she was. "Okay," said the doctor, and I closed my eyes tight, felt the jerk of her hand as the needle went in—"Ah!"—felt myself swoon a little, sickened, then caught myself. *Okay.* It was over. I could look again.

"It hurts," she complained in a small voice. "It feels . . . swollen."

Nope, couldn't look. Her left eye was bulging, just noticeably larger than her right. It gave her a demented expression. My knees wanted to buckle, but I locked them. "How long will she experience the swelling?" I asked the doctor.

"Well, it's going to be a little uncomfortable for a while, but we'll drain some of the fluid out of it in a few days, and hopefully we won't need another injection."

I took deep breaths, standing beside her, trying to concentrate on breathing from my diaphragm and not the image of them sucking eyeball juice out of her head with a needle. Sam looked up at me hopefully from her wheelchair. "Does it look weird?"

"Not so bad," I told her. "Hardly noticeable at all."

I left that evening, crossing paths quickly in the lobby with Maria ("How is she today?" "Well, her mood's pretty good, considering the *eyeball injection* they gave her"), my stomach crawling up into my throat, heart burning with acid reflux. Got home about ten minutes before Bill was due. There was nothing to eat in the house, and the place was a mess.

I heard the key in the lock, and Bill came in.

"Hey."

"Hey." He gave me a peck and went into the bedroom to take off his work clothes.

Bill was in a shitty mood, I could tell—working too many late nights, too many six-day weeks, so he could save up time off for the honeymoon—and I immediately felt defensive, resentful. *I* was the one in a shitty mood; whatever his day had been like, *mine* had been worse. I followed him into the bedroom.

"We don't really have anything for dinner," I informed him. "How was your day?"

"Long. How about yours?"

"Awful. She was feeling a little bit better today, but they had to give her an injection in her eyeball. And I was there for it. I thought I was going to collapse."

"Sounds pretty lame." He passed me, going for the kitchen. "So there's nothing to make?"

"Sorry," I said, following. My turn to get the groceries, and I'd missed it again. "How about takeout?"

Bill opened and shut the cabinets and fridge. His mouth was a flat line. "It's getting expensive, all the takeout every night. And I want to fit into my suit."

"Sorry. I meant to go yesterday, but I was wiped out."

He grabbed the take-out menus from their drawer. "So, what do you want?"

Um, I want you not to be mad at me. "I don't know," I said sweetly. "Whatever you want is good with me."

He sighed. He wanted a home-cooked meal, the way we used to make together. He wanted a conversation that wasn't "her T cells, her fungemia, her impending death." He wanted his partner back. "Oh, did you make the final arrangements with the florist?"

Shit. "Yeah," I lied. "I'm going over there, uh, Monday at lunch to approve everything. I still gotta call Sylvia, though. I'll do that after dinner."

"Please." He pushed the menu for macrobiotic food across the counter at me, not meeting my eye.

"I *will*," I said.

"All *right*."

I could tell he wanted to retreat to his computer, to avoid me, avoid the fight that was brewing—the fight *he* was starting, by being so pissy and abrupt. But now I was all engaged—I mean, was he really going to step to me for not doing the grocery shopping when my adoptive daughter was dying? I was in just as shitty a mood as he was; if he wanted to take his mood out on me, I'd be delighted to reciprocate.

I blocked his exit from the kitchen, frowning. "Is everything okay, honey?"

Bill let his breath go, and his shoulders slumped. "I'm just . . . this whole thing with Sam has just been really hard for everybody. Especially right now. I just wish it wasn't happening. That's all."

"Hard for everybody." I nodded seriously, frowning deeper. "You mean this has been hard for you?"

"Yes," he admitted, tense. "This has been hard for me."

I knew it was true. This was incredibly hard for Bill—he was watching this kid die, and he was losing a piece of me at the same time. And he couldn't complain; how could he say anything? Like, *Gee, honey, I sure wish we were just getting married like a normal couple, without the specter of death breathing down our necks.* This was a no-win situation for him, as much as it was for anybody else, and it was all my fault. I'd dragged us into this thing with Sam; our lives would have been so much easier if I hadn't. Knowing that I'd hurt Bill just made me angrier—strangely, at him.

"Hard for you?" I laughed a little, bitter. "What about for me? What about for *her*? She's fucking dying, Bill! Can you even imagine what that's like? She's lying up there with all of her organs failing, going blind in one eye, waiting to die, okay? And I'm holding her hand, trying to tell her, 'Go toward the light, Sam, we'll see you on the other side!' I'm telling her, 'Maria's right, Sam, you should get right with Jesus!' That's how bad this is! I'm telling her to embrace Jesus! Because she's *dying*, she is *facing imminent death*! And you think this is hard for *you*?"

His voice came back at me as loud as mine was, his hands flexing in frustration. "I know she's dying! Trust me, I know. There's nothing I can do about it, either. I wish she wasn't. We all wish she wasn't. I'm just saying, it sucks."

I burst into tears. "I know! I'm sorry. I'm fucking sorry, okay? I'm sorry I ever met her. I'm sorry we took her to Coney. I'm sorry she's not up there dying by herself right now, just like the twelve million other people who are fucking dying right now that we don't know anything about, okay? I wish it wasn't our problem. I'm sorry." I sobbed and heaved, covering my face with my hands.

Bill crossed his arms and sighed deeply. "Babe, calm down. I'm not blaming you for this. I'm not blaming anyone."

I kept crying. Maybe he wasn't blaming me for it, but I was—blaming myself, blaming Sam. *Damn you, Sam, why did you have to find me? I was fine before you came along. Now I'm going to have to mourn you for the rest of my life.* There was nobody to be angry with, and it was killing me. "It's my fault," I cried. "I'm ruining everything. I don't know why I signed up for this. You didn't ask for any of this. It's not fair to you."

He observed me as I wept, obviously beyond the point of reason, and sighed again. "You're not ruining everything. And you didn't ask for this, either. Come here." He opened his arms to me, and I wrapped myself around him, snuffling, hiding my guilty face. I'd somehow turned this from Bill airing a legitimate grievance to Bill comforting me. "It's okay."

I burrowed into him. "I'm sorry. I'm so sorry, honey. I don't know what to do."

"I know. I know." His voice was resigned; I could feel it through the ear pressed against his chest. "There's nothing we can do. That's what sucks so much."

I continued to cry for a while, because it was so hopeless, and he rocked me gently back and forth and said, "Shhhhh, it's okay." And I kept on crying, because we both knew that it wasn't, and that it wouldn't be—not until she died, and not even then. It was one thing that was never going to be okay again.

It was two days later, just after Bill had left for work, that Maria called with the news. "I just heard from one of the nurses. She's bad. She was bad last night, and she's worse now. The fever is really high, and they can't bring it down. I can't get there until this evening. I don't know, Janice, this might be it."

It. I started to memorize everything around me—*this is the rug I am standing on, this is the weight of the phone against my ear*—so I could describe it later. *I was in the living room when I got the call; the air was cooler than it had been in weeks, the sky was autumn blue.* I showered, dressed, got on the train. *The train was crowded, the newspapers spoke of terror.* I kept poking the idea like a bad tooth—*I'm on my way to see my dying friend; she's probably going to die today.* What was that going to be like? Impossible, that she would close her eyes and they wouldn't open, that I would come into her room and she would not be there anymore. The other riders stared at the subway ads, listened to their headphones; three teenage girls in tight acid-washed jeans pushed one another and giggled. They had no idea what I was riding uptown to do.

Sam was alone in her bed when I entered, her eyes shut, her color ghostly, her chest barely moving with each breath. Her eyes fluttered as I slid into my seat, took her hand, so thin and weak, with its familiar pink scar from the surgery nine months before. "I'm here," I told her, and her head lolled toward me, slumped on her spindly neck.

"It's okay," I said. "I'm here, and it's okay. It's going to be okay." She went limp again, her chest still. She wasn't breathing. The orange line on her breathing monitor went flat. "Sam." I jostled her, and the line started moving again. Her hand felt so hot in mine. I squeezed, and she did not squeeze back.

The breathing line went flat again. *Beeeeeep*, said the machine. I jostled her, more urgent. "Sam." The line moved again. I looked around helplessly for a nurse, the call button out of reach unless I dropped Sam's hand. The monitor beeped, the line flattened. "Sam."

The heart-rate monitor was beeping, too, the line there becoming more erratic. A gray-haired nurse hurried into the room, grabbed Sam's wrist, ripped open the hospital gown, and pushed hard on the electrodes on Sam's bony chest. Sam's head lolled again, and the lines on the monitors resumed their spikes and waves. The nurse frowned, checking the lines going into her arms, the antibiotics flowing into one side, the pain meds into the other.

"She's bad today," I said. My voice was surprisingly quiet and calm. I felt like I was hearing myself through a telephone.

"She's not feeling so good, no." The nurse stepped back and watched the lines on the monitors, moving in choppy waves. "If that beeps again, you call for me."

She exited the room. *Wait, come back. Help.* Sam's head lolled again, and her eyes fluttered open. "Hey," she managed to croak at me.

"Hey." I tried to smile. "Don't say anything. Just rest. I'm here."

"Thanks." She closed her eyes again.

This was how I spent the next few hours, sitting at her side, waiting for the lines on her monitors to fail. I picked up the book I'd been reading to her, *The Curious Incident of the Dog in the Night-Time*, stopping every few lines to look at her face. Was she struggling? Was she at peace? The waves of her breath, the spikes of her heartbeat— they were erratic, but they were still there.

And I prayed. *Don't fight anymore, Sam. It's going to be okay. You know what you told me about those photons, how they disappear, and when they come back they've aged years in a millisecond? And how that's proof of alternate dimensions? Well, I really believe that. I really believe there's a dimension out there, one where you never got HIV, and we're all there with you—me, and Maria, and Jodi, and Evan, and Bill, and your sister, Eileen, she's there, too. And your dead dog, Max. He's alive, and he's right there at your feet. And it's Christmas, and we're all at Jodi's house together, and we're opening our gifts. Look what you made for me, Sam; it's a drawing. It's a picture of us at Coney Island. There's you and me and Bill, and the water and the sand, and the Wonder Wheel, and the Cyclone. Your lips are blue from the candy. Look, Sam, look.*

Her lips were blue and purple. I could see the artery throbbing in the side of her neck. Her hands were as the nurse had left them, palms-up on the sheet next to her like they were waiting for nails.

Sam shifted her weight and blinked a few times. One eye opened slightly. "Hey," she croaked at me.

"Shhhh," I said. "Take it easy."

She tried to sit up, her eyes opening more and more. "What . . . when did you . . ."

"Shhhh," I said again, smiling at her. Here she was, awake. Alive. "You've had a rough night and day."

She shifted again, uncomfortable, and cleared her throat weakly. "I gotta . . . can you ask the nurse to come?"

She needed a bedpan, her least favorite thing to ask for. I put one on the bed next to her, and she grimaced as she tried to grasp it. "I'll go get the nurse."

I got the nurse and left them alone for a few minutes, pacing the hall right outside the room. Heard the sounds of Sam vomiting— sitting up didn't agree with her—and the nurse washing the basins in the sink. I reentered the room, pretending to knock as I came around the curtain.

"How's it going?"

Sam lay back against the pillows. She looked like she'd been flattened by a steamroller. "Better," she panted.

And she was, a little; she recouped somewhat that afternoon. By the time Maria got there that evening, Sam was propped up in bed, listening to me read aloud from *The Curious Incident*.

"How's our girl?" asked Maria, rushing into the room, hair flying behind her. "There she is. [*Smooch!*] I was so worried about you! They said this morning you were . . . not so hot."

"I'm a little better," said Sam, cracking a tired smile as Maria petted her hair.

Maria shot me a look over Sam's head. *And how are you?*

I shook my head at her. *Not good.* "Hi there," I said, outwardly jovial. "How's it going?"

"All right. I had to call in a bunch of favors to get out of work, but here I am." She spread her arms like the angel of good cheer and let them drop again. "So she's been resting today?"

"Nurse just took all her vitals; she said she's doing a lot better than earlier."

"Fantastic! Good girl." Maria pulled up a second chair, and Sam slowly turned her head Maria's way.

"So listen," I began.

This was always my exit gambit—*So listen. Maria, here's the baton; I'm passing it to you.* I was done for the day; I was more than done. Next time Sam was going to almost die, I wanted it to be on someone else's watch. "I'll see you tomorrow," I promised Sam. "Hang in there, okay?"

Tomorrow, and the next day, and the next. By September 12, Sam was starting to improve. Her fever was down, and she was awake, moving around; she even got out of bed so she wouldn't have to use the bedpan. September 13, she was sitting up, surfing the Internet, and eating solid foods. September 14, they had to do another spinal tap on her, to see if the infection had spread again.

Why did they put her through this, when her system was already so weak? And why did they always do it when I was there? A new doctor, an older guy, and a young dark-haired nurse whom I recognized from the floor came in with their torture tray, numbed Sam's back, and plunged in the pick. "*Ow!*"

I squeezed her hand and told her more about Disney World, per her request. "And then day two, we'll go to Epcot, and they've got this ride that's like you're hang gliding over California—"

"*Ow!*"

"*Ow!*" I echoed involuntarily. "It's okay, it's okay, Sam."

The doctor dug around in Sam's lower back, sweating and cursing under his breath. The dark-haired nurse looked at me with tears in her eyes. "You're a good friend," she said.

September 15 was a bad day, but not as bad as the week before. Sam was feverish, achy, anxious, angry; Valentina wanted to give up their apartment share and room with someone else, and the hospital's social worker, Felicia, told Sam that she wasn't going to file for benefits to cover home care. "Felicia said she won't file until they're sure I'm going to be leaving the hospital. *Of course* I'm leaving the hospital!"

Of course. It was this kind of thinking that was keeping Sam from signing the health-care proxy, which I'd left on her nightstand with a pen for the past week, with a Post-it note that said "Sign me." She didn't need a proxy—she was going to be fine. Look at how much better she'd gotten already! She wasn't supposed to live through the meningitis, but she did, didn't she? The doctors didn't know anything.

"Do you want me to try to talk to the social worker?" I asked. "I know it must be hard for you to deal with everyone, all the doctors and social workers and everything."

"Mmm, I can handle it. But thanks, Janice."

"No problem," I said, smiling through my disappointment. "Just part of my job."

Friday, September 16, she had another eye injection. The eye was practically dead by then, the retina floating in a sea of murk. It was unnerving, watching her go blinder by the day, watching her face grow a little dimmer from the bulb that couldn't be replaced. But she'd still smile, she'd still say things with remarkable force—"I'm *so* pissed at Valentina, I can't believe she's moving out," or "I *hate* the night nurse, she's such a bitch." She still wanted to play pranks. Maria called, and Sam whispered, "Tell her I'm real bad today. Tell her they moved me back to Intensive Care."

"I will tell her no such thing," I replied sternly. "She's fine," I reported into the phone. "She's even feisty today. She's going downstairs for another eyeball shot soon."

"Ugh. All right. Wish her my best, tell her I'll be down there this evening. And if we don't overlap, have a *great* wedding on Sunday. I wish we could be there!"

Me too. What I wouldn't have given to see Sam there, even in her wheelchair with an IV pole rolling beside her, but it was not to be. Instead, I spent the penultimate day before my wedding watching (or not exactly "watching," more like "cringing in the vicinity of") Samantha getting another eyeball injection. "*Ow!*"

Maria and I did in fact overlap that evening, and she gave me one of her smooches for luck. Sam grinned at me from her bed.

"Congratulations, Janice, it's gonna be so great. Bill's such an awesome guy. Remember, you said you'd save me a piece of cake!"

I held her hand, reluctant to let it go; her scarred and bony hand, so much bigger than mine. "Okay. But if I get a chance tomorrow, I'll call, and if anything happens—"

"*Go!*" said Maria, laughing. "And don't call. You have to get married this weekend; that's your job!"

"All right." I leaned in for smooches of my own, laughing back through the tears in my eyes. "I love you, and I love you. I wish you could be there on Sunday! I'll miss you!"

"Love you, too," said Maria, and Sam echoed it, waving good-bye like she was on the deck of a receding cruise ship.

"I love you, too, Janice. Bye!"

Chapter Thirteen

I Did

I woke up at 7 A.M. on my wedding day with a head-splitting fever, body aches, nausea, and chills.

I'd known it the day before, running around to get manicured, buying baby's breath for my hair and foot pads for my shoes: *I'm getting sick again.* I tried to write it off as nerves, as excitement, but I knew what was happening—I'd come down with this same virus twice in the past six months. I washed my hands constantly at the hospital, always made sure to dress in layers so I could go in and out of the air-conditioning comfortably, popped vitamin C and zinc lozenges that tasted like rust on my tongue. And still, it was my wedding day, and I was fucking sick.

I let Bill sleep and drew a hot bath, sat trembling inside the tub until the water cooled. Every swallow was a sharp pain, every sound and beam of light pierced me right through the sinuses. I struggled out of the bath and tried to down some Tylenol, only to heave it up five minutes later.

I redrew the bath and started to cry. This was so unfair; why today? I felt like I could barely move; couldn't we have this big party we'd been planning for months on Tuesday? I'd be feeling so much better by Tuesday. I just needed some antibiotics. Run me up to the hospital, stick Sam's tube in my arm for a day or two, and I'd be raring to go. *Fucking shit.* I felt so angry, so cheated, so sorry for myself. I didn't deserve this, not on the happiest day of my life.

Bill woke up, unhappily assessed the situation, tried to get me hydrated, watched me heave up the water. He called my folks. "Are you sure it's not just nerves?" they asked. "Maybe there's a doctor who makes house calls."

I dragged myself back to bed, my whole body throbbing. Slept for a fitful hour or two, woke up in a sweat. Tossed down the Gatorade Bill had supplied me, managed to keep the Tylenol down this time, and lit a joint. The all-purpose cure. My arms and legs still ached, clenching without my say-so, but I thrust myself into the shower and packed my bag for the hotel.

"I am going to get my hair done," I announced. "I don't care how shitty I feel—this is my one excuse in life to wear flowers on my head, and I am taking it. I will see you back here in an hour and a half, and then we're going to the hotel. Okay?"

Bill kissed me gingerly, his germy bride-to-be. "Sounds great, Shmoo. Call me from the hair place if you need anything."

My head was hot and pounding, but the lady at the hair place down the block made it look pretty nice anyway. I set off for home again holding it high, enjoying the looks I was getting on the street, in my jeans and sweatshirt and hairdo full of foliage. The spacey feeling of the virus was highlighted by the surreality of the situation— *This is it. I'm getting married today. Holy shit. It's happening.*

It seemed to be sinking in with Bill, too. By the time I got home again, he was looking a little pale and flustered himself, running around the house and double-checking his bag. "Cuff links . . . socks . . . collar stays . . ." My folks checked in by phone again. "Eat a banana," suggested Sylvia, an ex-nurse. "They're very hard to throw up." I ate a banana, waited to make sure it stayed down, then we summoned the cats with a handful of tuna-flavored treats.

"Mommy and Poppy are getting married today," we told the tops of their heads as they ignored us, crunching and snarfing at our feet. "So be good, and we'll see you in the morning."

Then we wheeled our bags across Union Square Park to the hotel. *Sam*, I thought, as we passed the dog run. How much I wished she was going to be there. I pictured Maria at her bedside, finishing off *The Curious Incident of the Dog in the Night-Time*, or maybe they were watching *Law & Order*. The doctors didn't tend to do too many tests or taps or injections on the weekends; it was probably an uneventful day. If I got dressed early enough, maybe I'd give a call.

We checked in to the bridal suite, toured the banquet room, saw the florist arranging the bouquets Sylvia had helped me choose. I clutched my vows, ink on my palms, muttering them to myself in a last-minute attempt to memorize them. *I never imagined that I would find a partner like you. You are everything I wish for everyone I love.* My folks arrived, as did Bill's family; they installed themselves in their respective rooms, and we started to dress for the occasion.

Whatever virus I had was now completely overshadowed by excitement and stage fright. Across the room, Bill buttoned his shirt, grinning at me. My hands were shaking almost too much to tie the strap of my dress behind my neck, and my feet wobbled in their high heels. I put in my earrings, and Bill came up behind me in the mirror, turned me around to face him. "You look so beautiful," he said.

It didn't strike me as bad luck to be seen by Bill before the wedding. Bad luck would have been being separated from him. I tried to hug him without getting makeup on his suit. "I love you so much."

He smiled down at me, my tender and true-hearted man. "Well, then, maybe we should do this after all."

We went downstairs to the banquet room with our families to greet our guests.

The next few hours were a dream. We were surrounded by dear friends and loved ones, all of them smiling—"We're so happy for you!" My brother looked so handsome and grown-up in his suit. Bill's best men surrounded him, clapping his back. About two hours into the affair, we took our places at the front of the room and exchanged our unofficiated vows.

Bill, you show me so much patience, caring, understanding, and appreciation; you inspire me and enrich my life. I promise to be the best partner I can be. . . .

Janice, I want to spend the rest of my life showing you, every day, how grateful I am that I found you. You are my home, and I love you. . . .

Jake brought us our rings—I'd been missing mine all day, fingering the empty space on my right hand where I'd grown accustomed to fiddling with it. Now Bill and I took the rings and placed them on each other's left hands.

"Here we go," he said.

"Here we go."

We kissed.

And so it was done. But not the party—the party lasted for hours more—and I danced with everyone without my shoes on, my face a collage of lipstick kisses, grinning until my cheeks ached. I toasted a hundred times with my water glass, still unable to eat or drink anything more than supplemental Tylenol, though I did manage to force down a few bites of wedding cake, for ceremony's sake. And when the aunts and uncles said good night, and the deejay and bartenders started packing up, we moved the party upstairs to the bridal suite, where it raged (quietly) for hours more. Then I looked over at Bill, and he gave a not-so-subtle yawn and stretch, and all of our remaining guests immediately realized they had pressing business elsewhere. They wished us one more round of congratulations and skedaddled.

We sat on the edge of the hotel bed, strewn with rose petals by my girlfriends, fancy chocolates in boxes on the pillows. This was life— roses and chocolates, and Bill by my side, my hand in his. He lifted my chin, looked into my eyes, and kissed me. The newlywed Mr. and Ms. Shmoo.

● ■ ●

There was no question, now—we were going on our honeymoon.

"Five days," I told Sam, calling from the waiting room at my doctor's office the next morning. "We're leaving for Bermuda on Saturday, so you better be feeling better this week."

"I am," she swore. "Yesterday was kind of crummy, but I'm a lot better today. When are you coming up? Did you leave the hairdo in? I want to see it. How was it? Do you feel different now? Did you save me a piece of cake, like you said?"

I laughed at the way she jumped all over me like a puppy, even over the phone. "Yeah, I saved you some cake. And yeah, I feel different. But I had to take out the hairdo—sorry. I'll show you the pictures, though—we took a bunch. And listen, I don't know if I should come up there today. I've got some kind of virus. I'm here at the doctor's right now. I don't want to add to your load. But I'll come up tomorrow, how's that?"

"All right," she said, a little dejected. "I'm sorry you're sick, that sucks."

"Yeah, I'm all right." I couldn't really complain to Sam about feeling sick, not when she'd spent the past seventeen days in the hospital again, getting spinal fluid scraped out of her back and needles stuck into her face, vomiting blood until it was almost banal, even for me— *Ho hum, bloody vomit again, I'll just stop up my nose from the inside and breathe through my mouth while I hold up this trough for her.* "And I'll see you tomorrow, I promise."

"Okay. But wait, one more thing . . ." And she went off on sixteen more things.

But she didn't disappoint me—she did start to get better. We'd all grown accustomed to a cycle: a few days of high fever, a new site of infection to treat, a shift or an increase in the medication, and then a few days of recovery. Then she'd crash again. But now she was managing to put together a string of mostly good days in a row. Her appetite was healthy, and the tests showed improvements in her organs.

"Doctors say I'm doing good," she reported when I saw her that Tuesday, and my visual assessment said the same—she was sharp, her color vivid, and her eyes clear, except for the one with the floating retina. "They say if I keep this up for a week or two, I can go from IV antibiotics to oral, and they'll start thinking about sending me home."

"That's great." She had ten times the energy she had last week. I missed three days of visiting her in a row, and look what happened— she improved. "I'm glad to hear it."

"Yeah, except right now I got nowheres to go. Valentina's moving out of our place this week. Maria's driving by there tonight to pick up all my stuff, just so it doesn't wind up on the street." Sam scowled. "Which is so fucked up, because Valentina never woulda been able to get that place without me, and without my friends helping her. I mean, if you didn't put down that deposit, we never woulda got that place, and is she going to pay you back now?"

"I'm not worried about that," I assured her. "And we can always find you a new place." I smiled, trying to hide my confusion. They were really talking about discharging her? Last time they checked her T cells, she had *twenty*. She shouldn't have been sitting up and chirping at me like a parakeet; they shouldn't have been talking about sending her home. To a hospice, maybe, but not home. "Has Dr. F. been by today?"

"No, she's off for the next few days for the Jewish holidays. But that reminds me." She reached over into the drawer of her nightstand, pulled out a sheet of paper, and presented it to me. "Here."

The health-care proxy. She'd finally signed it. My eyes lighted up, and my smile was genuine this time. "Oh, great! Great. I'll go tell them to put this on file."

Sam looked proud of herself for doing this thing that meant so much to me. "They already have one. This is my copy. But you can take it and make a copy for you, if you want."

"That's great." I beamed. I wanted to lean over and kiss her fore-head, but I didn't want to get germs on her. "Maybe when Dr. F. gets back, and I'm back from the honeymoon, we can all sit down with Maria and get up-to-date on everything that's been going on."

"All right."

I left the hospital early that evening, still exhausted from the virus and the wedding and the aftermath. Got home with time to spare and food in the fridge and started to make some vegetarian tacos.

Bill came home, and we kissed hello—a *married* kiss. "How was your day?" he asked. "How's the patient?"

"Recuperating," I said. "Amazingly. They're even talking about sending her home, if she keeps this up."

"Honey, that's great."

"Well, it would be great, except for the fact that Valentina moved out, and Sam's losing the lease on their room. So, aside from the hospital, she has no home."

"*Oy vey*," he said. "It never ends."

"I know." Bill washed his hands and jumped into the dinner preparations. "She's really pissed at Valentina, too, which I understand, but I also understand where Valentina's coming from—I mean, you have to figure she's seen people go down this road before. She doesn't want to sit around and wait for Sam to die so she can get a new roommate and move on with her life. Better for her to detach now, you know? She's got to take care of herself; she's had it tough enough. She's just trying to stay in school, and not go back to tricking full-time, I think."

"God." Bill shook his head over the onion he was chopping. "Poor Valentina Jesus Colón."

Yeah, poor everybody. "Poor Maria, is who's poor," I said. "She's all alone on Sam duty next week, while you and I go play in the ocean."

"Well, we'll send her a postcard," said Bill. "'Wish you guys were here! Not!'"

I biffed him in the shoulder. "Meanie."

"Sorry. I just can't believe I'm going to have you all to myself for a week. It's been a while."

Of course, the next day was a down day for Sam. Not as bad as the day when the monitors went flat—she was fully conscious, her eyes flashing with anger as she squeezed her arms across her chest—but she was feverish and cranky, she had no appetite and fierce pain in her abdomen and back.

"What's going on?" I asked, arriving at her room to find her glowering in the dark.

"I feel like hell. And I'm sick of it. And I wish these fucking doctors could do something for me, but they can't, because they're all a bunch of idiots."

"What happened?" I put my bag down, dropped into the familiar bedside chair.

"What do you mean, what happened? I got totally screwed! First I got a false negative last year, and I'm walking around thinking I'm fine—good thing I didn't have sex with anybody, huh? And meanwhile I keep getting real sick, and it took, like, sixteen doctors to notice, oh, maybe we should test her again! And then I find *this* out, and it's like they *still* can't even do anything for me! I mean, look at my eye, why'd they even bother doing all that stuff to it? I can't even barely see out of it anymore! All they keep doing is tests, and it sucks. I'm sick of it. I just want them to switch me to oral meds, so I can get out of here."

Meanwhile, her temperature was over a hundred, and the lunch tray on her table was untouched. The nurse came in with a new bag of antibiotics, and Sam glared at her the whole time.

"It's got to be frustrating," I said, trying to empathize. "They keep telling you conflicting things. I mean, are they really going to send you home with less than twenty T cells?"

She turned her glare toward me. "Why not? That's where I want to be. I don't want to be here anymore. However long I got left, I don't want to spend the rest of my life like this. I want to be outside; I barely got outside at all this summer. And now it's almost October." She leaned forward, frowning hard, hand on her belly. "This just sucks so bad."

I conferred with Maria by phone from the elevated-subway platform, waiting for my train downtown. "What the hell are we going to do if they really do discharge her?" I asked. "Go back to the barbershop Realtor and get her some crappy room, where they can eventually find her dead? This is crazy. This is the second time in three months she's been this sick. She can't go 'home.' I gotta talk to this Dr. F.; we've gotta get some answers."

"I agree." Maria's voice was quick and tense; she was catching a few minutes between rehab patients before she ran out to see Sam. "I mean, I can see she's gotten a little bit better than she was two weeks ago, but she's still . . . I agree. It doesn't make sense for them to send her home. Maybe I can get some answers while you're away."

The lights flashed as the train approached the station; I heard the shriek of metal brakes against metal rails. God, I was sick of this subway ride, of the hospital, of the whole rotten routine. "I hate to leave you alone at a time like this."

Maria scoffed, though I could tell she hated it, too. "Oh, it's as good a time as any. And Sam's adamant about you going. She told me so, more than once. She said, 'If Janice tells you she's not going on her honeymoon, you have to get her to go.'"

Once again, I was touched by the selflessness of our little girl. "Well, I'll be thinking of you guys. And I'll check in as often as I can. Listen, the train's here. Good luck with her tonight—she's moody. I'll talk to you tomorrow."

"All right, take care."

I spent the ride home brooding. They couldn't release Sam; they just couldn't. She needed round-the-clock care, and she couldn't get it from me. It wasn't just the medical inadvisability of sending her home that bothered me—though of course that bothered me, enough to inspire several impassioned rants on the state of health care in our country, where they'll drag you out of the hospital and roll you from a sheet into the gutter if your Medicaid runs out—it was the idea of Sam leaving the hospital, trying to live a normal life, getting a job walking dogs when she wasn't too weak, applying for school. It seemed like a cruel joke. *Sure, Sam, let's sign you a lease. Hell, let's buy you some furniture! What classes do you want to take your first semester in college? Oh, I'm sorry. You dropped dead!*

I scolded myself. Why was I so eager to forecast her death? It was like I wanted her to hurry up and die, like I was waiting like a vulture for it to happen, already. That's what it all felt like: waiting. I'd said as much to Bill that week—"I don't know. Part of me feels like, if it's going to happen . . ." *Let it happen already.* Which was awful. An unforgivable way to feel. And yet I wanted to know, how much longer was I going to have to do this? How many more days would I spend on that subway, at the hospital; how many phone calls would I get— *She's bad today, this might be it?* Would we cancel the trip to Disney in December because I'd be at her bedside, watching another spinal tap; would we celebrate her twenty-first birthday in April in an oxygen tent? Would she live a whole year—could I go on like this for another *year*?

I couldn't think that way. Every day with her was a gift. I would have the rest of my life to live without her. Right now, I had to be grateful for the time we had. Right now, I had to celebrate her life, to pack in the joy and fun and silliness she never had as a kid, to read her children's books and praise her drawings, to make her feel safe and loved. I had to soak up every word she said, every inflection and every gesture, and record them all, so when she was gone, I could remember her, and she'd continue to live. Right now, I had to be there for her.

Or, right after the honeymoon, anyway.

That Saturday morning I popped a Valium and strapped myself into the seat next to Bill's on an airplane bound for Bermuda. Bill held my hand as we took off, and—remember how loud I screamed on the Zipper?—I managed not to scream. But my terror of flying was still strong enough to chew through whatever soporifics I threw in its path; by the time we landed, three hours later, I was completely, mercilessly sober.

"We're here!" Bill cheered, relieved of the manacle of my clutching hand.

"God, this is *gorgeous*." And I thought the sky was blue in New York. That wasn't a sky, that was a sliver—*this* was a sky. It surrounded you in three dimensions, the florid breeze wafting over you, through you.

The resort was beautiful, the bungalow room enormous. We opened the sliding door to the patio, and the birds sang a welcome. *Greetings, Mr. and Mrs. Scurry!* said the brochure on the bedspread. "Oh my god," I said to Bill, pointing at it. "I think your *mom's* here."

Soon we were splashing in the ocean in the bright afternoon sun, the sand glowing pink on the shore. We were lying together in lounge chairs, wrapped in plush towels, awaiting the arrival of frosty drinks. We were showering, dressing for dinner, making eyes at each other across a linen tablecloth. Walking along the water's edge, as silver and slippery as mercury in the moonlight.

The week passed far too quickly. We rose late and ate enormous breakfasts, smuggling lox from the buffet for the posse of stray cats that prowled the resort's grounds; then we went swimming or snorkeling or sightseeing for the rest of the day, eating enormous lunches and dinners and desserts. Evenings, we sat on the beach and watched the sunset, talking about all the things we still planned to do: climb the lighthouse, go to the caves, swim with dolphins.

I called Sam's hospital room, interrupting her afternoon cartoons. "I been doing real good," she reported, her voice perky and high. "They're saying they might move me to a recovery hospital in Westchester next week. It's, like, a kids' hospital again, but I don't care, I'm used to it. And it's more flexible than a regular hospital—you don't have to stay in bed all day if you feel all right, they have activities and physical therapy and stuff. So they're saying I'd be there for a few weeks, and then they'd see if I was doing good enough to go home."

"That's great!" I cheered. "Where in Westchester?"

"Well," she said, a little hesitant, "that's the only thing. It'll be good for Maria, 'cause it's close to Larchmont, but it'd be a little harder for you to come visit. I forget the name of the place; I'll tell you when you get back."

"Okay." *Huh.* I couldn't help but think, if they moved her to Westchester, I'd have an excuse to visit less often—not only would she be doing better, by the doctors' estimation, she'd also be farther away. There was no way I could make it to Westchester every evening; no one could expect me to. "Hey, I'm so glad you're doing so well. This is great news."

"Yeah, I been a lot better. And me and Maria have been having a good time. Remember that night nurse I hated, the one who was a real bitch to me? Well, she was on days last week, and I started, like, fucking with the heart monitor. I made the leads real loose so it kept going flat, and she kept running in, like, 'What's happening? Why is your heart stopping?' It was so funny."

I remembered my own experience, watching the lines on her monitor flatten. "Hilarious," I said, sarcastic. "Listen, those guys are there to help you. Don't fuck with them, okay?"

I could picture her hanging her head with her naughty grin. "I know, I know." She changed the subject. "So how's Bermuda? Are you having a good time?"

"It's awesome," I reported. "It's so beautiful, I can't stand it. And I think we're getting ready for another swim, so I'm going to let you go. Say hi to Maria for me, and I'll give you a call in a day or two to check up on you, okay?"

"Okay." Her voice went sad for a second, then perked back up. "And hey, thanks for calling. It means a lot to me."

I smiled, my heart full. "I love you," I told her.

"Love you, too," she said. "Bye."

I hung up the phone, slid open the patio door, and found Bill a few yards away, sitting on the edge of a hammock, offering purloined turkey scraps to a ragged-eared orange-and-white stray. *Pss pss pss*, he said, as the little cat reached out to gobble a scrap from his hand. I approached slowly, and the cat swiveled around, prepared to flee, but Bill produced another scrap. *Pss pss pss*. The cat stayed.

I beamed at my beautiful partner, and he looked up at me over the cat's Creamsicle head, grinning.

"Everything's great," I told him. "What now?"

Chapter Fourteen

Revelations

We unlocked our apartment door that Sunday night, and all three cats ran to greet us and sniff our luggage. Bill flipped through the bills while I listened to the messages on the answering machine—our catsitter, welcoming us home; my folks, doing the same. Maria's perky, familiar voice: "It's me. Just wanted to see if you're back, catch you up to speed."

"Back to work," noted Bill.

I called Maria back the next morning and caught her between clients.

"You're back!" she exclaimed. "Oh, thank god. It's been a hell of a week."

"Really?" I asked, distressed. "I thought she was doing better."

I heard Maria exhale hard, or maybe she was smoking again— she'd quit for a while, but recently she'd confessed to cadging a cigarette here and there from a work buddy. "Physically, maybe, but psychologically, I think it's started to sink in, what's happening with her."

"She's starting to confront her mortality."

"You could say that." Maria took in a breath, and I could tell she was definitely smoking. "She spent most of last week in a suicidal rage, telling me she didn't want to go like this, and it isn't fair, and she's afraid of what's going to happen after she dies—she goes, 'What if hell is just the worst parts of your life, over and over?' She's really freaked out about dying. And I've got to say, so am I. You know, I signed up for this class at school called 'Grief and Grieving,' and let me tell you, Janice, I do not know what I'm going to do when this kid goes. I've been walking around like I'm all fine and dandy, got everything under control, but I *know* I am not going to be able to handle losing her. I'm going to fall apart."

Scary to hear Maria say it, in her matter-of-fact way—*She's going to die, and it's probably going to kill me, too.* Maria may have been younger than I, but ever since Jodi had had to back away, I'd still counted on her to be the primary adult in the situation, the sober professional with all the clinical experience. If Maria—tough, capable, pragmatic Maria—was going to fall apart, what was going to happen to me? "I know. Me too."

But for the meantime, the prognosis was okay—Sam was en route to the rehab hospital in Westchester, where she'd have teenage roommates, and arts and crafts, and a therapist to help her deal with what she was going through. The place had a good reputation, Maria told me. "And as for afterward, if she does recover enough for them to release her, I think we might have a short-term plan—I'm thinking of letting her stay with me for a few weeks, until I go away for the holidays, and then we'll see where we go from there."

"Wow." Just as I was thinking about cutting down on seeing Sam, Maria was talking about taking her in. The old jealousy, that tug-of-war feeling, sparked in my breast—Sam was closer to Maria than to me. I'd have to yank her arm to drag her back over toward my side. Instead, I put up my hands and let her go. "That's great," I said. "That's so huge of you."

Puff. "Oh, believe me, I wish there was another alternative. I can't even imagine taking her on full-time. But if we can't work things out with the social worker at this new hospital, and there's really no other way, at least we have a backup plan."

Thank god, again; thank god times infinity for Maria. Thank god, thank Jesus Christ, thank Jesus Colón. She was Maria, the Virgin Mother of Sam. "You're a saint," I told her.

Two days later, I got on a Westchester-bound train at Grand Central, on my way to the new hospital. I'd spoken to Sam the night before—she was enjoying her new surroundings, getting to know her roommates, excited about playing wheelchair basketball in the gym. "I'm real glad you're coming to visit," she said. "I feel like it's been forever since I seen you."

"I know." *Ugh.* I felt a pang of guilt, then a sliver of resentment. Reminded myself: *I didn't do anything wrong. I went on my honeymoon. She wanted me to go. I didn't abandon her.* "I can't wait to see you."

It should have been true—we hadn't seen each other in a week and a half, which was an eternity in Janice and Sam time. And yet I realized, watching the passing scenery from my window seat, the longer I went without seeing her, the more okay I felt about not seeing her. Weird. I used to get so antsy if she wasn't in touch; now I flinched when the phone rang. And then answered it: "Hi there! Just thinking about you." I was nervous about the visit. I didn't want Sam to sense how I was feeling, didn't want her to know that I was grateful for the distance of the hospital, the length of the train trip. Didn't want her to know that something had changed in me.

Do you feel different? she'd asked me the day after the wedding.

Yeah. I felt different.

I arrived at the hospital, asked for her at the front desk, and found her room down a corridor lined with children's artwork, passing kids scooting by on crutches, in wheelchairs, bald. I came into her room—big, airy, with three other beds, and throw rugs on the floor—smiling my widest smile. "Hey!"

"Hey!" She was sitting in her wheelchair by the window; she gave it an expert shove and twisted to face me. "Whoa, look how tan you got!"

"Oh, you should have seen me when we got back on Sunday." I stooped and kissed the top of her head. "And check you out—you're getting really good on those wheels."

She smiled at her lap, smug. "It's kind of like a skateboard, in a lot of ways." She tilted back, executed a few more sharp turns on her back wheels. "I'm looking forward to not needing it soon."

"Yeah, this is great—it looks like you're really recovering." I eyed her warily, following her chair over to her part of the room, where I pulled up a chair of my own. She looked good. She'd put on a few pounds again, and her color was back. The one eye still lagged behind the other, but if you didn't know to look for it, it might take you a minute to notice. More than that, she looked energetic, like the old days; she seemed raring to go.

"I am. I mean, I still feel real weak a lot of the time, especially if I walk a lot. But the doctors say the infection's getting better—even though my T cells are practically gone, the drugs are fighting it off, and the antivirals are finally getting a chance to work. At least my viral load's gone down." She looked up at me with her wide eyes— *Aren't you proud of me?*

"That's great news. Speaking of which, did they assign you a primary doctor? I was hoping I'd get a chance to speak to somebody today, or . . ."

She shrugged one shoulder. "They don't really have primary doctors here the way they did in the Bronx. But I'll ask who you should speak to—it's probably Dr. Eng, or Dr. Gambine. I'll find out, and I'll have them call you."

"Okay. Or I'll call them. Or . . . is either of them around right now?"

"Um, I don't think so. Probably not." She twisted her chair around again. "Hey, so do you want me to show you around?"

I followed Sam's chair into the hallway, trying not to show my irritation. I wanted to speak to someone, already, now that I had the health-care proxy; I wanted an actual medical professional to tell me what was going on. I'd had enough of pumping aides and technicians for answers—"Why are they doing another MRI?" "Did she eat anything today?" I was tired of trying to look things up online. The Internet was a lousy doctor.

Sam started giving me the tour, guiding me down the hall. "It's pretty cool here. I like it, so far. I wish some of my roommates were around. This one girl Kyla's all right. She's only, like, fifteen, and she has leukemia—this is the fourth or fifth time she's had to stay here for chemo. But they have, like, a school and teachers here, for the kids, and she works her butt off at it, 'cause she really wants to be able to graduate with all her friends and go to the prom and everything. Which is sad, because she's probably not gonna make it."

She hung a sharp left, leaving a short black skid mark on the tiled floor. "Okay, this ramp here takes you to the gym. Over there they got a pool *and* a whirlpool; they use it for physical therapy, but I can't go in, 'cause it's too dangerous, 'cause of the bacteria. And there's Tommy. Hi, Tommy!" A young kid wrapped in bandages cruised by on a motorized wheelchair. Sam dropped her voice. "He knocked over a candle and set his house on fire; he's covered in third-degree burns. His younger sister died. He's the *sweetest* thing. Everybody loves him."

We navigated through the doors to a grassy courtyard, and Sam parked in the sun. It was warm for early October; it felt like summer again—the summer we'd missed, indoors at Mid-Bronx Hospital for weeks at a time. "So," she said, facing me.

"So," I said. "So . . ."

Strange—there seemed to be nothing to say. We'd covered her health, her doctors, her new surroundings; now I couldn't think of anything to talk about. *So, how's that whole "confronting your mortality" thing going? Still in an existential panic over your imminent death?* This was supposed to be my moment as a mentor, where I said something profound and meaningful, where she let go of her terrible burden and cried to me and I comforted her. Instead, there was an awkward pause.

"Did you watch *The Amazing Race* the other night?" she asked. "It's so stupid, the family edition—they should have just kept it regular."

"Oh, yeah," I agreed, and we talked about TV for a while, until we hit a dead end and she tried a new tack.

"And . . . did you read the new Augusten Burroughs book yet? I want to read it, if you get it."

"Well, maybe I'll bring a copy next time I see you."

My leg was bouncing, I realized; it took effort to stop it. Sam flicked the brake of her chair on and off with her foot. "Did Maria tell you I'm gonna go live with her?"

I raised an internal eyebrow at her characterization of Maria's offer. "She mentioned you might stay with her for a few weeks, if push comes to shove."

She grinned at me. "I hope it works out. That would be so awesome. You know what's cool, this place isn't so far from her house. I think she's coming by later, if you can stay that long."

"I can't," I said, feigning regret. "I have, uh, a lot of work to catch up on."

"Oh." She wheeled around a little, gazed off toward the end of the courtyard, marked by a brick wall with a Dumpster in front of it. "That's cool."

I stayed for a while longer, talking about books and movies and Disney World. I asked about Valentina. "Did she ever call you, tell you where she wound up?"

Sam's eyes flashed. "Fuck Valentina. She ran out on me when I was real sick. I never want to see *his* ugly ass again."

Discomfiting, to see her snarl like that about her former friend. I thought of Sam and Valentina mucking around in the Bronx River, playing King of the Stairs at the halfway house; how they jabbered that day we found their apartment—"I want to put stars on the ceiling." "No, mirrors!" I hoped Valentina was all right, wherever she was. "I understand."

Soon I pulled out the train schedule and the number of the local taxi. "Well, I'd better be heading back—looks like there's a six o'clock train, and then nothing for an hour. . . ."

Sam slumped in her chair, crestfallen. "Already? 'Cause there was some stuff I wanted to talk to you about. . . ."

"Oh yeah?" I put on what I hoped was a patient smile. "What's that?"

"I don't know." She shrugged, like she was reluctant to get specific, started picking at stray threads around her pants pockets. "Just stuff I been thinking about. Stuff from my past."

"Uh-huh." *Goddamn it,* I thought. We didn't have time to get into "stuff from her past" right now; she should have brought that up an hour ago. "It must be hard, huh."

"Yeah." She looked up and met my eyes, the dull one wandering before it could fix on mine. "I mean, I'm still wondering, what if I'd done things different? Like, I always tried to bleach my needles, but what about those times I didn't? I keep thinking if I could go back . . ."

"Uh-huh." I had my hand on my phone, ready to call the cab. "But you know, we have to think about the future—there's a lot to look forward to."

Wow. That could not have sounded more hollow if I'd said it through an empty paper-towel tube. What was wrong with me today? I couldn't seem to muster the usual urgency, the overwhelming concern I needed to feel for her. This was Sam, I reminded myself; she was *dying.* I was supposed to feel anguished at the thought. Instead I felt fed up.

I faked another smile. Sam stared at me, frustrated. "I'm *trying* to stay positive," she said. "It's just hard, is all."

"I know. But right now, you're doing so much better—I have to say, it's great to see you with so much energy, and . . ." And I had to call my cab now. I had to go home, call Bill, smoke a joint, make dinner. "Hang on," I said, interrupting myself. "Just let me call the cab so they're on their way."

Sam folded her arms and tucked her chin to her chest as I dialed and made the arrangements. "Ten minutes? Okay. And do you think I'll be able to make the six o'clock train to the city? Great, thanks." I snapped my phone shut. "Okay. Sorry about that."

She scowled at her lap, arms crossed, as she spoke. "So . . . when are you coming back?"

In previous days, I would have been charmed by her pouting, flattered by how much she needed me; now I was annoyed, and angry at myself for feeling that way. "I'll come back next week, how about that? I'll check my schedule, and we'll pick a day. And this time, I'll make sure I can stay a little longer, okay?"

She nodded, chin still down. "Okay."

I rose from my seat, gathered my bag and jacket. "And don't forget to have your doctor call me. Or tell me who to call. Eng or Gambine, right?"

"I'll let you know." She looked like she'd shrunk in her chair, all of her limbs pulled in, her head dropped. "Here, I'll show you how to get back to the front."

I followed behind her as she rolled through the halls, quieter this time, going through the same internal tango of relief and guilt that I always went through with her. I professed to love her so much, and yet here I was, practically running down the corridor to get away from her, acting like it was a chore to come see her instead of a rare and extraordinary privilege. I should have been grateful for her presence— I'd be missing it soon enough—but right now, I couldn't wait to get home.

We made one last turn, and I was at the front door.

"Okay," said Sam, her voice small. "I guess I'll talk to you soon?"

"Of course you will." I leaned down and kissed her on the top of her head again, like a blessing. "And you know, you can call me anytime."

"I know." She picked up her head and tried to smile at me, making her jut-chinned brave face. "Well, thanks so much for coming, Janice, it always makes my day."

"Mine too." A cab rolled up to the curb outside, and I opened the front door, feeling the rush of the fresh air. "I'll talk to you soon."

Bye, she waved, as I stepped outside and into the taxi. Then she spun around on her wheels, and we both rolled away.

I got the message the next day.

"Hi, Janice, it's Maria. Listen, I just heard from the nurses at Westchester—Sam crashed again this morning, spiked a really high fever, vomiting, so they moved her back to the hospital in the Bronx. We should be able to see her tomorrow. I'll let you know if I hear anything else, and please call me if anybody calls you. Take care. I'll talk to you soon."

Not this again. I closed my phone, feeling the rage and frustration rippling through my body, like my muscles were expanding, ready to burst through my skin. I couldn't do this anymore. There was no way I could go back to the hospital in the Bronx. I physically could not get on that train, with the brakes shrieking as it pulled out of Union Square; I couldn't take that ride, trying not to count the stops, trying to steady my breathing when the train stopped between stations, as it always had to do, because god forbid it should just take me to my dying friend in the hospital, without stopping for a little *break* every now and then.

Bill was drying off after his shower the next morning, and I was doing my sit-ups, except today they were more like lie-backs—I was just lying there on the bedroom floor, completely lacking the will to move.

"I can't take this anymore," I called to Bill, eyes staring unfocused at the white ceiling. It looked so peaceful up there, uninterrupted and blank. "I'm serious. I can't."

Bill came into the bedroom, towel in hand, stood sadly in the doorway. "Oh, babe," he sighed.

My face crinkled into a crying face, but I couldn't even cry anymore. It was insincere. I wasn't sad, I was angry. At whom, I didn't know. At Sam's doctors, for not catching it sooner; at our government, for not taking this disease seriously years ago so we could have a cure by now. At Sam, as unfair as that was; I was mad at Sam, for being so sick.

I'm going to nail down the doctors today, I decided, and swung my torso to meet my knees. There it was—action. Action was what I needed. *Eleven, twelve* . . . Fuck Dr. F. and her vacation and "Oh, I don't know if it's Eng or Gambine"—today I was going right up to the nurses' station, and I was going to bitch at everybody in a lab coat until someone told me something I could use. *Thirty-three, thirty-four* . . .

I needed a deadline. A literal deadline. A line that demarcated when she was going to die.

Fifty.

It was this selfish, macabre, unconscionable thought that propelled me forward that morning; the only thing that got me through my shower, through getting dressed, to kissing Bill good-bye.

"Let me know what the doctors say," he said, his eyes drooping with the forecasted bad news. "And tell her . . . hang in there, from me."

"I will." I tucked my head into his chest for another hug. "I love you, babe."

"I love you, too."

Hang in there. But I didn't want her to hang in there, I thought, as the train shucked and lurched uptown. I wanted her to let go.

A few autumn leaves were starting to fall from the trees, I noticed, walking the familiar blocks from the subway to the hospital, though most of the leaves were still hanging on. Hanging in there. It had been a warm fall, so far; the leaves weren't so much bursting with autumnal color as they were giving up, turning pale yellow and dropping indifferently to the ground. Soon there would be a frost, snow on the ground; how many seasons would I see from the window of her hospital room?

My breath was coming shallow and fast in the elevator. *Calm down,* I told myself. I couldn't let her see how distraught I was over this latest setback, how little I wanted to be there today; I had to project warmth, love, and acceptance. I smeared a haphazard smile on my face, like cheap lipstick on a crazy woman. I hoped she'd be sleeping.

But it was even better than that—I opened the door to her new room, and she wasn't there. One of the orderlies I recognized from her last stay was changing the garbage. "How you doin' today?" he said, nodding to me. "Your girl's downstairs getting a test, should be back in a half hour or so."

"Thanks."

Perfect. I left my bag in her room and started trolling the hallways for more familiar faces. The short Indian nurse nodded at me when she saw me coming. "She's downstairs getting an MRI," she said, before I could say anything. "She'll be back up soon."

"Oh, thanks, but I'm actually looking for her doctor." I smiled, ingratiating. "Is there someone around who I can talk to about her condition?"

The nurse peered over her desk down the hall. "I think Dr. Rice is in the doctors' lounge." She pointed to an open door. "She should be there; if not, I can page her."

"Thanks." I headed toward the door she indicated. *Okay, Dr. Rice. Tell me something good.*

Dr. Rice was a tall, thin woman with straight, sandy brown hair and bangs, about my age, currently sipping a cup of coffee and glaring at the pager on her hip. I'd seen her around the floor, though we'd never had a chance to speak. "Excuse me, Dr. Rice, I'm a friend of Samantha Dunleavy, and I was wondering if you had a minute. I've been trying to get some information about her prognosis—"

"Oh, right, hi." She turned to face me. She recognized me, too; I was the girl in the chair by Sam's bedside all last month. "I'm sorry, what's your name again?"

"It's Janice Erlbaum. I'm her health-care proxy."

"Oh, her proxy, great. So, yeah, okay." She leaned one shoulder against the wall, and I faced her, doing the same. "So, the main problem she's having, obviously, is the recurring infections—the bacterial sepsis, the fungemia, the other opportunistic infections she keeps manifesting—and we've been throwing everything we can at them. We keep changing the antibiotics, you know, and for a few days she'll get better, but then she'll just . . ." Dr. Rice made a nose-dive gesture with her hand.

"Right," I agreed. "Which is why I was surprised that you guys had discharged her to Westchester. I mean, she keeps getting so sick."

Dr. Rice raised her eyebrows a little, defensive. "Well, she *had* made a lot of improvement, and you know we can't keep her here forever."

Well, you won't have to keep her here forever, I thought. *Just until she dies.*

"So what's the course of treatment now?" I asked. "Just continue to treat the infections, and . . ."

Dr. Rice turned up an empty hand in frustration, shook her head. "Well, if we knew the source of the infections, I might have a better answer for you. Unfortunately, we can't seem to figure out what's causing them. We're still waiting on the results of the lung culture, to see if maybe some of this was airborne. . . ."

I tried not to let my eyes bug out. She didn't know what was causing Samantha's *multiple opportunistic infections*? Did she need to go to remedial doctor school? "Well, it could be stemming from the AIDS," I suggested.

Dr. Rice frowned. "But she doesn't have AIDS. We've tested her twice, and she's negative. Believe me, that's the first thing we thought of. I mean, this would all make a lot more sense if she were HIV-positive, but she's not, so we've had to look for other potential causes."

"I'm sorry," I said, shaking my head. "You're telling me she doesn't have AIDS?"

Dr. Rice's eyes were as wide as mine. "Not to our knowledge, no. That's one of the first tests we ran. We even reran it two weeks ago, just to make sure. Because it's definitely an immune disorder, we've just never seen anything like it."

I interrupted her, stunned, my ears ringing like I was standing inside a bell. "You're saying she's HIV-*negative*?"

What had Sam just told me on our last visit? *My T cells are practically gone, but the antivirals are finally getting a chance to work—at least my viral load's gone down.* She couldn't be HIV-negative; she was dying of AIDS, and everybody knew it—me, Maria, the social worker who'd been wrangling with her benefits, the spinal-tap nurse with tears in her eyes.

I shook my head violently. "She's not HIV-negative. She can't be."

"So you're under the impression that she's HIV-positive?" Dr. Rice was looking at me, brow fully furrowed. "Because that would explain a lot. If there's been some kind of mistake—"

"There's *definitely* been some kind of mistake. There's *definitely* been a mistake." *This goddamn hospital*, I thought, my confusion flaring into anger. They probably mistested her, or the doctors weren't communicating. Samantha had AIDS; this was *obviously* a mistake on their part. It had to be.

Dr. Rice reached out as if to steady me. "Did she tell you that she'd tested positive in the past?"

I nodded. "First week of June. She was living at a halfway house in Brooklyn, and she was diagnosed at a hospital in Bushwick—"

"We'll get their records," Dr. Rice interrupted. "Go on."

"She was in Bushwick for a week or two back in April for acute pneumonia following a punctured lung, and she was doing follow-up there for her asthma and her kidney dysfunction, and they wondered why she kept getting hospitalized for infections, so they tested her. And they told her she had full-blown AIDS—multiple, virulent strains. They said she had less than a hundred T cells."

Dr. Rice's eyes were trained intently on mine. "We just tested her T cells the other day. They were normal."

"No." I shook my head, frustrated. "No. She just told me the other day, she's got less than twenty. She's been dealing with Dr. F. since she's been here, maybe if we call Dr. F.—"

Her eyebrows inched even higher. "Dr. F.?"

"Dr. F.—she has a long, foreign name, hard to pronounce. Samantha said they call her Dr. F. She's—"

"I don't know any female doctors on the floor named Dr. F.," said Dr. Rice.

"You don't . . . maybe she's . . . she's the AIDS specialist, she's . . ."

She's in her mid-fifties, blond, stout, slight accent, Eastern European. Of course I'd never seen her, but this is how I'd pictured her, every time Sam told me, "I spoke to Dr. F. this morning," or "You just missed Dr. F. I really wanted you to meet her."

Dr. Rice shook her head, looking almost as lost as I must have looked. "There's no Dr. F. here. Something very strange is going on."

Oh, yes, it was. Something very strange, supernatural, even. "I can't believe . . . this has got to be a mistake."

"I don't know what's going on," said Dr. Rice. "But I'm glad we're having this conversation right now. If you're telling me she's tested positive in the past, then we've got to retest her again, as soon as possible. All of her symptoms are consistent with late-stage AIDS, and if we've missed that somehow, then the whole strategy changes."

She'd already straightened her posture; she was looking over my head, ready for action. Her surge of confidence was inspiring. I straightened up as well, snapping to, all business. "So you think this is some kind of false negative test, you think this is a mistake."

She shook her head. "I don't know how, but it must be."

"Or . . ." Or what? There couldn't be another explanation; this had to be a mistake. And yet a nagging doubt was squirming its way from my queasy stomach into my brain. Sam and her pranks—the way she bragged to me, back at rehab, *I held my breath until I passed out—they thought I had epilepsy!* The day she told me, *Tell Maria I'm doing real bad, I'm back in the ICU.* And just last week, when I called from Bermuda—*You remember that night nurse, who was such a bitch to me? I loosened the leads on my monitors . . .* "I mean, she couldn't have . . . she couldn't have faked all of this somehow, could she?" I forced a little laugh, to suggest how crazy the idea was, but the laugh felt like a retch.

Dr. Rice smiled wryly. "Fungemia in her eyeball? No, she's definitely not faking it. Listen, I know this is confusing, but let us retest her, and you should be able to get the results when we do. If we can test her this evening before dinner, we should know something within twenty-four hours."

"Okay. Okay." I nodded. *Okay.* Twenty-four hours. And then maybe they were going to tell me that Sam was okay. They might tell me that she was all right, and she didn't have AIDS, and she wasn't going to die.

Which would mean that she'd been lying to me for the past four months.

Dr. Rice started to move toward the nurses' desk, but I stopped her. "Wait, if you could just . . ." Now I was scared that Sam would be angry with me, that I'd said too much and betrayed her confidence. She didn't want everybody to know about her AIDS; she could have been using the false negatives to lie to the doctors, to lie to herself. "Please don't tell her we had this talk. Samantha's incredibly protective of her privacy, and she hates talking about her AIDS. She's been in a lot of denial about it; she *hates* it when other people talk about it. If you could just tell her you need to retest her, okay, but don't tell her we talked—I've spent a lot of time trying to earn her trust, and—"

"I won't," Dr. Rice assured me. "But listen, you did the right thing. Now maybe we can get to the bottom of this and find out what's really wrong with her. She'll be up from her MRI soon, then I'll request the blood sample before dinner. You can wait in her room until she gets back, and neither of us has to say anything about this discussion. All right?"

Dr. Rice strode off to the nurses' station, picked up the phone, made a call. I was standing there staring at her, and she gave me a high sign with her chin—*I'm on the case; go wait for her in her room.*

In Sam's room: her messy sheets, a teddy bear from Maria, a children's library book about the building of the U.S. railroad spread open facedown on the night table. Her orange sweatshirt with the frayed cuffs and collar on the chair. It was like the scene of a crime—all the evidence of her life, but no her.

If I was panting when I showed up at the hospital today, I was hyperventilating now. I was dizzy from overoxygenation. I needed a paper bag, stat. I needed six or seven joints. I needed to sit down, but I had to pace. I pulled my phone out of my pocket and called Bill at work.

"Hey, babe," he answered. "What'd the doctors say?"

I braced one arm across my chest, smiled a vicious, hard-breathing smile. "Well, they say she doesn't have AIDS, is what they say."

"Wha-at?" His voice broke with surprise. "What the hell?"

"Yep. They say they've done two tests on her, and they're negative. *Negative.* They just did her T cells the other day, and they're *fine.*"

"What the . . . this has got to be a mistake. You're telling me she tested . . ." I heard his hand slap the desk. "No. They fucked up. The hospital fucked up." He'd called it—hospital error—and his voice went from bewildered to pissed off on my behalf. "No wonder they haven't been able to help her, they're a bunch of idiots who can't run a simple series of tests. Jesus, honey, that's gotta be—"

"I don't know, babe, I don't know." My stomach growled—fear, not hunger. I wished I was as desk-slapping sure as Bill was. Maybe it was a mistake, but whose? Dr. Rice's? Mine? I was pacing in the tiny room, my eyes lighting on objects I could barely identify anymore— a water pitcher with flowers from Jodi, half-deflated balloons that said GET WELL SOON. None of them meant anything. They were all props in a play.

"Look, it's got to be the hospital's error," Bill said again, in his patented voice of reason. He laughed a little, ironically. "Don't worry, honey, I'm sure she has AIDS."

"Hah," I said, mirthless. "She *better* have AIDS, or I'm going to kill her."

There were voices in the hall, getting closer; Samantha was back from her MRI. I promised I'd call Bill back as soon as I heard something, and signed off. "I love you."

I was looking at Samantha as I said the words, snapping the phone shut as one of the transporters wheeled her into the room. Sam looked groggy and pale, but she smiled at me under her heavy lids.

"Hey, babe," I said.

"Hey," she said thickly.

The transporter helped her into bed, her long, thin legs covered in scabs and scratches. He reattached her to the IV, the heart monitor, the breathing monitor. Her antibiotics were in a glass jar—they'd eat right through a plastic bag. On the jar, it said, DO NOT ALLOW CONTENTS TO COME IN CONTACT WITH MUCUS MEMBRANES OR EXPOSED SKIN. IF ACCIDENTALLY INGESTED, CALL POISON CONTROL.

Sam lay back against the pillow, her eyes glassy from the pain meds. I moved over into my usual position by her head, petted her hair for a minute. The familiar smell of her warm skin made my throat close. "How's it going today?"

"All right," she said, sniffling. They were giving her opiates again,

I could tell by the junkie sniffle. She scratched the side of her face. "Pain's been bad, but they gave me some meds. . . ."

"I can see that." I attempted a smile. "So how was the MRI? Did they tell you what they found?"

Something was wrong with my voice. That was supposed to sound sympathetic, and it came out suspicious. "It went okay," Sam said, looking at me with those penetrating, preternatural eyes, the dark bags beneath them. "I'm . . . it's been a hard day."

Yeah, I knew what she meant. The transporter finished adjusting the various tubes and plugs, pushed the beeping buttons on the IV, left us with a nod. Sam lifted her head to inspect the job, then sank back again against the propped-up pillow, let her head loll to the left.

"So listen," I said, "I want to have a talk with one of your doctors—"

"Can you hand me that pillow?" Sam interrupted, gesturing to the other chair, where an extra pillow sat next to a bag of Tootsie Pops from Maria. She wrinkled her nose like a rabbit, wiped it with the side of her hand, scratched her face. Just like the redhead on my corner would do, right before she started to nod.

"Sure thing." I passed her the pillow. I tried to meet her eyes, but they were off, unfocused. "So listen, I've been trying to get in touch with one of your doctors. . . ."

"Uh-huh." She put her hand over her stomach and sat up with a grimace. "Sorry, I'm just feeling so . . ." I reached out and stroked her back. She belched and scowled. "Uhhhh . . ."

Samantha looked over at the puke trough. My eyes followed hers, but I didn't reach over to get it for her, as I normally would, trying to anticipate her needs and meet them before she could even speak. She noted my negligence, pressed her hands against her stomach, and moaned some more.

"Should I call the nurse?" I asked.

She shook her head, dizzy and pained. "No, I'm . . . I'm okay, it's just—"

"Yeah." I cut her off. "You look awful. Listen, I definitely think we should get one of your doctors in here. I think we both need some explanations. They've got to do something to help you out."

"No-oo!" Her protest came out in a whine. I'd heard her whimper, during spinal taps and the like, but I didn't think I'd ever heard her whine. "I'm all right! It was just the test, and everything . . . just let me . . . I'm all right. . . ." She lay back weakly. "It's just been . . . a hard day. I think I just need to sleep. Maybe today's not the best day for a visit . . ."

Oh. No. I was *not* dismissed. I smiled a tight little smile. She was lying about something, and she thought I wasn't going to figure it out? I didn't care how much denial she wanted to be in, or how much she wanted to manipulate her own treatment. She was *not* lying to me and getting away with it.

"I understand," I said soothingly. "You get some rest. And I'm going to try and find one of these doctors, because I really think they need to give us some answers here. You shouldn't be suffering like this."

"No, but, the doctors, they're doing everything they can!" She was whining again, and her face was screwed up like I'd never seen it before. She sniffed, rubbed her nose, and scratched, more viciously this time. She was frustrated and high, she just wanted to lie up in bed and have someone read to her about the U.S. railroads, and I wasn't playing along.

"Well, I'd still like to talk to someone. I'll just ask the nurse who's on duty, and maybe we can all have a chat." I removed my hand from her mop of hair and strode with purpose out to the nurses' desk. *Action*. The watchword of the day.

"Can you please page Dr. Rice and ask her to join us in Sam's room when she gets a chance? Thanks."

The nurse gave me a quick nod, picked up the phone. "Dr. Rice to room 1015, please."

"Thanks."

Sam heard it, too. I reentered her room, and she was sitting up, scowling like a gargoyle. "I don't feel so good," she said, hand on her belly again. "I think I have to throw up."

I handed her the trough and assumed my usual position at her side, one hand patting her back as she dry heaved. "Oh, this sucks so much," I crooned. She heaved again, but it was forced; it wasn't coming from her stomach, she was just throwing her torso forward and pretending. Dr. Rice knocked and entered, looking concerned. She shut the door behind her.

"Hey, Samantha, how are you today?" Dr. Rice met my eyes as though we didn't just speak in the hallway ten minutes ago. "Hi there. You're her health-care proxy, right?"

"I am." I smiled. "Janice Erlbaum."

She shook my hand and took the chair with the bag of Tootsie Pops on it. I sat in the other chair.

"So how'd it go with the MRI?" asked Dr. Rice.

"Good," said Sam warily. She sniffled. "I mean, I'm kind of exhausted, but I'm glad it's done. Maybe they'll be able to tell me something."

"Well, that's what we're hoping for." Dr. Rice's eyes met mine, then flicked away to Sam's. "Anyway, I'm glad Janice is here, because I think it's good if we can all be up-to-date on everything that's going on."

Sam's glassy eyes were open about a foot high, and her skin was like wax. "Can we . . . do we have to talk about this now?"

"It'll just take a minute," Dr. Rice assured her. She turned to me, and repeated what she'd said in the hallway as though for the first time. "Of course, the main problem Sam's having is the recurring infections, which we keep treating with antibiotics, but they keep coming back. We're still trying to figure out why she keeps getting them, but—"

"Okay, but what about the antivirals?" I asked, wide eyed. "I mean, shouldn't they be helping to combat the AIDS?"

Samantha turned her head sharply my way, clenched her jaw and bugged her eyes out at me. *Don't say "AIDS" in front of the doctor.* The thin line of her mouth was menacing, and there was violence in her stare.

I bugged my eyes back at her, shocked by the ferocity of her look.

"Don't bug your eyes at me," I warned, my voice rising. "Have you been taking your AIDS meds, or not?"

Sam bugged her eyes again, wider this time. She was as hard and cold as marble. I'd never seen her like this; I could barely recognize this girl, staring at me with furious intent. This couldn't be Sam—not my kite-flying, birthday-card-sending Sam, who always looked at me with such gratitude and love. I stared right back at her, unflinching, even as my heart beat so loudly, the loudest thing in the room, louder than the beeping IV, louder than the nurse on the intercom: *Dr. Rice, please call Dr. Lashki; Dr. Rice, call Dr. Lashki.* Dr. Rice sat there, looking at the two of us, clipboard on her lap.

Sam turned her head away from me. "I want you to leave," she said coldly.

I laughed, and choked on it, *kah.* "You want me to leave?" I demanded, already rising. "You want *me* to leave?" I fumbled for my bag, shoving the chair back. My heart couldn't keep up with the pace it had set; the beats were stacking up, tripping. "You *bet* I'm leaving. Because *obviously,* I have been *in the way* here."

I was walking toward the door, though my feet didn't feel anything; I didn't feel anything but a rush of motion underneath me, like I was on a plane, on an escalator, like the world was moving for me. I stopped at the door and turned around.

"I will be right outside in the visitors' lounge," I said, "waiting for someone to explain to me exactly what the *fuck* is going on here."

Then I ripped open the door and stormed through.

The nurse gave me an alarmed look from her station as I heaved myself into the visitors' lounge, empty except for some chewed-up Styrofoam cups and a year-old copy of *Highlights Kids'* magazine. Ah, *Highlights!* How often I'd flipped through it during our stays here, reading about the twin brothers, Goofus and Gallant, one bad and one good—*Goofus lies about his HIV status and refuses to take his meds! Whereas Gallant acknowledges his AIDS and cooperates with his support team!* The room was barely big enough to pace; how could a hospital have a waiting room where you couldn't pace? What the hell was wrong with this place? What the hell?

Dr. Rice entered the visitors' lounge. "Hey," she said, her eyes wide. "So, Sam's revoked your proxy, and she asked me to have you leave the building."

I nodded, dumb with disbelief. "Okay."

"But before you go—I can't talk to you anymore, because she's asked me not to." She looked at me with extra meaning. "But *you* can still talk to *me*. So if there's anything we should know . . ."

Right. Well, you see, Doctor, I met this girl in a homeless shelter last fall, and I fell in love with her. Not like that. Real love, not romantic love—true love, family love. And she was sick, and then she got well, and she was high, and then she got sober, and then she got sick again, and she's stayed so sick. And I've just been here, for the past eleven months, loving her, and waiting for her to die.

"She's been in and out of hospitals all year," I began. Dr. Rice nodded and nodded as I went through the history. St. Victor's for the hand infection. Bushwick for the pneumonia. The phone call when she told me she'd been diagnosed HIV-positive. The weeks and weeks I'd spent here in the Bronx—meningitis and MAC, eyeball injections and spinal taps. And then I stopped, remembering how the doctor at the shelter had said that Sam might have sabotaged her infected hand because she didn't want to move on. I repeated this to Dr. Rice.

"This couldn't be her sabotaging her health," I asked, "could it?"

Dr. Rice tipped her head, considering. "Well, you know, I don't see how she could have sabotaged herself into fungemia, so I think we can rule that out. She's definitely been dishonest about something, though, and maybe this will give us some clues as to what's going on. Just let her calm down, we'll retest her, and I'll encourage her to be in touch with you, okay?"

"Okay. All right." I nodded. Okay. They'd retest her, and then we'd know. As long as she hadn't done this to herself, as long as Dr. Rice was sure about that. "Thanks, Dr. Rice, I'm really . . ." I fluffed my hands around in the air, unable to say what I was.

She smiled comfortingly. "No, thank *you*. I'm glad you found me today. And she's lucky to have you as a friend."

"Well . . ." I tried to chuckle. "We'll see about that."

We'd see. Was she really lucky? Was I really her friend? The test would tell. I turned to leave the lounge, and the room spun a little. My axis was off. I had to go by instinct, lumber toward the elevators, the mural of the solar system that greeted you on the floor. *Right.* I knew these double doors. I knew this place. I knew these hands. I knew what to do inside this metal box. Push the button, L. I knew what this buzzing thing in my pocket was—it was my cell phone. It was Maria. I walked out of the elevator into the lobby and answered the call.

"Hey," Maria said brightly. "How's it going today?"

I pushed through the lobby doors out into the brightness. It was so cloudless and clear blue—why were the most devastating days always so blue? It looked like September 11 today. "Well," I understated, "not so great."

Maria's voice dropped in sympathy. "She's had a bad day, huh? What's the latest?"

I had no idea how to put this. "Well, the latest is, I spoke to the doctor, and . . . you're not driving right now, are you?"

"No, I was just about to leave work." Her voice went grave. "Why, what's going on?"

I pulled over on the sidewalk and leaned back against a brick building. "Maria, they say she's HIV-negative. Her T cells are fine. They say they've tested her twice."

"*What?*" It came out as a glass-breaking shriek. "They said *what?*"

"I know. I know. And when I asked her, in front of the doctor, if she was taking her AIDS meds, she told me to get out of the room, and she revoked my proxy. I'm on my way to the subway right now. I'm in shock. I'm in total shock."

"*What? Wait . . . what?*"

It was like she was pulling dialogue directly from inside my head. "I wish I knew what was going on, Maria, but I really don't. All I know is, the doctor said she doesn't have AIDS, and Sam *freaked out* on me when I brought it up. But the doctor said it's probably a mistake or something. They're going to retest her, they should know something tomorrow."

I heard Maria taking quick, deep breaths. "I'm coming down there right now," she decided. "I can't . . . I have to hear this for myself. I don't even understand what you're saying. You're telling me they have recent negative HIV tests for her?"

"Two of them. And a T cell test last week. They were fine."

"Janice, that's *impossible*," she spat, furious with frustration. "What the *fuck* — "

"That's what I've been saying for the past forty-five minutes."

I heard the lighter click, the intake of breath as Maria lit a cigarette. *Puff. Puff.* I couldn't wait to get home for a smoke of my own; maybe drugs would make this situation make sense. "I'm coming down there," she repeated. "I'll be there in half an hour. And *somebody* better have some answers for me." *Puff.* "And . . . I won't tell her we talked. I'll act like I don't know anything."

I laughed my broken laugh. "Which we don't."

"Right?" She laughed, too, shrilly. "I mean, what the *hell*?"

I'd started walking toward the subway again — I could tell by the breeze against my face. "Look, it's probably a mistake. I asked the doctor a bunch of times if this could be a hoax, or anything else, and she said it's probably a mistake. They're going to retest her, so . . ."

"Okay," she said, in a warning tone. "But in the meantime, I'll be down there soon, and I will *certainly* call you if I learn anything new."

"Okay," I agreed. "I'll talk to you soon, then."

Snap.

I put the phone back into my pocket, took my MetroCard out. I climbed the stairs to the elevated subway station and took my usual place at the front of the platform. I stood there, waiting for the train, looking out at the trees with their yellow leaves. Waiting for the other leaf to drop.

Chapter Fifteen

Aftershocks

————————●———————— I got home, opened my notebook, and wrote:
This has been one of the top ten weirdest days of my life.

Then I wrote down everything that had happened since the morning: all the dialogue, all the action, all my impressions. A habit I'd
had for years, one I'd kept up through my association with Sam—it
always helped to unblow my mind, writing everything down where I
could look at it, judge it. I'd been keeping the current notebook for
the past three months, since she went into the hospital in July. When
I paused and riffled through it, I saw Sam's name on every page.

My cell phone buzzed: Sam's hospital phone. *Fuck you.* I didn't
answer it, didn't want to hear her pissed-off ugly voice, the voice that
went with that hateful face she'd made, telling me I was fired as her
proxy. She didn't leave a message. A minute later the phone buzzed
again. Again I didn't answer it. Again she didn't leave a message. It
buzzed a third time, then stopped halfway.

Good.

I turned off the phone and wrote until I caught up with myself in
real time. *And now I'm sitting here writing this, waiting for an update*

from Maria, waiting for the results of the retest. Waiting to find out if the past eleven months of my life have been a lie.

I closed the notebook, opened my laptop, and started a Google search for "Samantha Dunleavy." I didn't know what I thought I was going to find — I'd looked her up online before, to no avail. I'd even looked for her parents, her sister, and her brother, and never found them, either. Now I got the same old half page of results for my search: a genealogical record of the Dunleavys in Ireland, with a Samantha who'd died in the 1840s; an eighth-grader who'd recently won a prize for Excellence in Language Arts at a middle school in Virginia. Nothing that looked like Sam, nothing that looked like her family.

I stared at the useless results, unsure of what to look for next. I'd already looked up all the AIDS websites; I had a long list of bookmarks to which I'd frequently referred over the past few months as I'd tried to understand the course of her disease. They weren't going to tell me anything new. There had to be another diagnosis.

My hands hesitated, but I went ahead and typed it. *Faking illness.* Up came the results. The first page called it *Munchausen's syndrome — a psychological disorder whereby patients fake or induce illness in order to receive care and attention.*

I chewed at my lip as I studied the screen, consumed by a growing unease. I'd heard of Munchausen's before; I'd even read a book about it once. As a matter of fact, Samantha had mentioned it to me just three weeks earlier, a few days before the wedding.

We were in her hospital room, of course, and she'd been having a good day; she was propped all the way up in bed, her color high. "Valentina did this report for school about this thing called Munchausen's syndrome," she said, grinning. "Have you ever heard about it? Where people make themselves sick? It's so fucked up. They call themselves 'munchers,' and they, like, shoot *poop* into their veins to get sick on purpose. Isn't that the craziest thing?"

And I'd jumped right in. "Oh my god, I've heard of that, it's so crazy. And you know, there's also Munchausen's by proxy, where people's parents make them sick so they can get attention. I once read this book about this girl whose mom almost made her get heart surgery. . . ."

"Yeah," she'd said, serious for a minute. "That's so insane to me. Can you imagine *wanting* to feel this sick? I'd do anything to feel better."

Poor Sam. Maybe she could trade places with one of those munchers, and everyone would be happy. "It's crazy," I'd agreed.

Crazy. I stared at the blinking cursor, at the words on the screen. Munchausen's sufferers, it said, are exceptionally intelligent, and often claim to be the products of abusive homes. They enjoy being taken care of; they also enjoy feeling in control of others, especially doctors, whom they take great pride in outwitting. Sufferers have an unusual grasp of medical symptoms, treatments, and terminology. They are not deterred by unusual or painful procedures and will often have numerous surgical scars.

Sam certainly fit the profile: brilliant, abused, scarred all over her body. Able to toss around medical terms with the best of them; unafraid to get a needle stuck in her eye. I started to feel nauseated, reading the case histories—people who'd starved and bled themselves to mimic cancer, patients who'd infected open wounds with cat shit. And then this: *Munchausen's syndrome can be fatal. For most patients, there is little hope for recovery.*

I was trying to digest all of this when I heard Bill's key in the lock. He came in and I collapsed into his arms, grateful for his palpable, three-dimensional presence.

"This is some super-crazy *X Files* shit," he said, kissing the top of my head the way I'd kissed Sam's. "I can't wait to find out what's up."

We mixed some stiff drinks, made dinner, and discussed it. Bill was still going with the false-negative theory, whereby the hospital had somehow repeatedly mistested Sam and gotten the wrong results. Or maybe, he suggested, she'd manipulated the tests somehow, so she could hide her HIV status and stay in denial. If anybody could figure out how to screw up the tests, he said, it'd be her.

"I don't know," I said, frowning. I wanted to believe the false-negative theory, but I was leaning more toward the false-Samantha theory. I couldn't stop thinking about things she'd said and done: how she'd loosened the leads on her monitors to scare the night nurse; how she'd told me her sister was in a group home, then told me she was still in a coma. The grin on her face the day she asked me, *Munchausen's syndrome — have you heard of it?*

All I had to cling to was what Dr. Rice had said, standing there in the hallway: Sam couldn't have induced fungemia of the eyeball; she couldn't have done this to herself. She was, as Dr. Rice said, "legitimately sick." But again, if anybody could figure out how to make herself that way . . .

I looked at the clock: 10 P.M. Friday. Just that morning, I'd been lying on the floor in the other room, hoping she was going to hurry up and die. Now here I was, wondering if she ever really existed in the first place.

That weekend, Columbus Day, Bill and I tried to go about our lives as if nothing had changed. We went to the grocery store, where the ghosts of Sam and Valentina lurked in the dairy aisle; we went to the movies. We ran six laps around Washington Square Park, showered together, made lunch.

We looked at our honeymoon pictures again, downloading them from the camera to the computer—me in my swimsuit, posing like Bettie Page; Bill feeding the orange-and-white stray. The two of us with our heads together, Bill holding the camera at arm's length to take the picture, purple sky and pink shore behind us. It was only last Sunday—we'd woken up early in our hotel room, taken one last trip down to the beach, one last swim in the ocean before we caught our plane home. One last photo, in front of the hotel, big smiles on our faces. How happy we looked, except for that one thin line between my eyes.

There was an extra weight to the weekly Sunday-night sadness that week—*Oh, weekend's through, time to face reality again.* I didn't want to face reality. One way or the other, Sam had lied to us, or to the doctors—either way, she had lied. I put off the phone call I knew I had to make until after we'd eaten dinner, watched whatever was on TV, and I'd checked my e-mail for the fifty-fifth time. I went to roll a joint and stopped halfway—smoking didn't even get me high these days; it just made me depressed and sleepy. I couldn't avoid or procrastinate anymore. I picked up the phone and called Maria.

"Hi there." Maria sounded furious, her sharply musical voice a caricature of its former self. "How are you?"

"I'm . . . weirded out." I laughed. "How are you?"

"I'm not very good at all," she said. "But I can't talk about it until you talk to Sam. Did she call you yet?"

"She called on Friday, but I didn't feel like talking right then."

"Well, I think you should call her now."

"Why. Maria, what . . ." Her voice, so angry. A pit opened up in my stomach. This was bad news, this was the worst-case scenario. I wasn't even sure what that was anymore. "What's up?"

"You need to hear it from her. Then you and I can talk. All right? Call her, and call me back. I'll talk to you soon."

She hung up, and I looked over at Bill, lurking from the doorway. His face was grave.

"She wouldn't say," I told him. "I have to call Sam."

I dialed Sam's hospital phone, and she answered on the second ring, her voice low. "Hello?"

"Hey there," I said. "How are you?"

Surprisingly, my voice came out the way it always did with her— gentle, loving, concerned—asking the same question I always asked. *How are you?* As in: *How'd the tests go today? What'd the doctors say? Are you running a fever? Did you have anything to eat?*

"I'm all right," she said, hesitant. "Nauseous and achy, but the fever's down."

"That's good." I paused. Here was where she usually caught me up on the specifics—*I had an MRI earlier. They took blood before. Dr. F. says I'm doing real good.* Except now I knew that Dr. F. didn't exist. "So."

"So." Her voice was thick with dread. She knew what was coming, and so did I. I braced myself and asked the question.

"So, are you HIV-positive, or not?"

She took a deep breath. "I'm . . . not."

Boom. There it was. Good news, bad news, all in one. She didn't have AIDS; she was going to live. And she'd lied to me.

"Okay," I said, no big deal, as though she'd just told me she'd lost her cell phone. "And you've always known you weren't positive."

"Well . . ." Her voice got high and dodgy. "I mean, one time last year, I got this false positive, and I thought I was positive for a week or so, but then they retested me, and . . ."

I clamped my lips shut. She was lying again, and I didn't want to hear another lie. "Okay," I repeated. "So you didn't tell us the truth."

"I . . ." Her high voice broke, and she exhaled. The next word came out low. "No."

"Okay." I breathed in and out, in and out. "Okay."

One thing at a time—she wasn't going to die. Not this week, not next week, not next month, not next year. *She's going to make it to Disney World!* I thought, delirious. She was going to live! She'd be able to get a room and apply for school and work at a dog spa, write her book and ride her skateboard, do whatever she wanted to do. I laughed, relieved. "Well, so you don't have AIDS. That's good. I'm really glad about that."

"Me too," she said, high-voiced and uncertain. Waiting for the other shoe to drop, or hit her across the face.

"So . . ." I almost didn't want to ask the next question, didn't want to ruin the high of hearing that she wasn't fatally ill. "Why did you say you did?"

Her breath left her in a heavy sigh, her voice pained. "I don't know. I don't know why I said I was positive. It just . . . came out, and then once I said it, I couldn't take it back. I wanted to tell you guys so many times. I wanted to tell you right away, but I was afraid you'd hate me for it, and you wouldn't be my friend anymore. And then, it's like, I almost believed it, you know? Because I kept getting real sick, and I started to think maybe it was true—like maybe somehow God had punished me for lying by giving me AIDS."

I shut my eyes. I remembered junior high, when I was a habitual liar, lying compulsively to everyone, lying half the time before I realized what was coming out of my mouth. I'd learned to become a method liar, to have a full Sensurround story behind every lie, to be able to see every detail, hear every word, until I could have passed a polygraph; that's how much I believed myself. I understood lies you couldn't tell from reality anymore. I understood lies that got out of control, that stacked up, necessitating more lies. I knew that regret, *Why did I say that in the first place? I wish I could take it back*. When I was in my freshman year of high school, and still a virgin, I told my best friend, Karlina, that I was pregnant by a handsome older teenager I'd seen in our neighborhood—I even pointed him out to her on the street. *He wants me to keep it*, I told her. *But I don't know*. I had to lie for weeks on that one, months; had to describe the abortion clinic my mom took me to, and how I got stitches from the operation. Later, I discovered that you don't get stitches from an abortion. Karlina had known all along.

"I understand," I told her. "I do."

Bill shook his head from the doorway, still trying to comprehend what was happening. He looked at me, almost an appeal—*She didn't lie, did she? Tell me she didn't lie about having AIDS*—and I shook my head in return. *Sorry, pal*.

"I'm sorry," said Sam, almost whispering. "I really am."

"I understand," I said again. And then realized I didn't. I might have lied about getting pregnant, but my belly never swelled, I wasn't morning sick. I faked it, but Sam wasn't faking it. A team of doctors had observed her for most of the summer—meningitis, MAC disease, bacterial sepsis, fungemia—she was, as Dr. Rice had said, "legitimately sick." "But how did you get so sick?"

"I don't know," she said, miserable. "I mean, that's why I've been so confused."

She couldn't have done this to herself, said Dr. Rice. But the Internet told me something else. Munchausen's sufferers did it all the time—an injection of yeast or powdered cleanser; some fecal *E. coli* in her IV line—maybe she could have. "Well, now maybe the doctors will be able to figure it out, and you can really get well."

Sam was quiet, except for her quick, shallow breaths. I listened to her gather her thoughts, waited silently for her to speak. When she did, there was fear in her voice. "You must be real mad at me."

I laughed. "Well, I think I'm in shock." Yeah, definitely. I had that spacey, dreamlike feeling; I wanted to shake my head and wake my-self up. "And I'm just so happy to hear that you're not dying of AIDS. I mean, whatever the real problem is, now you'll be able to get some help for it."

And I won't have to sit there and watch anymore, if I don't want to. That weightless, drifting feeling I had—part of it was relief. I'd been looking for an excuse to pull away from her, and now I had two: She was going to live, so I didn't have to tend to her every want and need anymore; and she'd lied to me about it, so, shit, I didn't even have to *speak* to her again. I could walk away for good, if I wanted, and not felt guilty in the least; whatever promises I'd made to her were effec-tively annulled. This whole revelation was a real kick in the face, but it did have its upsides.

"I hope so." Sam breathed heavily into the phone, voice border-ing on squeaky. "I'm just . . . I'm real sorry, Janice. I don't want you to . . . I still need you to be my friend."

I bet she did. This was her worst-case scenario, losing me and Maria. She could break every bone in her body, and she didn't mind, as long as we were there to sign her casts. But to break our faith in her—that was a fatal blow. "I'm still your friend," I assured her. "And I'll call you tomorrow. But right now, it's getting late, and I need to think about everything we talked about, okay?"

"Okay. But . . ." Like always, she didn't want to let me off the phone. "Janice, I really am sorry."

"I know. And I'll talk to you tomorrow. All right?" I didn't wait for a response, just gave my usual sign-off. "Feel better, okay?"

I hung up the phone and turned to Bill. He shook his head at the floor. "No way," he said.

"Oh my god." I clapped my hands together in prayer, drew them to my lips. The stunned, dreamlike feeling was dissipating; the shame and the fury were starting to hit. "She fucking *lied* to me. She *lied*."

Bill kept shaking his head, arms folded across his chest. "I'm sorry, babe."

I shook this off, *pffft*. Why should he be sorry? *I* was the one who had screwed everything up; *I* was the one who'd gone out and dragged home this psychopath, this monster. I'd brought her into our *home*. With our *cats*. Anything could have happened—god, I was an idiot! I shouldn't have been allowed outside without supervision! "Jesus Christ, Bill, she's a psycho! She's a complete psycho!"

Bill continued to shake his head. "That's not who she is. That's not who I met. That's not who we went to Coney Island with."

"That person doesn't exist." Everything was whirling around in my head now, all the stories she told me—her family's meth lab, her mom the hooker, her violent past on the streets—probably all lies. Her name probably wasn't even Samantha. No, wait—she was on Medicaid; she had a Social Security card and a GED—she had to be using a real Social Security number. So at least we knew the name on the hospital bracelet was real. And her real birthday was April Fool's Day.

April Fool's! How perfect. My fist came down on the desk, *damn it*. And Bill had tried to warn me, months ago. *I'd hate to think she was playing you somehow*, he'd said, and I'd gotten mad at him. *She's not playing me!* How stupid I'd been, what a bleeding-heart liberal dupe. "My god, honey, I'm so sorry. I'm such an idiot."

"Stop. Don't blame yourself. It's her. She's even more fucked up than we thought."

We. At least he was still in this with me. With Bill, I could get through anything. I sat down on his lap in the chair and felt his arms close around me, comforting me. I held on to him, his firm chest, his strong arms. He was solid, he was real; our love for each other was real. This, at least, was real.

Somehow I managed to get to sleep that night, but I woke up at five in the morning, eyes wide open, heart pounding like I'd been running. Sam had lied to me for *four months*. About *AIDS*. And the timing—I told her back in May, on visiting day at the halfway house, that I was going to propose to Bill; not two weeks later, she told me she was diagnosed. I felt like spitting, thinking about the virus I had at the wedding, how I'd almost canceled the honeymoon. What if we hadn't gone to Bermuda; what if I'd made us stay because she was sick, she was dying? "She really wants you to go on your honeymoon," Maria had said. "She's adamant about it." And lo and behold, she'd hit an upswing, right on schedule; she'd recovered just enough so I could get married and leave town for a week. I guessed I should have been grateful—somehow, she'd been able to give me that.

I thought about the second phone call I'd had with Maria the night before, after talking to Sam and to Bill. She picked up her phone before I even heard it ring. "So, now you know." Maria was mighty, mighty pissed, she said, but she wasn't giving up on Sam. "I know she was brought into my life for a reason," she said. "I just don't know how to help this girl. I don't know what to do from here. I think I have to take a week away from the situation. I'm not abandoning her, I'm just . . ."

Thinking. We were both going to think about it, and we'd talk soon.

The sky was starting to turn umber, the cats stretching and climbing out of bed to see what I was doing awake, and if I had any food for them. I filled their bowls, then sat down at the computer and opened my e-mail. I started writing to Sam.

To: cypherpunk@_____.com
Subject: Hey there
So you lied about being sick. Which sucks for everyone, but especially for you. I'll say the same thing I said to you when I heard you were diagnosed with AIDS—this sucks, but I'm glad we found out, so you can get treatment for whatever your real problem is. Because I want you to have a long, happy life, free of sickness and pain of any sort. I know you must feel right now like your life is over, but it's not. This is a GOOD thing, that we discovered the real problem, and your life is going to get a lot better from here. Call me when you get this, and we'll talk some more.
Janice

Bill woke up, and we started our morning routine. He was still in disbelief—maybe there was something we were missing, he said. Maybe there was another explanation for her mysterious illness, besides *E. coli* in the IV. We kissed good-bye for the day, and he gave me an extra-long hug. "Let me know if you hear anything new," he said.

I worked as best as I could that day, stopping to check my e-mail every few minutes, waiting for a reply from Sam. I wrote to the friends I'd called over the weekend, gave them the breaking news: *So guess who doesn't have AIDS after all?* The replies came quickly and emphatically: *What the fuck? That's crazy! Are you sure?* And *I'm so sorry, for the both of you.*

At lunchtime I ran out to the bank, the copy shop, and the drugstore for my birth control—no kids for me today, thanks. I passed the redhead, slumped behind her battered cup in front of Anthropologie. She looked up as I walked by—maybe I'd buy her some cookies today, or a Snapple, like I had in weeks past. I felt like kicking her.

I walked past the bookstore, where Sam and I had spent so many afternoons. In the window was the Narnia collection I'd bought for her before the honeymoon, something for her and Maria to start reading while I was away. Last I checked, she was up to *The Magician's Nephew.* Automatically, I thought of myself at her bedside, starting the next chapter. *Oh, maybe tomorrow, we'll . . .*

Maybe we'll what, Janice? Maybe we'll nothing.

I had been wondering what it was going to feel like when she died. Now I felt like I knew.

Back at my desk, it was impossible to concentrate. This was always the part of the day when I'd be mentally preparing to go uptown, to sit by Sam's bedside, watch her face for signs of pain, or sadness, or fear, or boredom. Staring down the long afternoon without her, I felt eerily weightless, like an astronaut without a planet.

Impulsively, I picked up my phone and called her hospital room. She answered right away. "Hello?"

"Hey, it's me." I stopped. Now that she was on the phone, I didn't know what to say. I didn't even know why I'd called. Habit, probably. "I miss you."

"I miss you, too," she said, her voice so tiny and vulnerable. "I got your e-mail."

"You want to talk about it sometime?"

"Yeah."

Her gratitude was audible, and it was just what I needed to hear. Whatever else had changed, she still needed me, and I was still there for her—nobly, unselfishly giving. I was still the awesomest mom in the world, even more awesome than before; I was still caring for Sam, even if it was only for right this second. "Okay. How about I come see you sometime this week?"

"All right." Now she just sounded stunned. "I . . . I can't believe you still want to see me."

Well, maybe it would just be to say good-bye. But at least I'd say it in person. After everything we'd been through, I needed to look at her one more time.

We hung up and I turned back to my computer, staring blankly at the document on the screen. Bill was going to think I was crazy, calling Sam and offering to visit, when the last thing I'd said to him last night before bed was "I wish she were still dying." Well, I *was* crazy; if I hadn't had adequate proof before, now it was certifiable—I had lost my mind over Samantha Dunleavy.

I sat there at my desk arguing with myself like a hung jury—*fuck her, she conned you, cut her off already, don't be a jerk*. But she wasn't malicious, she was sick. She had a genuine disorder—I'd read about it online. And what did she con me out of, anyway? A month's rent, which she'd tried to refuse? A trip to Coney Island, which I'd begged her to take? She hadn't conned me out of my love—I'd loved her even before she got sick. I'd loved her since that first night, when she fixed me with those big, open eyes; since the first time I read her poem. And I still loved her. It hadn't gone away overnight.

"I don't know," I confessed to Bill that night, throwing myself at him the minute he got home, following him around the apartment as he took off his work clothes. "I don't know what to do. I know I have to take a huge step back, but I don't want to abandon her right now. I kind of want to see this through. Is that crazy?"

Bill shrugged at me, weary; he hadn't slept much better than me the night before. "I don't know, babe. I've been thinking about it all day." Like me, he'd been going back and forth between *Give up, it's a lost cause*, and *No, it doesn't have to be*; he'd been feeling sad, like someone had died. Bill's just as stubborn as me; he hated to admit defeat if there was still a chance things could work out. At the same time, he didn't want either of us to be a sucker.

Well, maybe it could work out after all, I ventured. Now that we knew her real problem, maybe we could find some kind of help for her; maybe a residential treatment program, where she'd finally go through the kind of intensive talk therapy she really needed, with the right medications, for a change. And I'd stay in touch with her like I always did when she was away—writing letters, calling, visiting on family day, sending packages with books and mixed CDs from Bill— and at the end of the term, maybe six months or a year, she'd be returned to us, fixed.

I watched Bill consider it, watched his dubious look turn wistful. "I don't know, either. My first instinct is, I want us to keep trying to help her." Then his look turned back to dubious. "As long as 'helping her' means 'sending her away somewhere for a good long time.'"

After an hour of discussion, we decided to try to stick by her, a decision I expected everybody to understand, including my folks, who were horrified by the news that I'd been lied to, duped—"conned," as my dad said over the phone when I told him.

Fortunately, I'd already argued this in my head. "But she didn't con me out of anything, Dad. Actually, in the worst possible way, she brought out the best in me. I never knew I could be so strong and competent. I never knew how I'd react if someone I loved were dying, and now I know—I'll be right there for them. And I don't think I'm ever going to have a kid, but if I did, now I know I'd be a really great mom. That knowledge, that opportunity—it's been an incredible gift."

"But she's so unstable," said Sylvia from the other extension. "Honey, I really think you should change the locks on your doors."

I drew in a breath for patience. "She doesn't have the keys, Sylvia. And she's not violent. She hurts herself, not others."

"But you *were* hurt here," my father insisted. "And Bill, too."

Now I set my mouth in a hard line. How dare anybody imply that I'd caused Bill to be hurt? "Bill agrees with me. We discussed it last night, and he wants to see if there's a way to continue to help this girl."

"Well, I don't scc how you can stay involved with her, after what she's done. . . ."

How absurd, to find myself back at the age of thirteen again—*You can't tell me who to be friends with! You can't tell me what to do!* "Dad, I'm not going to abandon her because she lied to me. That's what teenagers do—they lie. And instead of punishing her for it, I'm going to take the time to find out *why* she did it, and what I can do to help her, so she doesn't get herself into this kind of trouble again. Maybe if someone had done the same for *me* when *I* was a kid, I wouldn't have wound up living in a *shelter* for two and a half months."

Touché. "All right," he said stiffly. "Well, I hope it works out for you."

I hung up, furious, and started to pace. *Conned.* I hadn't been conned—I was the one who had busted the con! Well, my folks would see; everyone would see. I'd long ago determined that I was going to help Sam, and I was going to succeed in helping her, no matter what.

Bill gave me a sympathetic look. "You know they're just concerned, babe. You would be, too, if something like this happened to them."

"I know." They just thought I was an idiot, with no judgment. I sighed, hoping they weren't right. "I know."

So with my domestic partner's support, but to my folks' great dismay, I went to see Samantha that Wednesday after work. It was the first time I'd seen her since she'd thrown me out of her room five days earlier. I took that same old train ride uptown, wearing a light jacket against the chill of the late afternoon, unable to read, just staring out the window. Outside, the yellow leaves refused to fall from the trees.

I marched up to the hospital and into Sam's room, where she sat up in bed, an IV dripping toxic chemicals into her arm. But she was off the monitors—she'd been recovering from her mysterious infections since last week's revelation—and she looked flush, vital, like she was almost back to full-speed Sam.

"Hey." I came around her bed and gave her a hug, like always.

She gave me the whipped-puppy-dog eyes, the dying eye already going milky. Jesus, what she'd done to herself. "Janice, thanks so much for coming."

"It's good to see you," I said, smiling. "How are you feeling?"

"Well, mentally, not so great." She smiled ruefully back at me. "But I'm getting better, physically. The doctors say they think they figured out what's been wrong with me—they think it's an airborne virus or something. I got a couple more tests tomorrow."

I tried not to react with surprise. The doctors knew she'd been lying about her health, and they were still looking for the source of her infections? They should have come to me. It had taken me a little under an hour on the Internet to figure out how she could have given herself fungemia of the eyeball. But I had to go slowly, couldn't confront her head-on. All the literature warned me to be gentle and supportive, not harsh or accusing, or I could cause her to escalate, or flee.

I made a mental note to call Dr. Rice: *Um, you guys do realize that she's been causing her own illnesses, right?* "Uh-huh. But you're getting better, right? No fevers, nothing like that?"

"Yeah. I'm still real weak, and I need to be on the meds for a few more days, but then they said they might be able to discharge me soon."

"Oh really." And to where were they planning to discharge her? I wondered. She didn't have an apartment anymore, and I wasn't about to pay for another room deposit. Maria certainly wasn't letting Sam stay with her anytime soon—Maria was taking the week to think. When the week was up, we'd see how she was feeling. In the meantime, it was safe to assume that crashing with Maria was out of the question. "Where are you thinking you'll go?"

"I don't know. I was hoping maybe the social worker would help me find something."

Right. The social worker who'd supposedly been helping her arrange for her AIDS benefits. I'd actually met the social worker,

Felicia, so at least I knew she existed, though I'd never been privy to their conversations. I put Felicia on my mental list of people to call. "Huh. Because, you know, I've been looking into some options. I found this clinic in Illinois—here, I'll show you." I grabbed the wireless keyboard from her nightstand and navigated to the website of a clinic I'd found. *End the pain of selfabuse,* said the website. *Call 1-800-DON'T-CUT.*

"Huh," echoed Sam. She had a polite but skeptical look on her face, like a dinner guest presented with fried beetles. "I mean, I guess it looks interesting. I'm just not sure I need a place like that. I was kind of thinking I'd try to get my job back, or start at that dog-walking place, maybe find a place like the one me and Valentina had. . . ."

She looked at me like she was expecting me to support this idea—financially, even, the way I'd been doing for weeks, before Valentina gave up their room—but I wasn't reaching for my wallet today. Nor was I buying the idea of Sam living independently. "Sam, I think it's pretty clear that you need some kind of treatment program. I know it sucks, the idea of starting over from the bottom somewhere, but—"

"I don't know." Her nose was actively wrinkled now. Again, I tried not to gape at her. She had to be kidding me—she'd be lucky to get into a clinic like this one; she was lucky I was sitting next to her now, presenting her with the option. But again, I had to tread lightly.

"Well, you'll be here for a few more days, at least, yes? That gives us a little time to plan."

It was a strange visit, short and uneasy. There was no script for our new, post-revelation relationship, and the old one didn't work anymore. She wasn't going to tell me some new horror story about having to call 911 at the age of five because her mother was giving birth to her sister from the depths of a heroin blackout and her father was off on a meth rampage. I wasn't going to tell her about Disney World.

All right, I thought. This would take time, and patience. I didn't have a lot of either, but I'd see what I could do. I'd call Felicia the social worker, I'd call Dr. Rice; we'd get her into some kind of clinic, and they'd fix her. "All right," I said aloud, gathering my things.

And for once she didn't try to stall me on my way out the door. She was as relieved that I was leaving as I was. "Bye, Janice. Thanks for coming." But her voice was high and insincere. As was the hug I gave her.

I didn't say, "I'll see you soon."

Fuck her, I wrote in my notebook. *Fuck Samantha Dunleavy. I don't care if I ever see her again.*

So I'd moved past the denial phase of grieving and into anger. Which was good—now all I had to hit were bargaining and depression, and then I'd be on to acceptance. Except it seemed like I might stick around and hang out in anger for a while—for the rest of my life, maybe.

Maria's week of thinking was up; she gave me a call. "I feel better," she said, and she sounded it. "I feel like, all right. It's hard to deal with, but I'm ready to deal with it. I'm not giving up on her. I made a commitment, and I'm going to honor it."

"Fantastic," I said. "Because I'm ready to fucking quit. I can't deal with her at all. I'm so angry, I'm ready to bust through my clothes like the Incredible Hulk. You know she's denying she did this to herself, and she doesn't want to go to a treatment program?"

"I know, I spoke to her earlier. But she's going to have to go someplace, that's for sure. I'm looking into some other options, closer by— I think it'd be too hard to get her Medicaid transferred to Illinois."

"Well, that's great of you. Let me know how it goes." It was my turn to take a few days away.

I spent most of my time over the next few days researching fake illness and Munchausen's syndrome, reading online accounts from "munchers" of their ruses—how they tore ligaments to necessitate surgery, or convinced psychiatrists they had multiple personality disorder. They were all so smart, and so self-satisfied; they just loved outwitting the doctors and making people jump for them. I remembered the smug look Sam would get when she "played a prank," or manipulated someone into letting her have her way somehow, and I wanted

to reach through the monitor and wrap my hands around these people's necks, yelling, *Just fucking stop it!*

Then I looked at the joint in the ashtray next to me. If only it were
that easy to just fucking stop.

I was also tearing through a book I'd ordered online, rush delivery:
Dr. Marc Feldman's *Playing Sick? Untangling the Web of Munchausen's Syndrome, Munchausen's by Proxy, Malingering, and Facti-
tious Disorder*. Dr. Feldman was the country's foremost authority on
Munchausen's syndrome and faking illness, and he'd devoted a chapter in his book to people like me and Maria—the "casualties," as he
called them, of people like Sam. I underlined this passage:

> As a victim, your own therapy might focus on fully letting go
> of the other person. Although it may sound harsh, especially
> when you've been so close to a person, your own well-being
> may depend on your ending the relationship.

I started the next week singing an entirely new tune.

My dad and Sylvia were right. I *had* been conned. Sam had lied
to me, and I'd believed her. She'd jerked me around, and she'd enjoyed it. I'd been sick at my wedding, sick with worry on my honeymoon. What had she taken from me? Most of the past year of my life.
I didn't give a shit about the money I'd given her, the apartment deposit and the cell phone—it was the time I'd spent with her, the time
I would never get back. I didn't care if it was a disease that made her
act this way; she didn't have to infect me with it.

Every time I remembered something else she'd said, done, lied
about, I was refueled with fury. *I should hire a private detective*, I
thought. *I bet she's got hospital records all over the place. And I want to
find her real parents, the meth cooker and the prostitute. Maybe there
are some kind of criminal records.* I wanted answers, I wanted the truth.
And I wasn't going to get them from Sam.

I got a phone message from her, still recuperating from her self-
induced infections in the hospital—"Hey, Janice, just wanted to say
hi and thanks for everything. Um, hope you're doing okay. I guess I'll

talk to you soon." I heard the "poor, frightened, alone" sorrow in her voice, and I could have crushed the phone into dust. *Please, bitch, do not even* try *to guilt-trip me.* I sent her an e-mail in reply: "Hey there, it's been a busy week, but I'm thinking about you and hoping you're getting a lot better." It sounded much nicer than I meant it. I could lie just as well as she could.

I got another great big jolt of fury talking to Felicia, the hospital social worker. (Dr. Rice was no longer on Sam's floor—she'd rotated to another unit—and none of the doctors had permission to speak to me anyway). I'd left Felicia several messages; by the time I got her on the phone, I was already raring to yell at someone. "According to Maria, her other caretaker, Sam's almost fully recovered from her 'mysterious recurring infections.' Where do you plan to release her to, when she's ready to go?"

Felicia didn't have any good answers for me. "We're still working on that," she said, unconcerned. "I got your message about the place in Illinois, but I haven't had a chance to check into it yet."

"Okay. Well, I know they're talking about releasing her on Monday—that gives us today and the weekend to find something."

"Right." Felicia didn't care. So what if Sam was homeless and in need of therapeutic treatment? There were six people sitting in the emergency room right then who fit that profile. The hospital discharged people onto the streets all the time—it was a hospital, not a homeless shelter. Once Sam was healthy, she would not be their problem anymore.

I fumed, eyes bulging out of my head with frustration. "Felicia, she has been faking and inducing serious illness; she almost died from what she did to herself. She is an immediate danger to herself. You can't release her under her own recognizance, or she will flee, and she will injure herself again. Can't she at least be admitted to the psych ward while we find something?"

Felicia balked at my tone, clucking her teeth like she was annoyed. "Well, first of all, she denies making herself sick. And we don't tend to accept people with that kind of diagnosis anyway. There isn't really anything we can do for them."

"That's not true," I insisted. A week's worth of research, and I was an authority on the syndrome. "There's plenty they can do for her in the psych ward. Long-term talk therapy and the right mix of anti-depressants can be very effective in some cases. And you have to at least give it a shot—I mean, look at what the girl did to herself. She's *blind in one eye*."

Again, not Felicia's problem. "Look, I've already gone way out of my way to help Sam, and I'm going to keep looking on her behalf. But if we can't find anything, we still have to discharge her on Monday. She's recovered, and we can't keep her here."

I wanted to scream a string of profanities at Felicia, but I knew she was right—she'd done a lot for Sam already, a lot more than most patients required—and I needed whatever help she was still willing to give. "Well, I really appreciate your efforts on her behalf," I said, staunching the bile rising in my throat. *And if she hurts herself after leaving your hospital, when you've been explicitly warned that she would do so, I am so, so suing you.*

I hadn't even come close to finishing the anger stage of grieving when I started bargaining, which came with a side order of depression. Except depression wasn't a stage—it was a constant hum, a leaden feeling in my gut when I woke up in the middle of the night and the realization hit me fresh. Sam, as I'd known her, was gone. And this person was still here, this loathsome, whiny sack of neediness and deceit. *Please be my friend, Janice. Don't desert me.*

I would have been happy to grieve for Sam, if only she would go away, or drop dead. Instead, I was stuck with bargaining. And not with God, either—God wasn't changing anything about this situation to suit me, that was apparent. The only person to bargain with was Sam. She had to be talked into confessing what she'd done to herself and entering a treatment program, and it had to be now. Because she was going to be released from the hospital soon, and according to all of the research I'd read, she was going to bolt.

"She's going to take off," I told Bill. "I can feel it." As codependent as I'd become with Sam—cringing with pain when she got stuck with a needle, shivering in terror as she described her father's beatings—I could feel what she was feeling now: she was sitting in that hospital room planning to run as soon as the IV tube was out of her arm. Maybe she'd go to Oregon, or Southern California, and start over there; she'd find a homeless shelter or a church, someplace where Janices and Marias hung out. Maybe she'd break a bone on her skateboard and see who could resist her on crutches. She certainly wasn't going to stick around New York and face up to what she'd done; she wasn't entering any of the therapeutic programs Maria or Felicia would find. No, she was going to disappear, and I was never going to find her again.

So I steeled myself for one final journey, threw on my jacket, and headed up to the Bronx on the subway. This was really it, the last trip uptown. Sam was being discharged the next morning, and wherever she went from here, she'd never come back to this hospital again. They wouldn't let her; Felicia had said as much. They were finished with her.

Well, I wasn't finished yet. I came into Sam's room. She was flushed, her arms bandaged where the IV had been inserted; an empty dinner tray sat on the table next to her pencils and drawings.

She looked up with surprise. "Hey there," she said, nervous. "I wasn't expecting you."

. "I know." I smiled and threw myself into my usual chair, no hug. "Surprise visit, on your last night here."

"Oh, it's not my last night." Her eyes widened, so sincere. "They still haven't found a place for me, so they said they're going to do a 'social hold.' It's, like, something they can do to keep you in the hospital if you don't have anywheres to go. So I'll be here until, probably, Friday or something. But Maria's been working real hard on finding me a place—I may wind up going to that place upstate, the drug treatment program, DTP."

"Uh-huh." I rolled my eyes to myself. First of all, drug treatment? That wasn't what she needed. She needed psychiatric care. And DTP was one of the most emotionally abusive programs out there. It had been around since I was a kid—I'd almost been sent there myself—and had a terrible reputation; even Maria knew it was the pits. I'd never met a sober graduate of DTP. Also, I'd heard of a "social hold," but Felicia had made it clear to me that they were not extending Sam's stay in the hospital for any reason.

And I could see it all over Sam's face. Maria was wasting her time, making arrangements with DTP. Sam was leaving tomorrow.

Sam continued talking, unaware of my suspicions. "And I got good news—the doctors figured out where the fungemia came from."

"Oh really?" I asked dryly. "What did they say?"

Sam's eyes widened more at my skeptical tone. "Well, they think it was some kind of airborne contaminant that got into my lungs, and it spread from there."

"Uh-huh."

"So . . . that's good, because they were wondering how I got it, and now they know."

"Uh-huh."

I was looking straight into her eyes, the right one nearly dead in its socket. I switched my gaze to the good eye, and she flinched a little at my stare.

"So . . ."

"So," I said, leaning forward, my heart speeding up. "'Airborne' doesn't really explain how a contaminant got into your lungs. But I don't need anyone to explain it. Because I already know that you put it there."

She frowned and drew her head back. "What are you talking about?"

I smiled. "I'm talking about you putting a contaminant into your lungs. Probably yeast. Probably with your inhaler. Though you could have injected it—that's probably how it wound up in your eye." I looked at the dead eye, shook my head, switched back to the working one. She flinched again.

"What are you talking about? I didn't do that."

Her voice was alarmed, her face draining of color. I'd locked my gaze onto that one eye, and she couldn't get away. I laughed, though nothing was funny. "Babe, I have done way too much research. I know everything. I know how to give yourself bacterial sepsis with *E. coli*. I know how your hand got infected last year. You infected it. The doctor suspected it back then, but now we know."

"No." She shook her head. "I don't know what you're talking about."

This is how it went for the next half hour: I told her what I knew, ticking the list off on my fingers: "Symptom one: you feigned illness, which you admit. Symptom two: you waited too long to see a doctor when you knew you were sick, which you have also admitted. Sam, you *admitted* that you have Munchausen's syndrome—"

And she denied it: "I never said I had that!"

"Wrong." I smiled again. "You admitted it to me right in this very hospital. You said, 'They call themselves munchers, and they shoot poop into their veins.' And that's how you get bacterial sepsis every five days. Like clockwork. With *E. coli*, from feces." I raised my eyebrows at her, tipped my head to the side. *Huh? How 'bout that? I know about the feces, Sam.*

She was pale as the moon, agitated as a cat. "Just because I said I read about it doesn't mean—"

I shook my head. "It's not going to work. I know too much, and I've read too much. I know what you've done, and I know what you're planning to do." I paused dramatically, like a detective on her favorite show, *Law & Order*. "That's why I came to say good-bye."

Her eyes widened to an alarming degree, and her voice shook. "What? What are you talking about? Good-bye?"

I nodded. "I know you're going to leave tomorrow. And I wanted to say good-bye."

"I wasn't going to leave," she protested. "What . . . how . . ."

I kept the smile on my face. It was almost sadistic. After all she'd put me through, I couldn't help but enjoy watching her squirm. "Yeah, you are going to leave. I know you, Sam. I know what's going on. I know you can't wait to get out of this place, so you can go run someplace else and start this all over again. But let me tell you, it's not going to work. Because I know."

Now she was dropping the wide-eyed act, getting angry—she was being unjustly accused. "What are you talking about, Janice? You don't know—"

There was a hint of a sneer in her voice, which I matched. "Yes, Sam. I do know. I know everything you've been up to. I know you've done this before, and I know you're going to do it again. So when you take off tomorrow morning, thinking you're so ahead of everyone, remember—I know."

She stared at me with her one good eye, starting a slow burn as I continued. I wasn't smiling anymore. I leaned in closer, fixed my stare even harder, exhilaration coursing through my veins. I felt that life-or-death intensity between us, like when I'd held her while she sobbed, like when I'd prayed at her deathbed. Now it was the feeling of breaking her down.

"And I know you can't afford to keep doing this anymore. Because this time it almost killed you. You didn't mean for it to get this bad, did you? It scared you, didn't it? Got away from you for a minute there. You seriously almost died. The nurses were looking at me with tears in their eyes, Sam, because they knew how close to death you were. You almost shut down your organs and died."

She was silent, staring at me with her jaw clenched, lips pressed tight against her teeth. I stared back, and kept going.

"That's what happens to people who do what you do. They let the fever get too high, or they give themselves blood clots with their injections, and they die. You got lucky this time. You will not be that lucky next time."

Another flinch. I'd hit my mark, and I knew it. She recovered and tried to scoff. "Janice, I never injected anything. I don't even know what you're talking about."

"Sam, it's true, and you know I know it. And it's almost worse than admitting it, isn't it? Sitting here looking at me, knowing that I know? It's awful, right?" I tucked my chin, gave her a chiding look. "You might as well come clean."

It *was* awful, it was torture for her, having to look me in the eye, seeing the certainty there. She tried not to actively writhe under my scrutiny. "But . . . but it isn't true!"

"Riiiiight." I chuckled and shook my head. "Listen, babe. You don't know what's true. You do not know the truth from a lie. And you know, I think that scares you."

The bed shook as she brought her fist down on the mattress next to her. "I know the truth from a lie! I admitted I told a lie! What do you want from me? I admitted it and I apologized! And I'm sorry, but I—".

Now I outright laughed at her—she didn't *tell* a lie, she *lived* a lie. For *four whole months*. Everywhere she went, everything she did, she was wearing that lie like a blanket. And she believed that lie; even the part of her that knew it was a lie was getting washed away. She was starting to believe that God had given her AIDS, because she honestly did not know whether or not she had AIDS anymore. I cut her off from continuing to protest. "Sam, you do not know the truth from a lie anymore. But I do. And I came to tell you, you are in grave, grave danger. You cannot afford to walk out of this place and try to start over. It's not going to work this time. You're busted. I mean, you can leave, you can walk out and start this all over again someplace else. But it's not going to be the same. Because now I know. And just that fact in and of itself is going to ruin it for you."

She slit her eyes and crossed her arms, giving me her hardest glare. And I smiled again—I wasn't afraid of her anger anymore. I was the adult here; I was in charge. I had the truth on my side.

"Listen," I said. "I promised you once that I would stay in your life, for better or for worse. Now that promise is a threat. I am in your life, and you're not getting rid of me. You can run, but you won't shake me. Because I am a very smart woman, with a lot of resources, and I care about you too much to let this thing kill you. And it will kill you."

I was silent for a moment, and so was she. She was still looking at me, but her defiance had slipped, and she was breathing fast, like she was afraid. I narrowed my eyes and looked at her critically, assessing her.

"Which is a shame. Because you might even be able to kick this. I mean, you're young, and you're incredibly smart. If you wanted to, you *might* even have a chance at beating this thing. You *might* be able to live a normal life." I tilted my head, assessing some more. "Maybe. I don't know. I don't even know if you want to beat this. But if you did, maybe you could."

Sam broke the eye contact and stared glumly at the floor. She was cracking; I could see it. Now I just had to finish her off.

"But I'm betting you're going to bolt instead. Which is why I came to say good-bye. Because I wanted to tell you a few things before you go."

She looked up at me again, her eyes plaintive this time. *Don't go. Don't let me go.*

I launched into it, everything I'd prepared to say on the subway. "I wanted to tell you that I care about you, and I always have, from the first time we met. And you know what drew me to you? It was your writing. That's what I liked about you. Not your bullshit stories, not your broken hand. The best day we ever spent together was that day in Chinatown, do you remember? When we had lunch and talked about writing a book together, and then we went on the swings and flew your kite?" I felt such a pang, remembering that innocent day; I could see she felt it, too. "You were perfectly healthy that day, and I loved you."

And I still did. I loved the part of her that was really *her*—the brilliant, sensitive, ferocious part; the part of her that still wanted to live. The part, behind the clenched jaw and the steely glare, that I could see was terrified, as well she should have been. This was the worst disorder I'd ever heard of. AIDS would at least kill her—this just made her suffer and suffer. She couldn't even enjoy the caring she'd worked so hard to get, because it felt tainted. Nothing she did ever felt good for more than a few seconds at a time, and then it went back to being awful. I was flooded with compassion for her. Hers was no kind of life; it was a constant hell. It was like the Would You Rather . . . ? game—*Would you rather hide a deep dark secret from your loved ones? Or tell the truth and never see them again?*

My voice was soft but firm. "I still love you, Sam. I still wish I could help you. But you know, you have to decide that you want help.

And I came to tell you that, too. If you leave, and you decide later that you want help, I will still be here. Call me anytime. You have the number."

One last smile, and then I leaned down to gather my bag.

"Wait," she said to the floor.

I stopped and looked up at her. She met my eyes with hers. She'd broken.

"What . . . what do you think I should do?"

I rode the train home, my inner bad cop slapping palms with my inner good cop. *Yeah! We did it!* I'd sweated through my shirt *and* my sweater and was now dampening the armpits of my coat, just reliving the scene. But I'd done it, I'd gotten her to confess. We'd called in the young female doctor on duty, and Sam hung her head while I explained the situation: "She admits to infecting herself; she's at risk for further self-injury; you've got to put the social hold on her until she gets into DTP."

The doctor looked from me to her, her to me. "Is this true?" she asked Sam.

Sam nodded her hung head. *Yes.*

Yes! I called Maria, filled her in. She was confused—"What do you mean, she was going to bolt? She'd better not bolt, she's supposed to go to DTP on Friday!"

And now it looked like she might even get there. The stations flew by, 125th Street, 86th Street, 59th Street, Grand Central, Union Square. Once again, Sam was going to make it to rehab. And I was going to make it home.

Chapter Sixteen

Happiest Place on Earth

Two days later, Sam was transferred to DTP, a drug-treatment program in upstate New York, for an estimated yearlong stay.

So she wound up at the place I'd tried hardest to avoid as a teenager—DTP. Back in my day, they just called it "Treatment," and it was the worst punishment the counselors at the group home could threaten us with. Sadistic counselors berated you twenty-four hours a day, made you wear signs around your neck—LIAR, MANIPULATER, SLUT—and encouraged the other residents to tear you down every chance they got. This was confrontation therapy, or something; it was supposed to break you down so you could be rebuilt. Except the ratio of time spent breaking you down to time spent building you up was, like, a million to one.

Still, better DTP than the streets, or the shelter, or another hospital; better they break her down than she break down herself. We couldn't let DTP know the severity of Sam's real condition—Felicia had to fudge the application a little, or they never would have accepted her into the program. But in the meantime, at least she was being safely housed and monitored. She was being cared for by somebody else.

I was free.

Stillness—that's what it felt like, that first week she was gone. An electric, living stillness, the feeling of stasis rubbing against change. The hum you hear when you meditate, the loudness of nothing. I sat with my notebook open on my lap, not writing. I felt empty. It didn't feel so bad.

Strange, though, not to have Sam on my to-do list. I could sit in the easy chair in the evening, watch the cats follow the last shaft of light from the window around the darkening room. No phone calls to make. No hospitals to visit. Nothing to anticipate. I was at rest.

Bill and I were better than ever in the wake of Sam's departure— bonded by the trauma we'd endured, giddy from the relief of it being over. I hugged and kissed him with extra gratitude when he came home at night, and he hugged me gratefully in return, happy to find me at home, yakking with a girlfriend over the phone or sitting in the chair with a book and a cat vying for space on my lap. I'd never take Bill for granted again, I swore; I'd never stop marveling over the love I felt for him and from him—this deep, true, reciprocal love that bounced back and forth between us, gaining strength and momentum with every day. *This* was family.

Still, I thought of Sam constantly, wondering how she was feeling now that her disorder had been revealed and she was starting a new phase of her life. I wondered how she was feeling about me. I couldn't seem to write to her, though I kept meaning to. I knew I should have made sure to send her a letter or two in her first week at DTP, just to show her that nothing had changed—I was still on her side, still in her life. I wasn't flaking on my promise. But I couldn't seem to write and say so. I couldn't even return Maria's call—"Just calling to say hi, check in, see if you want to get together with me and Jodi sometime; maybe we could have dinner." I just listened to the message and deleted it.

One thing I could do: call Disney, cancel Sam's room, and get my deposit back. Bill and I were still going—I felt like we owed it to ourselves, after the way the wedding and honeymoon had been shadowed by Sam, and he'd even started, despite his lingering reservations about the place, to get into the Disney spirit. We referred to it as the Samantha Dunleavy Memorial Disney Trip, remembering how we thought we'd be flying down there with her ashes in an urn. The Disney operator was more than sympathetic — "Well, it's a shame that Samantha can't join you and William this year, but maybe on your next visit!"

If I thought about her for too long, if my mind wandered on my morning run and I found myself reliving things she'd said and done to me — the night she called and said she'd stabbed a pimp, the day I sat by her bedside and watched her monitors flatline — I found myself getting angry again; angry at her, angry at myself. But my anger toward her was the kind you might feel toward someone who broke up with you — the anger of being rejected. The anger of the bruised ego. Mostly, I felt hurt by her because she took away something important to me: herself. First she gave me this person to love, this person who loved me, and then she told me that person wasn't real. I was more angry at her because I missed her — or I missed the feelings I used to have about her — than anything else.

Three weeks had passed since she'd left, and I continued to get calls from Maria — "Just wanted to see if the seventeenth would work for dinner; hope all's well with you." Maria was still on the case, still a stalwart for Sam; she'd written her letters, though no reply had come yet. Somehow, Maria had been through everything I had, and she'd remained everything I was striving to be: compassionate, loyal, and loving. Not bitter, miserable, waking up in the middle of the night thinking of new things I wanted to say to Sam — *You're so sick and disgusting, I'm glad you're out of my life*. Maybe I could absorb some of Maria's conviction and faith.

I called her back, smiling at her familiar voice on her outgoing message. "Hey there, Maria, it's Janice. The seventeenth works great for me. Looking forward to seeing you and Jodi then."

November 17, 2005. One year to the day since I met Sam. And only one day shy of another anniversary: November 18 would mark twenty-one years since I'd left home for the shelter. Funny, I hadn't really noticed how close the two events were. My anniversary as a runaway meant less and less to me these days.

I stood outside the diner on Broadway by Astor Place, looking down the block, watching my breath make clouds in the cold air. Two girls in ripped tights and smeared eyeliner laughed and linked arms as they passed. I smiled at them indulgently, like a grandmother.

Jodi arrived first. I hadn't seen her in months, not since Sam's meningitis. She looked well, maybe a little grayer around the temples. Same firm hug, same arch smile. "How you doin', Bead Lady?"

We stood outside and waited for Maria; Jodi smoked a cigarette. We talked about her job, my work, the shelter. "I haven't been there in months," I confessed. "Not since I saw you last."

Jodi rolled her eyes. "Yeah. We were all getting a little burnt out around then."

We could see Maria bustling down the block, loaded down with her bag of schoolbooks—the youngest of us, and yet somehow our leader. Her indefatigable smile buoyed me right away. "Hi there, Other Moms!"

We hugged hello, Jodi stomped out her cigarette, and we went inside and got a seat.

So there we were. We'd never met like this before, the council of concerned elders. I felt very safe, sitting there at the table with them, listening to them chat about their various counseling and social work duties, figuring out where they overlapped—"I'm doing less case management and more hands-on these days." "Yeah, I prefer a lot of client interaction myself." I felt like a kid, swinging my legs under the table while the grown-ups talked about how to fix everything. Sam picked some good ones, I thought; when she went parent shopping, she got the best.

"So have you heard anything from Sam?" I asked.

"Well," Maria began. "I got the initial call from her saying she was at DTP, and she was okay. She told me there'd be no contact for the first thirty to ninety days, but as soon as she was assigned a primary counselor, she'd give that person permission to speak to us. And I've written her a few letters, but I don't think she can reply yet."

"Any word from her counselor?"

"No, but that's not a surprise. Her counselor probably wouldn't make contact with us unless we initiated it."

Jodi agreed. "Sounds like standard operating procedure."

"Huh." So all we had was Sam's word that she was going to keep us in the loop, that she wasn't going to shut us out now that she was in DTP. *As soon as she's assigned a primary counselor* reminded me too much of things she'd said before—*As soon as I know who's my primary doctor, Eng or Gambine, I'll have them call you.* "So do you think we should call her counselor? See how she's doing?"

"We could," said Maria. "I can put in a call sometime next week. But it's the holidays, so I wouldn't expect a call back right away."

Jodi and Maria both seemed so cool about the situation. Neither of them had a lot of confidence in DTP—"It's a last resort, but at least she's somewhere"—but they seemed to have confidence in Sam, confidence that she was committed to "working the program" and getting better. *Huh,* I thought. I'd read that some people with Munchausen's syndrome could be helped somewhat by modified 12-step therapy; maybe it wasn't so far-fetched that she'd manage to derive some good from this place. I perked up more and more, especially as we started talking about the good times, the Yankees games and the Coney Islands, and what we missed about Sam, how important she made us feel.

Then we started comparing her stories against one another. "Did you ever hear her play piano?" I asked.

Maria nodded. "She said she learned from a guy in Oklahoma City who owned a jazz bar."

"That's what she told me," Jodi confirmed.

So at least she was consistent, if not always truthful. I pressed on. "How about her sister in a coma? First she told me she'd recovered and moved to a group home, then later she told me she was still in a coma."

Maria frowned, looked from me to Jodi and back again. "I thought Eileen was still in a coma, last she heard. Are you sure she said she was in a group home?"

I pointed to my bag, indicating the notebook within. "That's what she told me back when she was at the psych ward. I wrote it all down, pretty much everything she said. I used to come home from the hospital and transcribe everything I could remember. Just because . . . I don't know. It helped."

The food came, and we went through the rest of it—living in Thailand, the pimp fight, the things she'd intimated to us about guns, and how she'd used them. All the stories matched, but there was no way to know if they matched the truth. Tentatively, I broached the subject I'd been obsessing over for the past few days: "I've been thinking about trying to do a background check on her."

Maria looked skeptical. "What do you want to find?"

Well, I *wanted* to find out that she hadn't been lying to us about everything. I wanted to find two criminal parents and a comatose sister and a brother in the navy who'd only been sober for the past few years himself. I was *afraid* of finding a suburban home, parents who'd paid for piano lessons, two healthy siblings, and a dog. Faking and inducing illness, Dr. Feldman's book said, often came with a corollary case of *pseudologia fantastica*—gratuitous, over-the-top lying. "I want to know if she is who she says she is."

Jodi tipped her head, considering it. "Understandable."

"Not the biggest vote of confidence, I realize."

"I don't know," said Maria, thoughtful. "It kind of seems like a violation of her privacy. I think we should give her the chance to tell us the truth herself. Otherwise, it's like, it doesn't really mean anything, you know?"

I nodded, trying to quell my discouragement at the veto. "I'd love it if Sam were able to tell us the truth herself. I mean, if there's anything to tell."

I was sure there was more to tell, but I walked away from dinner agreeing with Maria and Jodi—we'd stay out of Sam's treatment for now, give her a few more weeks to acclimate to DTP before we started trying to call her counselors. And we had to tread carefully, when we did finally speak to her counselors—if we told them how sick she'd made herself, how sick she remained, she could get booted from the program, and nobody wanted that to happen. Maria would be the point of contact with Sam's counselors, and if any of us got any reply from our letters (*"Our" letters*, I thought, guilty—*I'd better get busy writing her one*), we'd let the others know.

We kissed and hugged good-bye outside, in the glow of the green and red Christmas lights newly hung on the avenue. "Talk to you soon," we promised one another.

I walked away comforted, cheered, full of goodwill toward Sam.

Dec. 1, 2005

Dear Sam,
Hi. ☺

    I want to ask you all kinds of questions, like how are you, and how's it going, and what's it like at DTP, and stuff like that, but I'm pretty sure you're not allowed to write back— I'm not even sure if you'll be allowed to receive this letter, which is why I haven't written before this—I didn't want to send letters into The Void and wonder if you'd received them. But I saw Maria and Jodi the other week, and Maria said she was pretty sure you were allowed to get letters by now. So without further explanatory preamble, here it is: a letter.

    As I said, I had dinner with Maria and Jodi the other week, which was great—you picked some awesome ladies to be in your life, and I'm glad they're in my life too. Of course we talked about how much we miss you and love you, and how extraordinary you are and how grateful we are for your presence in our lives, and how concerned we are that you are getting the right kind of care. We also discussed our curiosity about you, and how much we are looking forward to the time when you'll be able to tell us more specific stuff about your past. Mostly, we wished that you were there having dinner with us, but we look forward to a time when all of us will be able to get together and hang out.

Anyway, since I can't ask you questions, though I am kind of dying to know how you are, I'll tell you stuff about what's going on here. Everybody's doing well—all the cats and the humans are okay. Bill and I are really enjoying being married, not that it's much different from living together, but it is—I don't know, there's just a really good feeling that comes from creating your own family (as you know), and in making those relationships "official."

I haven't gone back to the shelter yet, though I still plan to. I have a lot of great shelter memories from this time last year, especially because I was getting to know you. Last Christmas Eve, when I came to visit you in St. Victor's and then went uptown and brought Chinese food, was one of the best Christmas Eves I'd ever had—I'm glad you and I got to spend part of it together, and wish we could see each other this holiday season as well.

You know, I miss you so much, babe. I think about you a lot. I am so grateful and happy that you're alive, and that you're fighting to stay that way. I worry that it's hard and painful for you right now—I mean, of course it is, because life is hard and painful. I just hope you know that things can get a whole lot better than they are right now, and that I'm still here to try to help you make that happen. I'm always going to feel like you're my kid, for better or for worse, that's never going to change—I'll share you with your other moms, but I'm not giving you up. I love you, Samantha. You're just going to have to learn to deal with that.

Well, until you earn phone privileges or visits, I'll keep writing, and if you are allowed to receive books or CDs, I'll send some interesting stuff your way. I hope you're hanging in there, and I hope I'll hear from you soon. Until then, be

good to yourself, and remember your family here in NYC.
We can't wait to see you again soon.

Janice

I felt better after I wrote the letter—just the fact that I'd been able
to write it made me feel like a good person, as assuredly selfless and
moral as when I was visiting her in the hospital every day. I imagined
her receiving it and being so grateful that I was still on her side—
maybe she'd been worrying that she lost me, that I was no longer her
friend. Her eyes probably filled with tears when she realized how true
a friend I still was.

I dropped the letter into the mailbox on my corner, the hinge
groaning as the door snapped shut. *I love you, Samantha.* Then I
walked away, lighter all over, at peace.

The next Sunday, we got up at five in the morning and rolled our
suitcases to the curb for our second vacation in three months.

"Unconscionable," I said to Bill in the taxi to the airport. "I still
can't believe we're actually doing this."

"Oh, I know," he agreed. "It's totally obscene."

Which it was—educated liberals like us, going to Disney World,
spending our money to fund more globo-corporate hegemony—we
should have donated the cash to end genocide or breast cancer. "See,
that's why we needed Sam here. If she were here, this would all be
morally defensible."

Bill reached over and patted my hand exaggeratedly. "Well, she'll
always be here in our hearts. Did you take your Valium?"

I did, and I was pleasantly loopy by the time we pulled up to the
check-in counter. "Hello," I said warmly, presenting my e-ticket and
passport. The woman behind the counter checked our documents
and gave us our seat assignments.

"Is Samantha Dunleavy checking in with you as well?" she asked.

"No," said Bill. "She's not making it today."

"She wasn't feeling well," I added, mugging at Bill.

"Good one," he muttered as we walked away.

So there was an empty seat next to us, a Samantha-shaped absence on our flight to Florida. It should have been strange, taking this trip without her, when she and I had talked for months about how this day would go—*You'll meet us at our place, and we'll get a cab to the airport, and you can sit next to the window on the plane*—but it seemed natural to travel alone with Bill; it seemed right. I grabbed his hand, and he squeezed mine in return.

We collected our bags in Orlando and boarded the Disney Magical Express bus to the Disney Contemporary Hotel. "Space Mountain," I said, starting to bounce in my seat. Just like Sam and I had planned. "We're dumping the bags, and we're going straight there. Then over to the Haunted Mansion. Then Mickey's Philhar-magic show. I've never seen it, but the guidebook gives it four and a half stars. Then we're going to want something to eat. . . ."

From the minute Bill and I dropped off our bags at the hotel, we were in endorphin heaven: screaming on the thrill rides, gaping at the pageantry, stuffing our faces full of fried food. Maybe it was something they put in the air there—extra oxygen or laughing gas or something—or maybe it was the way everyone around us was smiling, the look of awe and wonder on the kids' faces—but we immediately regressed to the age of seven; we were overwhelmed with exuberance and joy. The place was even better than I remembered from my last visit with my mom and Jake, and Bill was loving it, too.

"The guidebook says they do special stuff for honeymooners," he noted our first night at the hotel. "We should get those buttons that say we're newlyweds."

"That's kosher," I reasoned. "We did just get married three months ago."

So we got the buttons, and now every single park employee was smiling extra-wide for us, and saying, "Congratulations!" and letting us ride things twice without waiting in line. It made the whole experience feel even more like a giant victory lap.

In fact, I almost had to stop and remember to think about Sam.

Bill and I would be running around, gawking and grinning, wolfing down ice cream between rides and attractions, and I'd realize, *We were supposed to be here with her.* But if I'd expected to miss her, I was wrong—all I could think while we were there was, *I am so glad Sam's not here. I'm so glad it's just me and Bill.* It never would have worked, I realized, the three-person arrangement; one of them would have always been the third wheel. I would have had to choose who to sit next to on every ride, and who would ride solo in the car behind, and what if she wanted to go to one part of the park and he wanted to go to another? Besides, she never would have made it through the week without pulling some kind of prank—trying to climb from balcony to balcony along the outside of the hotel, or setting off a fire alarm—and Disney doesn't take kindly to pranks. I could imagine the whole trip gone awry, Bill and I sitting in an office in one of the famed underground tunnels beneath the park, trying to get Sam out of Mickey Prison.

No, I didn't miss her. I wasn't sad she couldn't come. I even felt weird about how unsad I was. This trip was supposed to be poignant without her, tinged with melancholy—how was I supposed to come home and tell people we were overjoyed without her? A *good* person wouldn't have been overjoyed, a good person would have been missing her, thinking of what could have been. But I was too busy laughing my ass off with Bill, racing across Tomorrowland to get on Space Mountain for the fifteenth time.

It didn't hit me until our last night there, when we were shopping for souvenirs. Bill held up a T-shirt for his brother—"You think this'll fit Kevin?"—as I browsed the racks, thinking guiltily, *I should get something for Sam.* I hadn't mentioned Disney in my letter to her; I didn't want to remind her of what she was missing, the trip we'd been planning all year. But she must have been watching the calendar, thinking as she'd been thinking for months, *A month until Disney; three weeks until Disney; they must be there right now.* I wondered if it would be crappier to get her something, to rub the vacation in her face, or to get her nothing at all.

I fingered a Grumpy T-shirt. No, they'd never let her have that at

DTP; Grumpy represented negativism. Maybe Tigger was an acceptable role model for recovery. I grabbed a pair of Tigger boxer shorts, took them to the register. I imagined sending her a Christmas package with the boxer shorts, and maybe some books or CDs; I imagined her rueful smile as she put them on. I imagined the note that was probably waiting for me back home—*I'm doing well, I miss you, thanks for the letter.* I was glad I'd gotten her a souvenir.

We rode back to the airport the next morning hand in hand, five pounds fatter than when we arrived, a hundred times giddier. "That was unbelievable," said Bill, and I agreed.

"We'll have to do this every year. The *Annual* Samantha Dunleavy Memorial Disney Trip."

Maybe one year she'd even get to come with us.

We got home to the usual—sniffing cats, a stack of mail. No reply from Sam, I noticed. Oh well. She probably wasn't allowed to write back yet, or she was drafting a letter to me right now.

Or she'd crumpled up my letter and thrown it into the trash, unread.

We unpacked our suitcases. I put the boxer shorts for Sam in their bag on top of my dresser. *I'll send them soon,* I thought. As soon as I heard from her.

"Bead Lady!"

I walked into the lounge of the Older Females Unit at the shelter that Wednesday, bead bag on my arm, and Ashley the counselor gave me a big wave from the hallway.

"Hey there!" I waved and grinned back at her. "How are you?"

"Good! How've you been? We haven't seen you in . . ."

Four months. It had been four months since I'd been to the shelter, since Sam first went into the hospital in the Bronx; two months since we'd uncovered the true source of her illness. I'd gone back and forth about volunteering: one day I'd swear to Bill that I was never going back—"I've got to move on from that place one of these days. It's been twenty-one years, for crying out loud"—then the next day

I'd tell him how much I missed it, missed the girls, didn't want it to become something else Sam had taken from me. Then we got back from Disney World, and I don't know why, but suddenly there was no question—I needed the place, and it needed me.

I called the volunteer coordinator and left a message: I was coming back. No answer, and no head of the unit to call—after ten months, they still hadn't replaced Nadine. So I just showed up with my beads, waved to the guards at the desk—"Good to see you again!" "You too!"—and there I was.

"I know, it's been a while," I said. "I was doing some one-on-one mentoring."

Ashley nodded understandingly. "Well, it's great to see you. I bet the girls will be happy, too. Remember Ynnhoj, from last winter? She's back, and she asked about you. She goes, 'It's Wednesday; where's the Bead Lady?'"

"I'm right here," I told Ashley, smiling. "I'm back."

Chapter Seventeen

Family Day

Christmas again. A Salvation Army Santa clanged his bell on the corner where the redhead sat in the summer. No visit to Sam in St. Victor's this year, though I did go up to the shelter and reprise last year's Christmas Eve Chinese-food feast, celebrating another year of indoor living with a girl they called L'il Bit, a girl they called Stoney, and a girl whose parents had legally named her Bacardi.

Another merry Jewish Christmas with Bill and my folks; another happy-holiday visit with my brother, who was getting ready to graduate college and move in with his longtime girlfriend. Another bottle of champagne, to celebrate the coming of 2006. And another card to my mom—*Thinking of you, happy holidays, hope you're well.* No reply.

The Tigger boxer shorts sat on my dresser, unsent. Sam hadn't written, so neither had I. I traded calls with Maria and Jodi, exchanging warmest holiday wishes among our ersatz adopted family; they hadn't heard anything from Sam, either. *Fishy,* I thought; Sam had promised to stay in touch and have her counselors give us updates. She should have been past the mandatory no-contact phase by now; she should have called one of us, or written.

I waited until a few days after the New Year and called DTP, where the receptionist offered to take a message for Sam's counselor, Luwanda—"She's in a staff meeting right now, but I'll have her call you back." Then I watched three days pass, stewing with growing incredulity as I realized that Luwanda really wasn't calling me back. On the fourth day I called again; again Luwanda was "in a staff meeting." Again she did not return the message.

"Maybe Luwanda's busy," suggested Maria when I called to report my findings. "Maybe I'll try, too."

Maybe was not cutting it for me anymore. I'd lived with *maybe* for the past year—maybe Sam would make it to rehab, or maybe she would break a mirror; maybe we'd cancel our honeymoon; maybe she'd die. Maybe she wasn't who she'd said she was from the first minute I met her. I was sick of maybe; I wanted some certainty.

"I'm going to try to find Sam's parents," I announced to Bill, calling him at work with the breaking decision. "I know Jodi and Maria want the truth to come from Sam, but it's not going to, and I can't stand not knowing anymore."

"Great," said Bill, unsurprised. I'd been threatening to find her parents on and off since October; I'd only become more adamant about it as I waited for Luwanda's call. He and I were both curious; he'd just been waiting for my curiosity to outweigh my dread. "I hope you'll find what you're looking for."

What do you want to find? Maria had asked me back at the Meeting of the Moms. I didn't care anymore, as long as it was the truth.

I opened the folder where I kept all of Sam's writings, letters, and cards, pulling out the pages of the autobiography she'd been working on last summer. Edward Liam Dunleavy, she called him, the father who'd abused her since birth. Born in 1958, son of Canadian missionaries; met and married Ruby Delosantos, a teenage hooker whose family had emigrated from Bolivia. I opened my laptop and looked up "private detective," and found a page full of sites promising *background checks, all public records: criminal, assets, lawsuits*. I went to the first site listed and typed in "Edward Liam Dunleavy."

There he was. And for forty dollars, I could read his file. I typed in my credit card number and six pages of results unspooled onto the screen.

Edward Liam Dunleavy, age forty-seven, lived in Glendale, Colorado; the website gave his address. He was married to Ruby Dunleavy, also forty-seven—not thirty-seven, as Sam had often told me—*You're only one year younger than my mother*. Ed and Ruby owned their home, which was worth over a quarter of a million dollars—no bankruptcies, tax liens, or judgments. No criminal history for either of them—just one unspecified civil charge against Dad from April 2004. The report didn't say anything about their kids. I hit the "print" button, and the pages started spitting from the printer next to me.

My pulse pounded until I could practically taste it in my mouth as I opened another browser window: Google Maps. I typed in the Glendale address, and there it was—a satellite picture of a suburban subdivision, the aerial view of a bunch of look-alike houses on a winding, nondescript street. I zoomed in once, twice, three times, until I was as close up as I could get, looking at the roof of the Dunleavy house like I was Santa Claus sussing out the chimney. It was a nice-sized house. It didn't look like a meth cookery. And that was a swimming pool in the backyard. An *in-ground* swimming pool.

Goddamn.

I leaned back in my chair, smiling furiously at the screen. *Of course.* Here was the certainty I'd been looking for. Sam had grown up in a middle-class home with a pool and a piano, hardbound books on the shelves; she'd been driven to school in the SUV in the driveway. The ghettoes, the drug runs, the gangs, and the guns—they were all lies, just like the AIDS.

The search results listed a telephone number for the Dunleavys. I stared at it, willing myself to pick up the phone and call, unable to imagine what I'd say. "Hi there. I'm calling about your daughter, Samantha. I met her at a homeless shelter in New York; she said you used to sell her for drugs. Any comment?" I didn't know if I wanted to reach out to the residents of this house, now blown up to nearly full screen on my monitor—sure, they might have had money and a home, but they might still be sadistic, abusive creeps. It must have taken *some* kind of fucked-up parents to produce their daughter.

It wasn't enough information. It was the wrong information. I wanted to get information about Sam, what schools she went to, what hospitals she'd been in, but I couldn't—according to the record-search sites, that was kept private by law. Here were Sam's parents, but who was *she*?

She was someone who walked, talked, and acted like a hard-core street kid—the scars, the homemade tattoo, the same weathered clothes every day. The hunch, the quickness on the trigger, the instant rapport she had with other street people. She'd demonstrated her excellence at petty theft, breaking and entering, talking her way into and out of things; she had track marks and busted veins. The streetwisest of the street kids at the shelter gave her respect; they knew she was one of their own. I remembered her old roommate, St. Croix, telling me, "You know Samantha, she wouldn't sleep in a bed for the first few weeks. She slept curled up in all her clothes on the floor."

Can you really fake how you sleep?

Bill got home from work, and I dragged him straight to the computer. "Look," I said, showing him the aerial view of their house. "Her parents' house. With an *in-ground pool*."

Bill leaned over and peered at the screen. "Not exactly a drug slum." He straightened up and looked at my eager, angry face. "I'm sorry, babe."

"Hah," I huffed. I wasn't sorry; I was vindicated. I'd solved even more of the mystery—Nancy Drew and the Case of the Homeless Girl Who Wasn't. I *knew* she was full of shit, I *knew* it. This was why she hadn't replied to my letter; this is why Luwanda the counselor wasn't calling me back. Sam had to distance herself from me, before I caught on to who she really was, which she knew I would. "I'm just glad I found out. Knowledge is power, right?"

If only I knew what to do with all this power I had. I waited a few days for the shock and anger to subside, paging through Dr. Feldman's book, thumbprints and dog-ears on every other page. I'd hoped that finding Sam's parents would answer some questions for me; instead the questions multiplied. Maybe Sam was psychotic; maybe she was really beyond help—anybody who lied as thoroughly and consistently as she did had to be living outside reality. I was starting to think that faking illness was only part of her problem, just another symptom of some super-mega, never-before-seen, off-the-charts kind of craziness. Obviously, she lived inside a three-dimensional fiction that was as real to her as any schizophrenic's delusion—there's no way she could have sustained the ruse otherwise.

I fell into another funk. There really wasn't going to be a happy ending here. Sam wasn't going to leave DTP any better than she was when she arrived. She was up there right now, giving her counselors the same bullshit stories she'd fed me and Jodi and Maria. She wasn't telling them about the subdivision in Glendale; she was feeding them jazz bars in Oklahoma City, street rapes in Boston, shivering in a doorway in Cheyenne, Wyoming, thinking, *I want to get sober and change my life*. And who even knew what she was telling them about me? I'd probably molested her, or tried to. She had to discredit me somehow. She knew me well enough to know that I was onto her by now, and she couldn't risk my contacting DTP.

I called DTP yet again and asked for Luwanda. "She's in a staff meeting," said the receptionist. "I'll have her get back to you."

I rolled my eyes with disgust. No matter what time of day I called, the counselors were "in a staff meeting." Even Sam knew how to switch up her lies, throw a little variety in there for verisimilitude's sake. "Please do," I said, testily reciting my name and number for the third time. "I have some important information for her about Sam's health."

But Luwanda did not call me back. Luwanda was too busy "in a staff meeting." She was too busy sitting in session with Sam, listening to her tell stories about forced prostitution, comforting her through imaginary flashbacks. Luwanda was wasting her time, at the expense of other patients—at her own expense, no doubt. It looked like I was going to have to hire a blimp if I wanted to get her my "important information."

Maria, meanwhile, had better luck. She called to fill me in.

"Hi, Janice, just wanted to let you know that I heard back from Luwanda. Sam gave her permission to give me a quick update, and she says she's doing fine. She had some adjustment problems to start, but she's been doing well for the past few weeks. No health issues, as far as she mentioned. I tried to press her for more information, but she wasn't all that forthcoming, and I didn't want to say anything that might jeopardize Sam's spot there."

"Oh." I smiled tightly. So Sam was still playing favorites—Maria got a call from her counselor, but I didn't—and it still somehow managed to irk me. "So, she's basically not letting her counselors talk to us, like she promised."

"Correct," said Maria. "It's a little frustrating. And I've kept writing to her every week, but I haven't received any letters from her. I'm not sure exactly what's going on, but . . ."

My smile got even tighter. "Well, I think I might have a clue."

"Oh yeah?"

"Yeah." I paused for a second, gathered my nerve. Maria hadn't asked to have her faith in Sam shattered again; that was me. "I looked up her family online. And I found them. And they're not who she said they were."

"Okay." Maria's voice dropped an octave. "Who are they?"

"They live in a quarter-million-dollar house, that they own, with an in-ground pool, in Glendale, Colorado. They're both forty-seven—so Sam's mom aged ten years overnight. No criminal records. They look like upstanding citizens. No information about their kids."

"Wow." There was a pause, and then her voice came back, harder and more peeved. "I wish I were more surprised."

"Me too."

"Have you contacted them?"

"Not yet."

"Do you plan to?" Her words were clipped, terse.

"I don't know." I knew Maria was angry about the revelation—it was another bitter pill to swallow, after all the ones we'd already choked down—but it sounded more like she was mad at me. "Look, I know we were going to wait for Sam to tell us—"

"Well, like I said, I wish I was more surprised." Maria exhaled wearily and tried to turn her tone back to upbeat. "Anyway, I just wanted to let you know that I'd heard from Luwanda. Oh, and she mentioned family day, it's the third weekend of February. So, you know, maybe Sam's not cutting us off just yet."

"I hope not," I said. "I guess the call's a good sign." *Or*, I thought, *a defensive maneuver, to head us off before we got too close.*

I promised to call Maria before doing anything else that would preclude Sam's own spontaneous confession about her past; then I hung up, feeling alienated and shitty. Even in absentia, Sam was still managing to play me and Maria against each other, to keep us in competition instead of cooperation. Even in absentia, she was still running the show. I pictured her up in DTP, humming to herself as she went about her chores, those enormous eyes of hers narrowed with satisfaction.

I hadn't cracked her after all.

Two weeks passed, and the Dunleavys' phone number sat on the pad next to my laptop, mocking me in my own handwriting as I tried to ignore it. I didn't need to call them, I told myself, because I'd already learned everything they would possibly tell me. They weren't going to talk to a total stranger about their estranged daughter; it was a fool's errand. Besides, if they were anything like the kid they'd produced, I didn't want anything to do with them. They were probably psychos themselves. I was afraid that calling them might only expose me to further misery.

Which was backward—*they* were the ones who should have been afraid, if they'd neglected their parental duties to the point where their baby girl was running around the country shooting heroin and faking AIDS. I'd been one of the primary adults in her life for the past year; I was entitled to contact these people and request information about the girl I'd nearly adopted. My back got straighter, my resolve more firm, the more I thought about it—maybe I could do this after all. I remembered my first days of volunteering: how afraid of

Nadine I'd been, how tentative I was around anyone who smacked of authority. And look at me now: yelling at hospital social workers, getting Sam to admit her medical deceptions, facing the information none of us really wanted to hear. This was how parenting Sam had changed me.

I rehearsed potential phone openers with Bill, finessing them through a few iterations—"Hi, Mrs. Dunleavy, my name's Janice, and I met your daughter Samantha last October at a homeless shelter—*while I was doing arts therapy* at a homeless shelter. Mrs. Dunleavy, when was the last time you heard from Samantha?"

Bill nodded, gave me notes. "Don't give away too much. Hang back a little and see what she says."

Right. I went through it over and over, out loud and in my head. If I got a machine, I'd hang up and call back. If I got the father, same. And if I blew this, I'd be back at a dead end; the only avenue of information about Sam would be permanently closed.

The next day, I psyched myself up for the phone call, pacing around the living room and swinging my arms. Then I picked up the phone, punched *66 into the keypad to block the Dunleavys from seeing my phone number, and dialed the number on my pad.

Ring. Ring.

A young woman answered, her voice upbeat and carefree. Eileen, Sam's sister. Not in a group home, not in a coma. On the phone with me. "Hello?"

"Hi," I said, in the smooth tones of a newscaster. "Is Ruby Dunleavy there, please?"

"Sure, one minute, please." So chipper, so polite. Barely a hint of Sam's strange 'hood-inflected accent, but I could hear the similarities in the clear, high tone—she sounded like Sam at her sweetest. "Mom!"

It was too easy. Too fast. All of a sudden, Sam's mother was on the phone, the famed junkie hooker who whored her kids out on Christmas Eve. She was a middle-aged housewife from Colorado. "Hello?" she said.

"Hi, Mrs. Dunleavy." I could barely recognize my own voice, my mind was so blown, but it sounded good to me, it sounded assured.

"My name is Janice, and I'm calling from New York City about your daughter Samantha."

She sipped in a small breath. "Oh my." Her voice trembled, wary. "All right."

I started into the pitch I'd prepared. "I met Samantha a little over a year ago, when I was doing arts therapy at a homeless shelter here in New York, and she and I became friends. It's been a hard year for her—she had some problems with her health—but I just wanted to call and let you know that she's all right."

"Oh my," her mother said again, and gasped. "Oh, this is . . . so she's all right."

"She is." I closed my eyes. I could hear her mother practically sob with relief, and I wanted to cry with her. She'd been worried about her daughter for who knew how long now, suffering so much grief and anguish, while Sam and I were browsing bookstores and swinging on swings. I should have suspected her parents might be decent people who'd been worried about her; I should have found them and called them weeks ago, *months* ago, for everybody's sake. "It's been a tough year, but she's been getting better and better. And she's had lots of people looking out for her. She's a very special girl, and I care for her very much."

"Oh, oh my." I heard Eileen in the background: "It's about Sam? She's all right?" Mrs. Dunleavy tried to compose herself, but her voice continued to shake. "You say you're calling from New York?"

"That's right. I met Samantha at a homeless shelter here last November, and—"

"That's when we last heard from her," she interrupted. "October, 2004. She wouldn't tell us where she was. She was still using drugs. We begged her to come home, try and work things out with us, but she wouldn't. We haven't heard from her since then. And now . . . now you're saying she's all right."

"That's right. She's been in a drug treatment program for the past three months, and she's doing very well."

"Oh, this is an answered prayer. Oh, thank the Lord. I just . . . I don't know . . ."

This was overwhelming her, I could feel it. I was dizzy and over-whelmed, too, though I was doing my best to sound like this was something I did all the time, calling strangers out of the blue to tell them their missing children were alive. "I'm sorry if this comes as a shock, Mrs. Dunleavy. I know it must be a lot for you to deal with at once." I said it as much to myself as to her.

"It is, but I'm very glad you called."

"I care very much for Samantha," I told her, "and I'd love to help you work things out with her, if that's possible."

Her voice fluttered. "That's . . . all we've wanted."

I dropped my voice, tried to make it soothing and kind. She was talking to me, this was working—I could push, but I'd have to push gently. "Mrs. Dunleavy, can you tell me what happened with Samantha?"

She let out a long breath, like she was hoping I could answer that question for her. "I just don't know," she said, honestly perplexed. "I mean, we've always lived a very normal middle-class life. We had the three children, Sam and her brother and her sister; we went to church, and everything was fine. Then when Samantha was eleven, we moved to Thailand for two years for my husband's job, and when we came back, she had some trouble readjusting at school. But then she started to do quite well again. She won the physics award at her high school."

I flashed back to the day Sam showed me her GED, how proud she was. The girl who'd supposedly dropped out of the seventh grade, winner of the physics award.

"And then something happened around her junior year of high school. She developed a drug habit, and we weren't fully aware of it at first. We just knew she was acting strangely, lying about things, very defiant. Then when she was seventeen, she came to me and told me she had been raped the year before, but when we tried to find out more about it, we found out it wasn't true."

What do you mean, you found out it wasn't true? I wanted to inter-rupt with a million questions, but I didn't want to disrupt her flow—I wanted her to tell me everything she could, then I'd ask more. I could hardly believe she was being so forthcoming, reporting all this like she'd reported it before, but I was all gentle reassurance and singsong niceness, coaxing it out of her, pacing around the room with one hand clamped under the other armpit, shaking my head with disbelief.

"And then she was causing so much distress and disruption in the house, we told her she had to stop using drugs, or she couldn't live at home anymore. So she went to live with some family friends who ran a youth ministry while she finished high school and enrolled in college. But she was still using drugs, it was getting worse and worse, and at some point, right around her eighteenth birthday, she ran away again. And we didn't know where she was for a while. . . ."

Her voice trailed off; I could hear her quick breathing in the background. "That must have been terrible for you," I said, sympathetic.

She continued. "It was. And then we got a call from another family in a nearby town; the mother said they found us in the phone book. They'd met Samantha at their church, and she told them she was very sick and needed a kidney transplant, and they took her in. She lived with them for two months, right up to the day she was supposed to go into the hospital for the transplant, and then she disappeared."

So she'd done it before, suckered people into thinking she was dying and then ditched them. Part of me was vindicated—I'd guessed that she'd pulled this trick before—another part of me was just horrified. Well, I'd wanted to know who she was, and now I was learning. I couldn't wait to get this family's phone number from Sam's mom, call them and compare stories. "My goodness," I murmured.

"So then we didn't hear anything for months, and then, completely without warning, she filed a restraining order against my husband. That was April of 2004—we hadn't even seen her for over a year—and the day she was supposed to show up in court to enforce it, we were there, but she wasn't. And then that was the last we heard of her for six months or so, until that phone call last October. And then nothing."

Until today. "And that's when I met her." I picked up the story where she had left off, told her how Sam and I had met at the shelter around Thanksgiving, how Sam had claimed to have been homeless since she was twelve, and using drugs for most of her life. How we became friends when she was in the hospital for her hand, and how our friendship continued after she left the shelter, through rehab, to the halfway house, and then the hospital in the Bronx. "She's all right now," I assured her mom. "But she had made herself very sick intentionally, and she lied about her illness."

"Like she did with the other family," said her mother, still quavering. "But she's recovered—she's better now?"

"Yes, she is. We caught on before too much damage was done, and now she's in a long-term therapeutic rehab program, and she hasn't suffered any health issues for a while now. So things are stable, and she's getting help for her problems."

"Oh, thank the Lord. This is the news we'd prayed for."

I could hear the relief in her voice and Eileen chattering excitedly in the background—"Say to tell Sam I miss her!" However happy or unhappy I was to hear about Sam's past, these people were overjoyed to hear about her present, and it was starting to rub off on me. Sam was okay, and I'd helped make her that way; I was a hero again, I was the angel of good news. And everything would only get better from here. This phone call would be the start of a fresh era in Sam's life, and in mine. There was a whole new "other mom"—her *real* mom— who was going to take care of this.

"I really appreciate everything you've told me," I said. "It's been a confusing time for me as well, trying to figure out what's real and what's been the product of Sam's imagination." I chuckled a little, because now Mom and I were old friends, on the same team. "I'm actually delighted to hear Eileen sounding so well—Sam told me she was either in a coma or a group home following a suicide attempt, so hearing her voice is—"

"Well," Ruby interrupted nervously, "Eileen did try to kill herself a few years ago, and she was briefly comatose, and then she was living in a group facility, yes. But she's much better now."

"Oh." *Nice family*, I thought. I tried to keep the surprise out of my voice, but Ruby's tone had become defensive, so I changed the subject back to Sam. "Mrs. Dunleavy, do you think Sam is psychotic?"

She let out another deep sigh—the good news was over; now the hard facts remained. "I don't know. At first we thought it was the drugs, but now I think it's something more."

"But it definitely started around age seventeen."

"Yes, that's right." She cleared her throat nervously. "But . . . but you say she's been to drug treatment now?"

"Yes, she's there right now. And I'd give you the phone number of the program, but it's impossible to contact her right now anyway. Besides, I think it might be upsetting to her if she knew we spoke. She seems to be doing well at this program; she's been there for a few months now. I'm hoping we can proceed slowly, so we don't spook the horses, you know?"

Her mother agreed right away—too fast, almost. She'd just gasped with relief to find out that Sam was alive; I'd have thought she would have wanted to contact her right away, but she seemed almost afraid of her daughter. "Oh, no, I wouldn't want to . . . I mean, I'm just so grateful that she's all right, and that she's getting some kind of help. I wouldn't want to do anything . . . and I have to talk to my husband, you know, this is all very . . ."

She trailed off again, like she was at a loss for what to say or do next, and I realized I didn't know, either. I hadn't thought this far ahead; I had no idea how to reunite Sam and her mom when I was being blockaded from Sam myself.

"Well, maybe you and I can figure out a good way for you to reestablish contact with her—you can talk things over with your husband, and I can try to figure something out on my end, and we can talk again in a few days. Does that sound like a good idea?"

"Yes, I think we should. I definitely need to speak with my husband, you know, this is such a surprise. . . ."

Ruby Dunleavy sounded like she really needed to sit down, maybe take a Valium. I hoped Eileen was standing by, ready to make her mother a nice cup of tea. "I'm sorry," I said again, reassuring. "I know it's out of the blue."

"Oh no. You're an answered prayer. We've just been hoping that she was . . . being taken care of somehow."

"She has been," I told her. "She's had a lot of people who have cared very much for her." Talking about her with all this warmth and love in my voice made me feel it again. I thought about the Sam I'd met that first night at the shelter—her wide, open smile, her look of satisfied concentration as she strung beads on a key chain for Jodi. "She's a very special and talented young person, and I'm very dedicated to seeing her get well."

I gave her my name and number, and Mrs. Dunleavy wrote them down. "Well, that's just wonderful, and we thank you so much for calling."

"I'm glad I called, too, and we'll talk again in a few days."

We hung up.

Well.

I put the phone down, exhilarated. I'd done it, I'd made the call, and it had worked out as well as it could have, better than I'd imagined. She'd talked to me, she was going to work with me. As shattered as I was by the truth, I was also satisfied, my curiosity sated, my ego somewhat restored. I'd been right about Sam—she was a middle-class suburban kid, as I'd suspected, but she'd also been a runaway junkie—I hadn't been wrong to believe that. And I was right when I said she'd pulled a stunt with her health before. God, I loved being right. Sam had made me wrong there for a while, she'd made me mistaken, but now I was back to being right.

I called Bill at work. "Just had a chat with my new best friend, Mrs. Ruby Dunleavy."

"*And?*"

I recounted the highlights of the conversation, Bill stopping in the same exact place I had. "So wait, one of her daughters tried to kill herself, and the other one . . . is Sam?"

"I know. Something's rotten in that house. But listen, her mom is totally relieved and grateful to hear that Sam's all right, and she's committed to getting back in touch with her and helping her get better. I can't help but think this is a good thing, you know?"

"I hope so," he said. Then, "Wow, a kidney transplant. The kid's got balls."

"Yeah, no kidding. I can't wait to talk to that family. I'll ask Ruby for their name next time we talk."

So much to ask, so much to discuss. But first I had to sit down with my notebook and write down the conversation before my short-term memory failed me. I hung up with Bill and picked up the pen. *Her sister Eileen answered, sounded perfectly fine, handed me over to Mom. . . .*

For once, writing about it was making me feel worse. The more I wrote, the more the initial elation of the phone call wore off; by the time I was finished, I was angry again, feeling ridiculous, feeling this tremendous sense of loss. Had I actually thought I was going to become this girl's mom? How stupid of me, how vain. She already had a mom; I'd just spoken to her. I thought of Sam sitting on that log that summer day, considering my offer to be her guardian, smirking into her knee because she knew she already had a mom, worrying about her, waiting for her, back in Colorado. I wasn't her mom; I was nobody. I was nothing special. She'd duped whole families full of people like me before.

So I'd solved the mystery—big deal. I was only a year too late. And it wasn't like I was such a supersleuth; it doesn't take an advanced degree to use the Internet. Anybody with forty bucks and a bug up her ass could have found Sam's parents—she gave me her father's middle name, for Christ's sake. Now I knew the truth, but what good was it going to do me? I couldn't confront Sam with it. I couldn't tell DTP—they wouldn't listen to me, they were too busy in "staff meetings." I couldn't even tell Maria. She was going to kill me for digging around when I'd said I'd leave the revelations to Sam.

I was still gloomy the next morning, even after my run, when the home phone rang. "Hello?"

"Hi, Ms. Erlbaum. It's Ruby Dunleavy."

Her voice was even more nervous and stressed than when I'd spoken to her the day before. I looked at the clock and frowned. It was only 9 A.M.—7 A.M. Colorado time. We'd spoken less than eighteen hours ago. She didn't wait for me to acknowledge her before rushing ahead.

"Ms. Erlbaum, I've spoken to my husband, and we've decided that we can't allow Samantha back into our lives until she's well. She's just caused too much damage to our family. You know, we have to protect Eileen, because this has just been so damaging. I hope you understand; we can't have anything to do with her at all."

"Of course," I said automatically, my voice reassuring, even as I re-coiled in confusion—surely she didn't mean she wanted *nothing* to do with Sam. She was so agitated; if I could just calm her down, maybe I could get her to explain. "I understand, it's a very difficult—"

"It is," she interrupted quickly. "And I have to ask you, please don't call here again. Please remove our number from your records. My husband and I just can't allow Samantha to disrupt the family the way she has in the past. Maybe if she gets better someday, but not now."

"Okay, I understand," I said again. "Of course, if you want to reach me at any time, you have my number. But—"

She didn't stop to hear me out. "All right, well. Thank you for un-derstanding. Good-bye."

Click.

Bill came into the room. "Who was that?"

I stared at the mute receiver in my hand, disbelieving. "That was Ruby Dunleavy. She says they're done with Sam. She doesn't want me to call them anymore."

He looked dumbfounded, then disgusted. "So much for her Par-ent of the Year award."

"Really."

I couldn't fathom it—Sam's mother was giving up; she'd quit. I felt my chest swell with indignation. What kind of mother gives up on her kid? Sam wasn't even mine, she'd tortured me for a year, and I still couldn't fully let her go.

So Ruby had spoken to her husband—I bet he was behind her drastic change of heart. In fact, I bet he was behind a lot of things. I bet he was a big part of the reason both his daughters wanted to die.

Him, and his frightened, hiding wife. Sam had filed a restraining order against him, right around the time her sister had tried to kill herself—I saw it on the background check, the civil charge from April 2004. Ruby herself admitted it. But there was something else she wasn't admitting.

I put the dead phone back on the cradle, frowning. Something had happened in that house, that quarter-million-dollar house with the in-ground swimming pool—something that had helped make Sam very, very sick.

The second meeting of Sam's three remaining moms took place two weeks later, at a chain restaurant in Midtown.

"Well, here we are again," Maria said brightly, unwrapping her scarf, kissing me and Jodi hello. "Good to see you, ladies."

It was good to see her, too, her cheeks pink from the cold outside, drops of melted snow in the curls of her dark hair. It had been more than two months since we'd seen one another, after months of seeing one another almost every day; it was a relief to see her now, and Jodi, too. They were my touchstones, my witnesses; this hadn't all been a figment of my imagination. The past year and a half had actually happened. As unreal as she was, Sam wasn't just a dream.

Jodi turned to me, gave me her pursed-lipped smile. "So, have you heard from Sam's mom again?"

"Nope. And I doubt I ever will. It sounds like her husband put the kibosh on her speaking to me; she said they want nothing to do with Sam."

"Unbelievable," said Maria, shaking her head. "Just unbelievable."

I'd called Maria and Jodi after talking to Sam's mom and told them what I'd discovered: the physics award, the other family and the fake kidney transplant, Eileen's very real suicide attempt, Mom's overnight change of heart after talking to Dad. It took a few days for Maria to get over the shock and upset—she'd suspected the truth about Sam's past, but she wasn't entirely delighted to have it confirmed, especially after I'd said I would let the fact-finding mission lie for a while. But ultimately she agreed that it was better we knew than not. She and Jodi also agreed that the Dunleavy family stank of something rotten.

"That father," said Jodi.

I threw my hands up. "Don't get me started. Out of all the lies Sam told, I believe that her dad's a total creep."

"Well, *I* got an interesting phone call the other day." Maria unfolded her napkin with a flourish, placed it on her lap. "Sam called to ask me about family day."

"Really."

And my stupid heart raced, that old adrenaline shot I got whenever Sam drew nearer. I shouldn't have been surprised that she'd called Maria; Maria had remained a relentless supporter, sending unanswered letters every other week for four months now. Sam must have thought Maria could still be won over, drawn in, emotionally useful somehow. I wondered what it would be like to talk to Sam after all this time, knowing what we knew now. I didn't know if I could do it, didn't know if I could approach her with the care and compassion I was still trying to feel for her. Family day had been on my calendar since I'd heard about it from Maria last month, but I hadn't yet decided whether or not to attend.

"How did it go?" Jodi asked.

"Hard," said Maria bluntly. "It was really hard. She was talking to me like normal, like nothing had changed, and I was just . . . I didn't want to tell her, 'Listen, I know everything, tell me the truth.' I still want her to own up to it herself, you know? But it was hard, not saying anything. It's like, I still love her, I still care for her. I still want to support her so she can get better. But hearing her voice like that . . . it was hard."

I could only imagine—that clear, piercing voice, so full of need. And so full of shit. "Are you still thinking you want to go to family day?" I asked.

"I am," she said, resolute. "Especially since she called and asked me to. That had to be a big deal for her—calling me, after what we went through last summer, knowing that we know she lied about

AIDS. It's almost like, if she's willing to admit part of it, maybe we can get her to tell us the rest."

"How about you?" I asked Jodi.

"I'm ready to go," Jodi said, shrugging. "I'm curious, as much as anything. And I still care about her, as crazy as that sounds. She didn't call *me*, but if she wants me to go, I'll go. It'll be interesting, at the very least."

I nodded. "I'm still not sure," I told them. "Part of me kind of feels like I have to go—not just to be supportive of her, but for clo-sure's sake. Like maybe if I saw her again, I'd feel more settled about the whole thing." Instead of unsettled, wildly ambivalent, alter-nately infuriated and depressed. The truth was, I didn't want to go to family day. I couldn't imagine being around Sam without wanting to grab her throat and squeeze it, and that impulse made me dislike both her and myself. "I don't know," I concluded. "Jury's still out, for me."

"Well, I think I can help you make that decision," said Maria. She hesitated for a second. "But I don't think you're going to like it."

"Okay." I wondered what Maria could tell me that would be worse than what I already knew. "What's that?"

"You're not on the list of approved visitors." She wrinkled her nose and cringed a little. *Sorry.*

"Really." I broke into a manic grin, blood rushing to my head. *She didn't*, I thought. Sam *didn't* block me, and allow Jodi and Maria to come. "And why's that?"

Maria hesitated again, and her cringe got deeper. "Because . . . she told them you're a drug user."

I stared at her, incredulous, then laughed.

"Oh, no," said Jodi, drawing back. "She didn't."

"I'm sorry," said Maria. "I really am."

And I laughed again, because it was perfect—for once, Sam wasn't lying. I *was* a drug user; I smoked pot all the time. Maria and Jodi knew it, I'd never kept it from them; as ashamed as I was of my immature habit, I didn't hide it from the people I loved. And now Sam was telling the truth, wielding it just as skillfully as she wielded lies, slashing at my Achilles heel the way hers had been slashed, exposing me as I'd exposed her.

At the same time, in disowning me, she'd made my decision for me. I hadn't wanted to go to family day, and now I didn't have to. I could walk away from the situation with no remorse—in fact, I had no other choice. I hadn't been able to cut myself loose from her, so she'd done it for me. Almost a kindness, like when she'd recuperated so I could go on my honeymoon. She'd released me.

"I'm sorry," Maria said again. "I feel awful. I can't believe that she said that, but—"

I waved it off—we could all believe that she'd said that. "Oh, I figured she'd told them something. I thought maybe she'd say I tried to grab her boobs or something. At least this is the truth, right?"

"Well, I'd be pretty angry," said Jodi, looking offended on my behalf. "After all you've done for her . . ."

Right—after all I'd done for her. Which was what? I wondered. I'd listened to her, like the nun on the shelter's videotape told me to, and I'd believed. But that wasn't what she needed. She needed someone to *not* believe her, to see through her, and I'd been too busy seeing a reflection of myself. What *had* I done for her, after all? I'd rewarded her for being sick; I'd absolved her of guilt for any harm she'd done to others. I'd bought all the bullshit she'd sold me, until supply couldn't keep up with demand anymore, and she was forced to take her ruse to new heights.

But I'd loved her. Or I'd loved the way she made me feel about myself. I'd loved the person I was when I was with her—competent, maternal, adult—but had I ever really loved *her*? How could I? I didn't know anything about her. And once I did, I didn't love her at all.

Jodi and Maria were still looking at me, waiting for my reaction with concerned faces.

"Good luck at family day," I blessed them. "Hope it goes very well."

I trudged out of the restaurant after the meal, down a dripping concrete corridor to the subway, mulling over this latest development. The relief I'd felt started to melt as I sat in the overstuffed train, boiling in my layers of wool; now I was starting to feel distinctly itchy—chafed, even. So what if I was a pothead, what did that matter? It had never inhibited me from acting as her guardian before. Stoned or sober, I'd been there for Sam, through rehabs and hospitals, lies and revelations; stoned or sober, no matter what she'd thrown at me, I'd been there. But Sam wasn't finished punishing me, trying to humiliate me, trying to make me wrong; she wasn't going to let me have my say. She was going to deny me closure. She would have the last word, and the last word would be *nyah nyah*.

No. I got home, ripped off my coat and sweater, and called DTP. I wanted to get Luwanda on the phone. Or somebody. This was not going to end with Sam blowing me off. This relationship was not over until I said it was. I didn't care if it *did* jeopardize her spot there—I was going to talk to someone about Samantha Eliza Dunleavy, the piano prodigy, winner of the physics award. If she was suddenly going to start telling the truth, then so was I.

"Hello, DTP, Samantha speaking, can I help you?"

That high, clear voice, the 'hood accent smoothed over for receptionist duty. I couldn't believe my luck. "Samantha Dunleavy?"

"Yes?"

"Janice Erlbaum." I smiled hugely. "How are you?"

She didn't skip a beat. Her voice stayed smooth, dispassionate, like I was any other caller. "Oh, hey. I can't talk right now, I'm at the switchboard."

She was a cucumber. The smile on my face withered and died. I'd wondered what it would be like to talk to her again, and now I knew—hollow. There was no feeling in her. It was like talking to the automated voice on the phone with the bank: monotone, bland, detached. This was not the Sam I'd loved; this was not the Sam who'd said she loved me. The person I'd loved was gone, if she'd ever been there at all.

I heard her hovering over the disconnect button. "So, when should I call back?" I asked quickly.

"Listen," she said. "I gotta go."

She hung up.

It was the last time I would ever speak to her.

Since U Been Gone

Listen. She had to go.

It's May again—over a year since that last phone call, a year since I started writing this book. Plenty of time for me to figure out what really happened with me and Sam, to figure out how I feel about it. Right?

It depends on the day, I guess. Some days, I'm grateful for what she did for me, how she caused me to grow up and let go of my adolescence, how she cured me of my need to play savior. Other days, I'm horrified at what she had to resort to in order to feel loved. But I'm not angry anymore—not at Sam, and not at myself. She was sick, and her sickness went untreated. All I could do was stop using her to make myself sick, too.

I don't know where Sam is today—if she graduated from DTP last October, or if she eloped before then; if she's somewhere in California right now, or Texas, or Maine. I don't know if she's in a hospital or a homeless shelter. I don't know if she's dead. I suspect that she's still out there, running her scams, ruining her health; I don't think anything has changed for her. I know I promised to stay in her life, whether she wanted me to or not, and I've thought about calling her mom again, or trying to find her somehow.

But I don't want to find her.

Life's been good since Sam's been gone—my family is well, my friends are great, and I love being partnered with Bill. I started teaching for a living, and I wrote a book, *Girlbomb*, about my experiences as a halfway-homeless teenager. I'm not volunteering at the shelter these days; I might go back to it someday, but I think that chapter of my life might finally be over. I'm not looking for Little Janice anymore. She's here inside me, where she's always been. And she's happy.

A funny thing happened: Bill and I went back to Disney World this winter—the Annual Samantha Dunleavy Memorial Disney Trip—and we had just as much fun as we did the year before, except for the bronchial infection I picked up on the plane ride home. I couldn't smoke pot while I was sick; it made my chest hurt and my heart race. So I stopped. It's been five months now, and there are days when I crave it like crazy, but I haven't smoked a joint since.

I don't know what happened to Valentina or any of my old favorites from the shelter. I don't hear from Jodi anymore. But I spoke to Maria the other day—we're in touch every few weeks to catch up and say hi. She's still working at the rehab in Larchmont, just finishing grad school; she's in love with a great guy who loves her back. She's been reading this book as I wrote it—"I was never a junkie," she says, laughing. "Where did Sam come up with that one?"

Maria hasn't heard from Sam, either, not since she and Jodi went to family day, over a year ago. Sam was like a stranger that day, says Maria; there was nothing behind her one good eye. When Maria got into her car at the end of the day, she broke down and cried.

And the redhead is missing from my corner; she's been missing since last fall. Last time I saw her, I almost didn't recognize her—she wasn't sitting in her usual spot. She was standing upright, waiting for the light to change at Fourteenth Street, wearing a long strapless dress and flat shoes, grinding her teeth. Her arms were as thin as soda straws, but her chin was up; she was still fighting. The light went green, and she took off across the street.

I wanted to follow her, but I didn't. Now I don't know where she's gone.

THANKS

This book is for Bill. Of course.

Thanks to my editor and friend, Bruce Tracy; to my agent and advocate, Alice Martell; and to my shrink and hero, Judith Fleisher. Thanks to my beloved father, Larry, and my wonderful stepmom, Sylvia. Thanks to my brother, whose name is not Jake. Thanks to my writers' group: Anne Elliott, Virginia Vitzthum, and Cheryl Burke. Thanks to Eric Nelson. Thanks to my great friends Emilie Blythe MacDonald, Amanda Stern, Sarah Fisch, Steve Fine, M. David Hornbuckle, Dave "luckydave" Memory, Kat Fasano, Naomi Rivkis, Stephanie Reisin, and Dana Piccoli; to my stepsister, Satia Renée; and to the posters on girlbomb.com, especially Éireann Laskey, C. S. Norman, Katie Foley, Kirsten Fitrell, and Jennifer Glick. Thanks to Joy Parisi and Lila Cecil of Paragraph NY, and Bill Ottignon of A Summer Place. Thanks to the amazing professional support of Lauren Cerand, Patty Park, Avideh Bashirrad, and Debbie Aroff. Thanks to Dr. Marc Feldman. Thanks to "Maria," "Jodi," "Nadine," and "Ashley." Thanks to all of the staff and residents of the shelter.

Finally, thanks to "Sam." I hope you will be well.

Have You Found Her

Janice Erlbaum

A Reader's Guide

Questions and Topics for Discussion

1. In *Have You Found Her,* Janice has returned as a volunteer to the shelter where she once lived. She also voluntarily accepts a great deal of responsibility for Sam's care and well-being. How else does the theme of volunteering apply in this book? Some self-help books discuss the notion of "volunteering for victimhood." Can either Sam or Janice be seen this way?

2. Another theme of the book is addiction. Both Sam and Janice have drug addictions, but they also exhibit other addictive behaviors. Can you identify them? How do these other addictions affect their lives and the events of the story?

3. Janice often mentions her own skin color, ethnic background, and economic class, as well as the color, ethnicity, class, and sexual orientation of the girls at the shelter. How do you think color, ethnicity, class, and sexuality play into the events of the story? Do you think such issues are handled sensitively in this book?

4. In the book, Janice admits to lying, taking drugs, and evading rules a number of times. Does this influence your perception of her as a reliable narrator? Why or why not?

5. Janice is a writer, as is Sam. How do you think Janice's being a writer affected the events of the story? Does this make her more or less reliable as a narrator?

6. Were you surprised by the conditions of the shelter as Janice describes them? What do you think of the shelter system, and how do you think it could be improved? What kinds of services do you think should be available to homeless and addicted youths?

7. Have you ever known someone like Sam? Is there anything about her behavior that you recognize in other people, or even in yourself? How do you think her behavior differs from that of "normal" people?

8. On page 336, Janice writes, "Something had happened in that house . . . something that had helped make Sam very, very sick." Do you agree with her assessment? Do you think Sam's sickness is a product of her upbringing or do you think it is biological in nature? Are her parents responsible for making her the way she was?

9. One title that was suggested for this book was "Sucker: A Love Story." Do you think that title is apt?

10. What do you think happened to the redhead who panhandled on Janice's block? What about the other graduates of the shelter? What kinds of outcomes do you imagine for these girls?

PHOTO: RICHARD KERN

JANICE ERLBAUM is the author of *Girlbomb:
A Halfway Homeless Memoir*. She lives in
New York City with her domestic partner,
Bill Scurry, and their three cats. You can find
her at www.girlbomb.com.